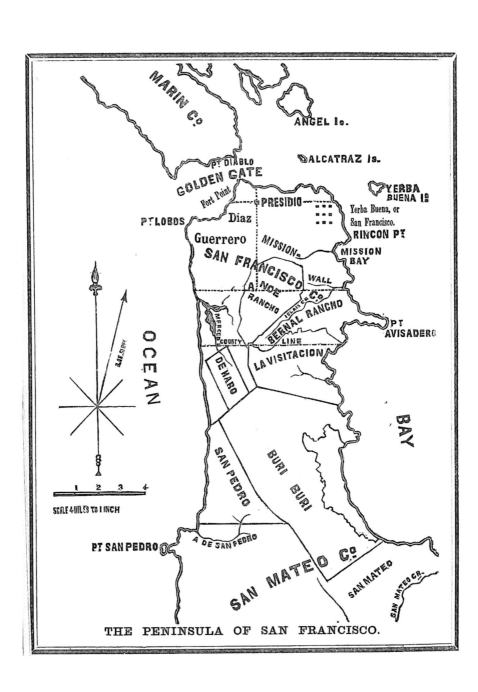

THE PENINSULA OF SAN FRANCISCO.

APPLEWOOD'S
AMERICAN FRONTIER
SERIES

The Colonial History

Of San Francisco

WITHDRAWN

John Whipple Dwinelle

APPLEWOOD BOOKS
Carlisle, Massachusetts

The Colonial History
was originally published in
1863

ISBN: 978-1-4290-4570-4

APPLEWOOD'S AMERICAN FRONTIER SERIES

Thank you for purchasing an Applewood book. Applewood reprints America's lively classics—books from the past that are still of interest to modern readers. This facsimile was printed using many new technologies together to bring our tradition-bound mission to you. Applewood's facsimile edition of this work may include library stamps, scribbles, and margin notes as they exist in the original book. These interesting historical artifacts celebrate the place the book was read or the person who read the book. In addition to these artifacts, the work may have additional errors that were either in the original, in the digital scans, or introduced as we prepared the book for printing. If you believe the work has such errors, please let us know by writing to us at the address below.

For a free copy of our current print catalog featuring our bestselling books, write to:

APPLEWOOD BOOKS
P.O. Box 27
Carlisle, MA 01741

For more complete listings, visit us on the web at:
www.awb.com

Prepared for publishing by HP

THE

COLONIAL HISTORY

OF

THE CITY OF SAN FRANCISCO:

BEING

A SYNTHETIC ARGUMENT IN THE DISTRICT COURT OF THE UNITED
STATES FOR THE NORTHERN DISTRICT OF CALIFORNIA,
FOR FOUR SQUARE LEAGUES OF LAND
CLAIMED BY THAT CITY.

BY JOHN W. DWINELLE,

COUNSELLOR AND ADVOCATE.

SAN FRANCISCO:

PRINTED BY TOWNE & BACON, BOOK AND JOB PRINTERS,
No. 536 Clay Street, opposite Leidesdorff.

1863.

PREFACE.

It is hoped that the title given to this volume will not be considered pretentious, when it is stated that it resulted from an afterthought, based upon the following considerations: The discussion of the case was thrown into a narrative form, for the reason that although often treated analytically with great ability, and with a conclusive result, still a class of persons has existed ever ready to resist the conclusions of the argument by the cry: " There was never any Pueblo of San Francisco !" thus endeavering to evade the result by forcing a re-examination of the main fact in the case. A chronological narrative, weaving into itself in their appropriate places the organization and acts of the Pueblo, and its constant and often repeated recognition by the executive, the Legislatures, and the citizens of California, both before and after the conquest by the Anglo-Americans, seemed the appropriate and only means of silencing this clamor, and of utterly and forever establishing the indisputable fact of the existence of the Pueblo, in such a manner that whoever hereafter shall assume to deny it will render himself ridiculous. When the work was nearly finished, the suggestion occurred that it was too valuable to be thrown as a mere waif upon the stream, as law-briefs and other pamphlets commonly are, and that whatever its merits or deficiencies in point of execution, the narrative, with its documents entitled Addenda, were not without a permanent value as the first essay towards the " Colonial History of San Francisco." It has therefore been honored with a title page, received an appropriate title, and been elevated from the low estate of a pamphlet to the dignity of a book. The documents in the Addenda contain precious *matériaux pour servir*, and present a view of the wise and beneficent colonial policy of Spain and Mexico, which will repay the study of the historian, the ethnologist, and the statesman.

NOTICE.

THE narrative proper contains one hundred and eight pages, and immediately afterwards is placed the ADDENDA with a paging of its own, and each document designated by its number in Roman numerals. The Addenda are cited each by its number, to which is generally added the page *of the Addenda* to which reference is made.

In the District Court of the United States,

FOR THE NORTHERN DISTRICT OF CALIFORNIA.

The CITY OF SAN FRANCISCO

vs.

The UNITED STATES.

ARGUMENT OF MR. JOHN W. DWINELLE FOR CLAIMANT.

STATEMENT OF THE CASE.

§ **1.** This is a claim by the City of San Francisco for four leagues of land, including the present site of the City, and the lands immediately adjacent sufficient to make up that quantity. The law and the facts upon which this claim is based are stated in the two following propositions:

"FIRST: On the seventh day of July, in the year 1846, and long "before that time, a Hispano-Mexican PUEBLO or town existed within "the northern limits of the present City of San Francisco.

"SECONDLY: That this PUEBLO or town, by virtue of the ancient "and immemorial laws of Spain, and of the modern laws of Spain and "Mexico, was vested in proprietorship, in trust for the inhabitants "thereof, with four leagues of land, including the said PUEBLO or "town, and the lands in the immediate vicinity of the same.

"THIRDLY: That the said four leagues of land are to be determined "by taking all the land included by the natural tide-water boundaries "of the northern portion of the peninsula upon which the present City "of San Francisco is situated, and proceeding within those natural "boundaries south to a parallel of latitude, which, with those natural "boundaries, shall, when surveyed according to the Spanish and Mex- "ican lands, include the full quantity of four square leagues."

These three propositions will be discussed together.

The United States, on the other hand, insist that there was never an organized PUEBLO of San Francisco; that an attempt was made to convert the neighboring Catholic Indian Mission of Dolores into a PUEBLO, but that it was never accomplished.

A HISTORICAL STATEMENT NECESSARY.

§ **2.**   The discussion of this case cannot be confined to the presenta- tion of a few sharply-defined propositions.   The history of the whole country of California is involved in that of the City of San Francisco. It will be remembered that the proposition of the United States is, that there never was a PUEBLO or organized town of San Francisco, and that the claim of four leagues of lands for such PUEBLOS is a modern invention, never heard of among the Hispano-Californian population, nor among the Anglo-Americans until within the last few years.   On the other hand, it is contended, on the part of the City of San Francisco, that there was here a PUEBLO of San Francisco fully organized and in operation in its Political and Municipal capacity, and that to this PUEBLO or town, AS SUCH, and without any special grant for that purpose, belonged four leagues of land, including its site, and the lands adjacent to it.   To demonstrate the facts which sustain these last propositions requires an extended historical disquisition, detailing the origin and progress of the SPANISH LAWS OF COLONIZATION which have from time to time been in force in California, their gradual development and improvement, and their application to the colonial establishments which grew up under them.   It will require a critical sketch of the development, decline and final extinction of the plan of CATHOLIC MISSIONS among the Indians of California; of the system of PURE PUEBLOS; and of the military establishment of PRESIDIOS which were finally converted into PRESIDIAL-PUEBLOS.   But before entering into this argument, it will be well to ascertain with precision the definition of certain terms which will be frequently employed in the discussion.

MODERN MUNICIPALITIES OR COMMUNES.

§ **3.**   No portion of history is more interesting than that of the rise and development of modern Municipalities or Communes, or, in the better understood American terms, ORGANIZED VILLAGES, CITIES or TOWNS.   At the same time no portion of history is more obscure. While it is evident that MODERN COMMUNES originated in the instinct of association and protection among the weak against the strong, the indigenous conquered serf against his robber lord,—and became salient points of reaction for the democratic element in society against the aristocratic,—still the time, place and exact circumstances under which they were formed cannot be definitely ascertained, and are even difficult of conjecture. As the darkness of the middle ages recedes before the dawn of the new civilization, the modern *commune* EMERGES from the obscurity, perfect and mature, but with unknown antecedents. It is only until lately that history has busied itself with these democratic organizations: formerly they were beneath its notice. It is highly indicative of the small value attached to the municipal institutions which lie at the base of the liberties of the British races, that in the histories of the English law, written by Hallam, Reeves, Crabbe, and Blackstone, we find no account whatever of the rise and development of the English COMMUNE, although the House of Commons (*communes*) has for more than a century and a half been the most powerful branch of the British Legislature. Robertson was the first writer of eminence who considered the subject worthy of his research and illustration; Guizot and Thierry have exhausted the subject. Robertson's Charles V, Vol. 1, Proofs and Illustrations Notes XVI–XX; Guizot Hist. de la Civilization; Thierry, le tiers-Etat; Maddox, Firma Burgi, and Merlin, Questions de Droit, titres *Commune* et *Communaux;*—may be consulted with interest and profit by the archæologist, and even by the general reader, but the present discussion does not demand any critical research of that nature.

SPAIN FIRST ORIGINATED A System OF COMMUNES, BURGHS, OR LOCAL MUNICIPALITIES.

§ 4. As Spain was the kingdom under whose laws was first built up, codified and published a complete system of civilized and Christian law [LAS SIETE PARTIDAS, enacted by Don Alfonso X in 1260,] so it was the country where the COMMUNES, whether called cities, villas, or towns, first obtained a representation in the Cortes, the National Legislature. The Hispano-American Communes are legitimately descended from those of Spain, but although resembling them in many features, yet in others they differ from them almost as widely as it is possible for two species of the same class of plants or animals to differ from each other. Guizot specially notes this great difference between the colonies of Greece and Rome and those of modern Europe, that the founders of the former carried with them and planted in the new colony the political distinctions of class, and the social distinctions of rank, so that the new city was a complete copy of the parent one; while the modern *communes* were all pure democracies, or nearly so. But the European *commune*, translated across the Atlantic, experienced the same enfranchisement which has attended most other civilized institutions in the like transit. If we bear in mind that the Hispano-American colonies or pueblos were *communes* entirely *sui generis,* built up from an uniform basis, perfectly resembling each other in *all* their features, and wholly emancipated from the irregularities, uncertainties, and servitudes which deformed European communes, and even prevented them from attaining the dignity of a System, we shall comprehend in the outset why so little of the law applicable to the PUEBLOS of Spain will be of use to us in this discussion, and also avoid the bewildering labyrinths of useless law-learning. For example: suppose a dozen European communes,—each a city of refuge from the exactions of titled robbers,—had established themselves in fact upon certain lands,—one holding the lands occupied by it as its own in full property; another holding the same description of lands under a mere usurpment; another in common with the neighboring *lord*; another in common with the adjoining bishop, or monastery, or convent, or church; and others holding the same kind of property in trust for all comers;—what uniform rule of property, what system, could be evolved from such an aggregation of *exceptional* cases? Happily when we come to the Spanish Pueblos established in America, we shall find a Perfect System of Homogeneous Pueblos, sometimes differing in rank, but never in kind, or in organization.

DIFFICULTY IN ARGUING THE CASE.

§ **5.** A serious difficulty in arguing the case arises from the fact that it has repeatedly been decided by the Supreme Court of the State of California. It could not be expected that land litigation should not attend the sudden growth of the City of San Francisco. Accordingly, the Supreme Court of the new State was called upon in the first year of its existence, to decide whether the Hispano-American town of San Francisco had such a proprietary interest in the lands lying within its limits as to constitute a source of title. This question was before that tribunal for several years, with various elucidations and solutions, until finally, in the year 1860, in the case of Hart *vs.* Burnett, 15 Cal. Rep. 530, it was decided in the affirmative, after such thoroughness of research and force of argument as to render it almost impossible to treat the question again in a purely forensic manner. I propose, therefore, to discuss the case in another manner, and to weave the proofs and illustrations into a chronological narrative of the HISTORY OF THE PUEBLO OR TOWN OF SAN FRANCISCO; and I hope in this manner to construct a SYNTHETIC ARGUMENT which shall lead conclusively to the same result that is reached by the admirable ANALYSIS in the case of Hart *vs.* Burnett.

CHARACTER OF THE TESTIMONY. LOSS OF PAPERS. DOCUMENTARY EVIDENCE—" ADDENDA."

§ **6.** I shall rely almost entirely on documentary evidence, and shall make little use of parol testimony, except to show the loss of documentary evidence. The testimony of Hispano-Americans has been found to be proverbially unreliable for many reasons, and under no circumstances could stand in the face of authentic official documents. That most of the authentic official documents relating to the history of San Francisco, have been lost, is too well established by the testimony, both documentary and parol. Among the documentary testimony is an original authentic document, annexed to the testimony of R. C. Hopkins, as Exhibit No. 1, containing an "inventory of all the documents con-"tained in the Archives of the Juzgado of San Francisco de Asis," from the year 1829 to 1839, during which period the Ayuntamiento of San Francisco was organized, and finally superseded. Hardly any of these documents are to be found. They are not in the custody of the Mayor or of the City Clerk; they are not in the City Archives; a few have been produced from private hands; and only a few are in the California Archives. See testimony of R. C. Hopkins, keeper of the California Archives; of A. F. Teschemacher, Mayor of San Francisco; of J. W. Dwinelle. In the California Archives the official correspondence of the Governors of California from about 1834 to 1839, the most interesting period of the history of the Pueblo of San Francisco, is wanting. See R. C. Hopkins's testimony, *ut supra.* Whenever a trace has been found in this inventory of a document of peculiar interest in the case, and which from its nature must have shed light upon the points to be investigated, in almost every instance it has been found that this document could not be found either in the archives, or any where else. See testimony of Hopkins and Dwinelle. That the government itself is answerable for this loss of documents, is very easily demonstrated. On July 11th, 1847, a few days after the Americans took possession of San Francisco, Lt. J. S. Misroon, U. S. Navy, dating from Yerba Buena, reports that he had visited the Mission of Dolores, and adds :

"A collection of public documents was made and carefully brought "to town, where they were packed, sealed, and superscribed, by Mr. "Leidesdorff and myself, and witnessed by Don Andres Hoepender, "(sealed with the consulate seal), and placed in the Custom House un-"der charge of Military Commander Watson, subject to such disposi-"tion as you may be pleased to make." Executive Document, 2d Session 30th Congress, Vol. I, pages 1021, 1022. And J. B. Montgomery, the Commander U. S. Navy who took the town of San Francisco for the Americans, under date of July 20, 1846, reports to his superior :

"I sent an officer on Friday to the rancho of Don Francisco Guer-"rero, late sub-prefect of this department, who came in on the summons, "and having delivered the papers of his department, which appeared "to be of little importance, was permitted to return on his parol of "honor not to go beyond the limits of this district without my pass-"port; neither to instigate, take part in, or in any way to countenance "movements or designs against the existing government or peace of "the country." Exec. Doc. as above, pp. 1029, 1030. That the United States Government thus got possession of the archives of the Mission and of the Sub-Prefecture of the Juzgado of San Francisco, thus appears very clearly. That the documents thus obtained were the very documents most needed to elucidate the history of the Pueblo of San Francisco, is very evident from the inspection of the document Exhibit No. 1, annexed to the testimony of R. C. Hopkins, as above mentioned. What has become of these documents? Where are they? *We trace*

*them into the possession of the Government; what has the Government
done with them?* Happily the existence of the PUEBLO can be clearly
and indisputably established by the authentic original documents which
have not been lost or mislaid, many of which we have discovered and
produced for the first time in evidence. The most important and interesting of the proofs and illustrations in the case are printed and annexed to this argument under the designation of ADDENDA. They are
published in full, because their purport could not be easily understood
from selected extracts; and their length is amply compensated by their
value, especially since it is graphically asserted in these latter times
that the claim of Hispano-American Pueblos to four leagues of land is
"a new pretense never heard of until since the conquest of California."
These documents will ever remain monuments of the wise and pious
benevolence which characterized the Colonial Policy of Spain. The
original Spanish has been interjected in many phrases which are made
the subject of comment. Many of the translations are absolutely gro-
tesque in their solecisms and want of accuracy, frequently obscuring,
and often reversing the sense of the original; but these are the translations which both suitors and the United States were formerly obliged
to accept at the hands of some of the official translators, who, it is to
be hoped, understood Spanish, for they certainly did not understand
English. These remarks do not apply to the early translations furnished by Hartnell, Halleck, and some others, which are admirable,
although sometimes liable to criticism when we descend from generic
to specific terms.

DEFINITION OF TERMS.

§ **7.** Before proceeding to the argument of the case, it is necessary
to define certain terms which will be of frequent recurrence, and some
of which have no exact synonyms in the English law. I shall make
my own definitions, giving my authority for each of them, reserving,
of course, to my opponents the right to criticise, to invalidate, and to
destroy them. As I have chosen a synthetic form for my argument, I
shall make no excuse for following that form in all its exigencies,
among which I include those of definition. Says Locke: "Before
"entering into a discussion, be sure that you and your opponent are
"agreed as to the meaning of the terms employed, for I have known
"persons engaged a full ten days in discussing topics, and have finally
"found that they were perfectly agreed, only that they differed in the
"meaning of the terms employed."

DEPARTMENT—DISTRICT—PARTIDO.

§ **8.** Sometimes the Mexican Republic was under a Federative
Constitution, and then the Californias were called DEPARTMENTS, a
designation corresponding to the TERRITORIES of the United States;
at others, the Constitution of Mexico was centralized, and then, also,
the Californias were called DEPARTMENTS. Each Department was
divided into Districts; and each District into two Partidos. Under

either form the actual division of the Californias was the same. A Prefect presided over the District, and a Sub-Prefect over the Partido. See Constitutional Laws of 1821—1822 ; Constitutional Laws 1836, ADDENDA No. LXIX, page 100. Leyes Vigentes, 45.

PUEBLO.

§ 9. The term PUEBLO answers to that of the English word Town, in all its vagueness, and all its precision. As the word town in English generally embraces every kind of population from the Village to the City, and also, used specifically, signifies a town "corporate and politic," so the word PUEBLO in Spanish, ranges from the hamlet to the city, but, used emphatically, signifies a town "corporate and politic." San José was a pure pueblo, organized as such ; so was Los Angeles, until raised in 1835 to the rank of a city. (Recopilacion de Arrillaya, A. D. 1835, p. 189.) We contend that San Francisco was a PUEBLO especial, a body politic and corporate, or *quasi*-corporate, thoroughly organized as a politico-economical Municipality, and the word PUEBLO, employed without any restriction, is used in this sense in this argument. At the same time the word PUEBLO was often used, and will often be found used in the documentary evidence in this case, in the sense of village. Thus the miserable, abandoned, forfeited Indian hamlet at the Mission Dolores, is sometimes called "Pueblo of Dolores," which is an instance of the application of the word in its generic sense of settlement. The Spaniards preferred the word LUGAR to that of PUEBLO. The Hispano-Americans commonly used the word PUEBLO, probably because the American PUEBLOS differed so much from the Spanish LUGARES, as we have before shown : the variation in the terms denoted the specific varieties of members of the same general family, and the word PUEBLO as used in America, denoted one of the emancipated, homogeneous, American PUEBLOS which owed their existence to the experience, wisdom, piety, and bounty of the Kings of Spain. See ante §§ 2 to 5 of this argument.

But, without some further distinctions, we shall mislead ourselves. A PUEBLO manifested itself in various ways. It had a *political* jurisdiction, embracing all the *legal voters*, within a certain territory. It had a *judicial* jurisdiction, as "by 'termino Jurisdiccional,' Jurisdiction, "'Partido,' or 'Distrito,' is understood all that is comprised within the "limits to which the *jurisdiction* of the Alcalde or Judge of the Pue-"blo extends." Governor Gutierrez, Jan. 25, 1836, ADDENDA No. XXXIII, page 51, 3d ¶ from the foot. It had also a *proprietary* existence, embraced in the phrase "termino municipal," "fundo legal," "the lands owned by the corporation:" "that land which has been "assigned to the PUEBLOS for the relief of their herds, within which "neither the cattle nor inhabitants of neighboring PUEBLOS can enter, "for the purpose of grazing or cutting wood, without being denounced, "[prosecuted?] unless they have some letter of commonalty." Governor Gutierrez, Jan. 25, 1836, ADDENDA No. XXXIII, page 51, 2d ¶ from the foot. So far as the documentary testimony throws any light

on the subject, the *political* and *judicial* authority of the pueblos seems
to have extended to the same district or territory, and the *proprietary*
ownership to have been restricted within narrower limits, namely, to
the four leagues of land belonging to the pueblo, the "termino municipal." We shall see, in the course of this argument, how far these distinctions are justified and maintained.

PROPIOS AND ARBITRIOS.

§ **10.** The PROPIOS were such lands, houses, or other property of
cities and pueblos as were rented, and the proceeds thereof applied to
the payment of municipal expenses. Salvá, Dic. Esp.; Escriche, Dic.
de Legis. in verbo. ARBITRIOS, as applied to cities and pueblos, are
taxes, licenses, and other impositions laid upon certain trades, occupa-
tions, pursuits, conveniences and luxuries, in order to defray the municipal expenses. Escriche, Dic. de Legislacion; Salvá Dic. Esp. in
verbo. Febrero Mejicano, vol. 1, pp. 304, 305, etc. Escriche says :
" This property is a part of the patrimony of the Pueblo, and is ad-
" ministered by the Ayuntamiento, or a special board established for
" that purpose :—estos bienes patrimoniales del Pueblo se llaman *Pro-*
" *pios* y se administran por el Ayuntamiento ó una junta especial estab-
" lecida al intento :" in verbo *Bienes concejiles.* Says Governor Gutierrez, over the date of January 25th, 1836 : " The *terrenos de Propios*
" are lands assigned to the Ayuntamiento, so that by leasing them to
" the best bidders, for a term not exceeding five years, they may de-
" fray their expenses by the proceeds ; and the Ayuntamiento may
" propose the amount of rent, mentioning it in the petition which is
" presented." See ADDENDA, No. XXXIII, page 51, last ¶ on the
page.

SUERTES, SOLARES, SITIOS.

§ **11.** SUERTES were the cultivable lots of land granted to colonists in California, near the Pueblos, and within the four leagues assigned to the Pueblo. Each SUERTE is defined by the Regulations of
Colonization of Felipe de Neve of 1779–1781, to consist of two hundred varas in length, and two hundred in breadth. See ADDENDA, No.
IV, § 5, page 4. The Spanish vara or yard, is 33 inches long. In the
Plan of Tepic, A. D.. 1789, the suertes are designated as being
200 × 400 varas. See ADDENDA, No. VII, Art. 14, page 13. But
their area is of no consequence ; it is sufficient for our present purpose, that they were tracts of cultivable lands granted to colonists.
SOLARES, [*Solum, area, Salvá,*] building lots, granted to colonists, and
which were to conform to a precise plan, and to the designated squares
and streets. Regulations of Felipe de Neve of 1779–1781. ADDENDA,
No. IV, § 4, page 4 ; Plan of Pitic. ADDENDA, No. VII, Art. 8, page
12. The word sitio originally meant only a " place," " *situ,*" and when
a person petitioned for a " sitio of land," he was understood to ask for
a " place " to live upon. But afterwards it came to have a more specific meaning : a " sitio de ganado mayor,—a sitio of large (neat) cattle," signifying a square of 5,000 Spanish varas, or yards ; and a " sitio

de ganado menor—of smaller cattle—sheep, etc." signifying a square of 3,333⅓ Spanish yards. Exec. Doc. 1st Sess., 31st Cong. Doc. 17, page 145. But "sitio," without any qualification, is generally understood to signify a square league of land, and will be so used in this argument.

AYUNTAMIENTO — REGIDOR — PROCURADOR — SINDICO — MUNICIPALIDAD.

§ **12.** The word Ayuntamiento is best rendered by the English term Common Council, [*commune* Council,] to which it exactly corresponds. If we restore the word to its barbarous Latin etymology, *adjungamentum*, its force becomes at once apparent. "AYUNTAMIENTO: el " congreso ó junta compuesta de la justicia ó alcalde regidores y demas " individuos encargados de la administracion ó gobierno economico-po- " litico de cada pueblo. Suele llmarse tambien rejimiento, cabildo, con- " cejo, *municipalidad* y cuerpo municipal. Escriche Dic. de Legisla- " cion, in verbo. Ayuntamiento : the body or legislature composed of " the justice, or alcalde, the regidores, and the like persons who are " entrusted with the administration or politico-economical government " of each pueblo. It is also called Regimiento, [decurionum consessus ; " Salvá] Cabildo, [Senatus municipalis ; Salvá ;] concejo, [council ;] " Municipalidad, [Municipality ;] y cuerpo municipal, [municipal " body.] Salvá gives the term the same substantial definition, and adds the Latin definitions : *Congressus, Senatus, Coetus.*

REGIDOR, a common Councilman ; an Alderman. " Cada uno de " los individuos del Ayuntamiento encargados del gobierno economico " de los pueblos. *Decurio.*—Each of the persons belonging to the " Ayuntamiento who are entrusted with the economical government of " the Pueblos." SALVA Dic. Esp. in verbo.

" PROCURADOR SINDICO. El sugeto que en los ayuntamientos ó " concejos tiene el cargo de promover los intereses de los pueblos, " defiende sus derechos, y se queja de los agravios que se les " hacen. Tiene asiento en los ayuntamientos. *Procurator syn-* " *dicus, municipii tribunus.* Procurador sindico : the person who " in the Common Council is charged with promoting the interests " of the Pueblos, defending their rights, and complaining [remedy- " ing by suit] public injuries when they occur. He has a seat " in the Common Council." SALVA, Diccionario Espanol in verbo. The functions of Procurador really answered to Fisc and City Attorney. So here we have Ayuntamiento, or Common Council ; Regidores, Council men or Aldermen ; and Procurador Sindico, or City Attorney, and Fisc, in exact correspondence to the organization and officers of an American or English Municipality. But it will be observed and hereafter shown, that although a PUEBLO could not have its Ayuntamiento, Councilmen and Attorney, without being fully organized and entitled to all the rights of a Pueblo, yet the converse was not true, and a Pueblo might be fully organized, and entitled to all the rights, political and proprietary, including its four square leagues of land, without having an Ayuntamiento. Or, it might have an Ayuntamiento, and lose it, without losing its political or proprietory rights. for the basis upon which an Ayuntamiento rested was that of population; a basis often numerically changed by positive law, and often shifting from various causes. See §§ 47, 89 to 92 of this argument.

"MUNICIPALIDAD. Vos que va introduciendose sin necesidad en "lugar de Ayuntamiento ó Concejo—a word which is unnecessarily "getting itself introduced in place of ' Common Council.' " SALVA, Dic. Esp. in verbo.

BIENES CONCEJILES. [TOWN PROPERTY.]

§ 13. " BIENES CONCEJILES—Los que en cuanto á la propiedad "pertenecen al comun ó concejo de una ciudad, villa ó lugar, y en "cuanto al uso á todas y cada una de sus vecinos; como las fuentes, "montes, dehesas, pastos, etc. Partida 3, tit. 28, Ley. 9. TOWN " PROPERTY. That which in respect of ownership belongs to the pub- "lic or council of a city, villa, or town, and in respect of its use belongs "to every one of its inhabitants, such as fountains, woods, the pas- "tures, etc." Escriche, Dic. de Legislacion, in verbo. " Town Property," is the English synomym which both popularly and logically includes the definition.

EJIDOS, OR EXIDOS.

§ 14. EJIDOS or EXIDOS, [*Exitus*, Salvá, Dic. Esp.] The vacant *suburbs* of the PUEBLO. Our English word *commons* well translates this term, and I should employ that word exclusively were it not that it seems to have misled some of our early translators, who, with a stupidity which seems almost malicious, have translated *ejidos* by " common lands," as if it included the pasture grounds of the PUEBLO, as well as the "commons." Instances of this mistranslation will occur in many of the documents in this case which both parties have been compelled to accept at the hands of the official translators. But it simply means the *vacant* suburbs, and nothing more. Says Governor Gutierrez, in 1836: " By Ejidos, are understood lands that are immediate to and in "the circumference of the Pueblo, which serve both for the relief and "the convenience of the inhabitants, who may keep therein a few "milch cows and horses for their use, and to form walks or alleys which "may adorn the entrance of the place, so that the ejidos may have a "quarter or half a league around the town, which is sufficient for its "ventilation, and the Ayuntamiento may dispose of these lands for "building lots, [solares.]" See Expediente of the Presidial-Pueblo of Monterey, respecting its Ejidos, or Suburbs. ADDENDA, No. XXXIII, page 52, ¶ 2d. " EJIDOS—El campo ó tierra que está á la salida del " lugar, y no se planta ni se labra, y es common para todos los vecinos. "Viene de la palabra latina *exitus* que significa *salida*. Los ejidos "de cada Pueblo estan destinados al uso comun de sus moradores: na- "die por consiguiente puede apropiarselos, ni ganarlos por prescripcion, " ni edificar en ellos, ni mandarlos en legado. EJIDOS: The field or land

"which is at the exit of the town, and can neither be planted nor cul-
"tivated, and is common to all the citizens. It comes from the Latin
"word *exitus*, which signifies the exit, or suburbs. The *ejidos* of each
"Pueblo are designated for the common use of its inhabitants: conse-
"quently no one can appropriate them, nor acquire them by prescription,
"nor build on them, nor devise them." Escriche, Dic. de Legislacion,
in verbo. These *ejidos* are recognized in the Regulations of Felipe de
Neve, 1779—1781. ADDENDA, No. IV, § 4, page 4, and receive the
same definition above given, in the Plan of Pitic, 1787. ADDENDA,
No. VII, Art. 11, page 13. They were, therefore, a portion of the
most inalienable patrimony of the Pueblo; they could be alienated
only for the purpose of granting solares, or building lots, as Governor
Gutierrez says above, and this only from absolute necessity, for the
growth of the Pueblo would otherwise be circumscribed. By Law 13,
Title VII, Book IV, of the Leyes de los Indias, each Pueblo was
entitled to have its ejidos assigned out of its domain. This peculiarity
of the vacant suburbs often appears in comparative jurisprudence. On
this subject we can consult with interest and profit "Le Recueil Alpha-
betique de Questions de Droit," par Merlin, Tome III, page 396, aux
titres COMMUNE et COMMUNAUX, (biens,) for a résumé of the French
jurisprudence on that point, which, it may well be presumed, has
repeated itself throughout all modern Europe. The same inviolability
was early recognized in the Hebrew theocracy: "the field of the suburbs of their cities may not be sold; for it is their *perpetual possession.*"
Leviticus 34.

These PUEBLOS were usually called *Pueblos de Españoles*—Spanish
Pueblos, or *Pueblos de gente de razon*—*Pueblos of People of reason*—
to distinguish them from those of the Indians, who were not supposed
to have that faculty. Concerning *Indian* Pueblos, see § 17 of this
argument.

DEHESAS.

§ **15.** The Dehesas were the *great* Pasture grounds where the
large herds of the Pueblos roamed and grazed. An attempt has been
made to confound them with the Ejidos (respecting which see ante
§ 14), and "ejidos y dehesas" are often translated in one phrase as
"commons" or "pasture grounds." But *dehesa* receives its definition
in the Plan of Pitic (see ADDENDA No. VII, Art. 13, page 13, where
it is designated as "la dehesa ó Prado Boyal—*"Pratum bovinum*—
the GREAT HERD PASTURE. In this same article it is also contradistinguished from the ejidos: "los ejidos y á la dehesa, the ejidos *and*
"the dehesa." In the Regulations of Felipe de Neve, the same contra-
distinction is observed: "exido competente para el pueblo, y Dehesas;
"ejidos *and* dehesas;" § 4. See ADDENDA, No. IV, § 4, page 4, and
in § 8 of the same we have again "exido y dehesa." As we proceed
in the course of this narrative we shall find that *ejidos* has often been
translated "commons, common property and landed property;" that
"dehesas" has often been rendered by the same terms, and "ejidos y
"dehesas" again translated by the same terms, as if they were equiva-

lent. But as we have seen, ante §§ 13 and 14 and in this section, although both these terms were *generically* included in "commons," "landed property" and "town property," yet *specifically* they were different. *Ejidos* being those commons or vacant suburbs at the exit of the Pueblo which could never be sold, and *dehesas* the great cattle pastures in which the inhabitants had a right of commons, but which the Government could dispose of,—which the Government at one time *did* order to be sold,—and the greater part of which belonging to the Pueblo of San Francisco, the Government did actually grant to set- tlers, while at the same time the *ejidos* were positively forbidden to be granted or sold. See ADDENDA, No. XI, page 20, § 1, etc. By Law 14, Title VII, Book IV, of the Leyes de las Indias, each Pueblo was entitled to have its dehesas assigned.*

HOW THE PUEBLO LANDS MIGHT BE DIVIDED.

§ **16.** Assuming that a Pueblo was entitled to four leagues of land, these lands were *capable* of being divided into several portions, each assigned to its respective uses. FIRST, the site of the town proper, including the public square and streets, the building lots fronting on them, and the *propios* to be rented for public revenue. De Neve's Regulations, ADDENDA, No. IV, § 4, page 4 ; Plan of Pitic, ADDENDA, No. VII, Art. 8, page 12. SECONDLY, the vacant Suburbs, or Ejidos, lying next to the Pueblo. See Ejidos, ante, § 14. THIRDLY, the Suertes or sowing grounds granted to each inhabitant. See ante, § 11. FOURTHLY, the Dehesas, or Great Cattle Pasture, lying beyond. See Dehesas, ante § 15. Common, everywhere, were the Montes y Aguas, the woods and waters. But although these four leagues *might* be thus divided, I do not find in the original law granting them to the Pueblos, nor in any subsequent enactment, any provisions imposing a forfeiture of the lands in case this division was not made. In fact the division depended upon the convenience of the Pueblo. It might or might not be made. But still the four leagues of land belonged to the Pueblo.

---

* NOTE.—DEHESAS.—We read in Catullus, LXXXII :

> " *Ch*ommoda dicebat, siquando commoda vellet
> Dicere, et *hin*sidias Arrius insidias.
> *   *   *   *   *   *
> Ionios fluctus, postquam iliuc Arius isset
> Jam non Ionios esse sed Hionios."

The introduction of the aspirate by the Latin provincials, the supplanting of a letter by the aspirate, and the final softening and disappearance of the aspirate itself, with the substitution of cognate letters, will solve many etymological mysteries in French and Spanish. Thus CABALLUS, *ch*aballus, *ch*eval. CASA, *ch*asa, *ch*ez. FILLUS, *fh*ilio, hilio, hijo. CONCILIUM, concilio, concejo. CABALLUS, caballo, cabayo, cavayo. But *dehesas* presents an unusual modification of the original word : DEFENSAS, def*h*ensas, dehesas, and sometimes deesas. Our English word "fence " is of the same etymology as dehesas. Says Escriche, Dic. Razonado de Legislacion : "Dehesa viene del verbo " latino *defendere* que significa defender ó prohibir"—"It comes from the Latin word *defendere*, which signifies to defend or prohibit." This was because neighboring pro- prietors were *prohibited* to pasture their flocks on the *dehesas*.

COMUNIDAD—COMMUNITY. INDIAN PUEBLOS.

§ **17.** By the term Comunidad—Community, as used in the Spanish and Hispano-American law, I understand to be primarily designated a " body or congregation of persons who are united under certain consti- " tutions or rulers, such as convents, colleges and other similar bodies : " la junta ó congregacion de personas que viven unidas bajo ciertas " constituciones y reglas, como los conventos, colegios, y otros cuerpos " semejantes." Escriche Dic. Razonado de Legis., et Jurispr. in verbo comunidad. In England, where religious communities have for the greater part been abolished, and in the United States, where they have scarcely ever existed, the term community has become expanded into an indefinite application. But I shall insist, and hope to demonstrate, that in the Hispano-American law, the term " comunidad " never ceased to preserve its specific meaning, and was always applied to a body of persons living in " community " in the proper sense of the term. Thus we shall see that while the body of the citizens of the Pueblo of San Francisco was styled " the Municipality," " the Corpo- ration," " the Public,—*el comun,*" the Mission of Dolores was styled " the community,—*la communidad,*" that being the very term of law which defined the body of the Indian residents there, and their rights and relations to each other. The *Indian* Pueblos were of early origin. It was the policy of Spain, adopted as early as the year 1551 by the Emperor Charles V, and never departed from by his successors, that the Indians should be induced and compelled to live together in villages, this being considered the only possible condition of their becoming civilized. The ordinances decreed for this purpose are exceedingly minute and well digested, and are principally to be found in the Leyes de las Indios, Lib. V, titulo III. It was decreed that the Indians should be settled in villages ; that churches should be estab- lished for them ; that they should be governed by *Indian* Alcaldes, and *Indian* Regidores (council-men) ; that no Indian should remove from his own village to another, nor live outside of his own village ; that no Spaniard, negro, mestizo, or mulatto should live in an *Indian* Pueblo, even though he bought lands there ; that no Spaniard should sojourn in an *Indian* Pueblo beyond one day after the day of his arrival, and other like provisions of police. *Ibid.* It will be difficult to recognize any of these features in the PUEBLO of San Francisco, upon whose history we are about entering. The interesting fact of *Indian* Alcaldes and *Indian* Common-Council men will among others, be entirely wanting. The lands belonging to *Indian* Pueblos were called *Tierras de Comunidad.*

ESPEDIENTE—EXPEDIENTE. INFORME. VISTA. BORRADOR.

§ **18.** The first two of these terms, which are of the same ety- mology,—*negotia* EXPEDIRE—signify that collection of papers or docu- ments which shows the despatch or *expedition* of a matter in hand. In an ordinary grant of lands the *espediente,* or collected documents will generally consist of :

FIRST : The *petition,* setting out the situation, qualifications and claims of the petitioner.

SECONDLY: The *informe* or marginal order of the Governor, directing the respective (proper) inferior officer to *inform* himself and report to the Governor.

THIRDLY: The report of the respective officers.

FOURTHLY: The vista, or order of the Governor upon the report, so called because it almost always begins, "*Vista—having seen*," etc., which contains the grant or refusal of the Governor, and the *borrador* or rough draft of the grant, if one is made.

FIFTHLY: Any proceeding taken afterwards by the Departmental Junta, or Assembly, approving or disapproving the action of the Governor.

But in relation to any proceedings, the whole bundle (or, as the French say) the "dossier" of all the documents relating to any executive or administrative proceeding is called the "espediente," or as we say in Anglo-American English, "the Documents." Thus when the Ayuntamiento of the PRESIDIAL-PUEBLO of Monterey, in the year 1836 applied to have the EJIDOS of that PUEBLO assigned, the *whole series of documents* promoted (instituted) on that occasion are called ESPEDIENTE—EXPEDIENTE. See ADDENDA, No. XXXIII, page 49. So when certain citizens of the Department of Upper California wished, A. D. 1836, to separate themselves from the jurisdiction of the Ayuntamiento of the PUEBLO of San Francisco, and attach themselves to the jurisdiction of the PUEBLO of San José, the whole bundle (*dossier* en Français) of documents relating to that proceeding is styled in Spanish, the "*Espediente.*" See ADDENDA, No. XXIX, page 44, etc. "ESPEDIENTE," Spanish, the bundle of papers showing how the matter was *expedited;* the *dossier* in French, the papers whose *endorsement* sufficiently indicated their contents; the "documents," as the Anglo-Americans expectorate the term; the "Record," in legitimate Anglo-Norman English; the papers showing "what it is all about" in the language of the frontiers. This term will be of constant recurrence. The Hispano-Americans, among other traditions, had that of order, association, and arrangement. They attached each "document" to the one which immediately preceded it in its respective series. Consequently their Archives have an extraordinary reliability, always excepting the case of theft, or of a systematic spoliation. As this argument is cast in a narrative, or popular form, it does not seem amiss to define anew this familiar law term.

THE PUEBLOS OF CALIFORNIA.

§ **19.** Historical events, arranged and narrated in the order of their respective dates, follow each other in a natural logical sequence, and as the strength of my argument is derived from the constantly-recurring recognition of the Pueblo of San Francisco by all the legislative. executive, and ministerial authorities of California during a long period of years, I shall content myself by presenting, FIRST, a succinct history of the colonization of this country, and SECONDLY a specific history of the settlement and progress of this PUEBLO.

The Pueblos of California originated in three different ways. FIRST, there were PUEBLOS which were founded *as such:* the Pueblo (after-wards city) of Los Angeles, the Pueblo of San José, and the Villa of Branciforté were of this class.

SECONDLY : PUEBLOS which originated in the settlement of the PRESIDIOS, and grew up under their protection. Of these PRESIDIAL-PUEBLOS there were four, namely : the PUEBLO of San Diego, the PUEBLO of Santa Barbara, the PUEBLO of Monterey, and the PUEBLO OF SAN FRANCISCO.

THIRDLY : PUEBLOS which grew out of Mission establishments. Of these last, a few struggled into a transient existence, but under such circumstances as to leave the circumstances of their origin in great obscurity. See ADDENDA, No. LXII, page 89, § 2.

THREE-FOLD PLAN OF THIS COLONIZATION OF CALIFORNIA : MISSIONS, PRESIDIOS, AND PUEBLOS, INCLUDING PRESIDIAL-PUEBLOS.

§ 20. The plan for the colonization of California was, therefore, three-fold : RELIGIOUS, MILITARY, and CIVIL.

" At the same time that the monks established MISSIONS to civilize " the Indians, the Governors founded military posts called PRESIDIOS, " and PUEBLOS (villages) composed of married soldiers and white " colonists who were brought from Sonora, Sinaloa, and Lower Califor-nia." 1 De Mofras, 261. A description of each of these establish-ments will show how impossible it is to confound the PUEBLOS of the whites with the missionary establishments founded for the christianiza-tion and civilization of the Indians, and particularly how distinct a PRESIDIAL-PUEBLO,—a PUEBLO growing up under the protection of a PRESIDIO and becoming an off-shoot from it,—was from any and every form of organized population which could result from either the success or the destruction of a MISSION of christianized Indians.

A. D. 1642—1773.
FOUNDATION OF THE MISSIONS. JESUIT VOYAGES.

§ 21. " In 1642, the Viceroy, the Duke of Escalona, sent into " Lower California the Governor of Sinaloa, with some members of " the Society of Jesus, to found missions there, and civilize the Indi-" ans." " Exploration de l'Oregon et des Californies pendant les années 1840, 1841, 1842, par M. Duflot de Mofras, attaché à la Légation de France à Mexico,"—Vol. I, p. 102. M. Duflot de Mofras, an attaché of the French Legation at Mexico, was detached from that service in 1840, by Marshal Soult, at that time President of the Privy Council of Louis Phillippe, for the purpose of making a thorough reconnoissance of California and Oregon. This work he accomplished in the most faithful manner, and the results, embracing the most extended and accurate description of California, its natural history, climatology, social condition, politics, legislation, and religious institutions, and containing even plans and soundings of its harbors, with sailing directions for entering them from the ocean, were published at Paris by order of the

King, in 1846, in two volumes, 8vo., being the book above cited. It is a work of the highest authority, and was doubtless prepared as a *hand-book* for the acquisition of California by the French. De Mofras does not profess to have been in California later than 1842; and his work contains internal evidence that that year terminated his visit to that country.

"In 1683, the Admiral Atondo went to La Paz, (on the eastern "shore of the Gulf of California), with the Jesuit Fathers. Salva-"tierra and Eusebius Kino, (Kuhn) a learned astronomer from Ingol-"stadt. It is from the date of this epoch that the regular clergy *(reli-"giosos)* were invested with the ecclesiastical, civil, and military ad-"ministration of the missions. In a short time they succeeded in con-"verting all Lower California, (the peninsula), and the plan which "they adopted will always serve as a model." De Mofras, Vol. I, p. 103. "In 1701 and 1703, Father Kuhn made his celebrated explora-"tions to the north of California, and on the river Colorado. King "Philip V granted to the Jesuit Missions in California an annual "pension of $13,000." De Mofras, Vol. I, p. 104. "In 1719, Fa-"ther Guillen, and in 1721, Father Ugarte, extended the domains "of their Missions, by means of several expeditions by land in Califor-"nia." De Mofras, Vol. I, p. 105. "In 1746, Father Consag ex-"plored the river Colorado, with the design of organizing other mis-"sions, which should render an overland route practicable from Sonora "to California." De Mofras, Vol. I, p. 106.

THE JESUITS SUPPRESSED. THE MISSIONS CEDED TO THE FRAN-CISCANS.

§ 22. The Jesuits continued to extend their geographical limits, and to govern their missions in the most paternal manner until the year 1767, when they ceded them to the Franciscans of the Royal College of San Fernando at Mexico. De Mofras, Vol. I, p. 106. "By "order of Charles III, King of Spain, the Marquis de Croix, Viceroy "of Mexico, and the Inspector-General (Visitador) of that Kingdom, "Don Joseph de Galvez, on the 25th of June, suppressed the Society "of Jesus, and entrusted to the Franciscan Monks of the College of "San Fernando at Mexico, the administration of the Missions which the "Jesuits up to that time had managed with so much wisdom and suc-"cess. The various donations and real estate which constituted the "'Pious Fund of California' passed into the hands of the Franciscans, "*(fondo piadoso de California)*. Sixteen of these monks, by direction "of their Apostolic Prefect, the Reverend Father Junipero Serra, em-"barked at Loreto, Lower California,. in April, 1758. On July 16, of "the same year, the Inspector-General of New Spain, arrived in per-"son, bearer of a royal order commanding him to found a missionary "establishment either at the port of Monterey, or at that of San Die-"go." De Mofras, Vol. I, p. 255.

A. D. 1772.

THE FRANCISCANS YIELD THE MISSIONS OF LOWER CALIFORNIA
TO THE DOMINICANS, AND ESTABLISH THEMSELVES IN UPPER
CALIFORNIA.

§ 23. But this success of a rival order excited the zeal of the
DOMINICANS, who demanded a share of this new field of missionary
labor; the result of which was that the Dominicans of Mexico obtained
a royal rescript, by which the FRANCISCANS were ordered to surren-
der to the DOMINICANS the administration of one or two Missions.
"The Reverend Warden of the College of San Fernando, remarked,
"with reason, that the province of Lower California (where most of
"the Missions were at that time,) could not be divided; that its limits
"were well defined; and that serious inconveniences would arise if the
"two orders were found in competition in the same territory. He con-
"cluded by offering to the Dominicans, in case they would take exclu-
"sive charge of the whole province (of Lower California) from Cape
"St. Lucas to the port of San Diego, to cede to them, together with
"all the Missions then lately administered by the Jesuits, also that of
"Fernando de Vellicata, and the five others which were yet to be es-
"tablished there. The Viceroy assembled the Council, and on April
"30th, 1772, decreed that the above agreement should be carried into
"effect. It was not, however, until the 1st of May of the following
"year, that the Dominicans entered into definitive possession of Lower
"California, and that the Franciscans retired into Upper California,
"where, being able to concentrate all their efforts upon a territory less
"extensive and more fertile, they soon obtained results which command
"admiration. At the end of fourteen years, Father Junipero, who
"died in 1784, had already founded fifteen Missions of Indians, or vil-
"lages of Spanish colonists." 1 De Mofras, 259. In the printed AD-
DENDA at the end of this argument, No. LXVII, page 97, will be found
a tabular statement of the foundation of all the Missions of Upper California, as well as a succinct history of their greatest prosperity and
subsequent ruin.

DESCRIPTION OF A MISSION.

§ 24. DE MOFRAS takes as a type of the Missions, that of SAN
LUIZ REY, which was like the others in its management and discipline,
and differed from them only in a superior architecture and extent of
decoration. "The building is a quadrilateral. The church occupies
"one of its wings; the façade is ornamented with a gallery. The
"building, raised some feet above the soil, is two stories in height. The
"interior is formed by a court. Upon the gallery, which runs around
"it, open the dormitories of the monks, of the major-domos, and of
"travellers; small work-shops, school-rooms, and store-rooms. The
"hospitals are situated in the most quiet parts of the Mission, where
"the schools also are kept. The young Indian girls dwell in the halls
"called the Monastery (el monjero) and they themselves are called

2

" nuns, (las monjas); they are obliged to be secluded to be secure from
" outrage by the Indians. Placed under the care of Indian matrons,
" who are worthy of confidence, they learn to make cloths of wool, cot-
" ton, and flax, and do not. leave the monastery until they are old
" enough to be married. The Indian children mingle in the schools
" with those of the white colonists. A certain number, chosen among
" the pupils who display the most. intelligence, learn music, chanting,
" the violin, the flute, the horn, the violincello, and other instruments.
" Those who distinguish themselves in the carpenter's shop, at the
" forge, or in agricultural labors, are appointed Alcalde's, or chiefs,
" (overseers), and charged with the direction of a squad of workmen.
" Before the civil power was substituted for the paternal government
" of the missionaries, the administrative body of each Mission con-
" sisted of two monks, of whom the elder had charge of the interior,
" and of the religious instruction, and the younger of the agricultural
" works. In order to maintain morals and good order in the Missions,
" they employed only so many whites as were absolutely necessary, for
" they well knew that their influence was wholly pernicious, and that
" an association with them only developed among the Indians those
" habits of gambling and drunkenness to which they are unfortunately
" too much inclined." 1 De Mofras, 261 etc. " The regulations of each
" Mission were the same. The Indians were divided into squads of
" laborers. At sunrise the bell sounded the angelus, and every one
" set out for the church. After mass they breakfasted, and then went
" to work. At eleven they dined, and this period of repose extended
" to two o'clock, when they returned to labor until the evening angelus,
" one hour before sunset. After prayers and the rosary, the Indians
" had supper, and then amused themselves with dancing and other
" sports. Their diet consisted of fresh beef and mutton, as much as
" they chose; of wheat and corn cakes, and of boiled puddings (or por-
" ridges) called *atole* and *pinole*. They also had peas, large or small
" beans, in all an ' almud,' or the twelfth part of a bushel (fanega) a
" week. For dress, they wore a linen shirt, pantaloons, and a woollen
" blanket; but the overseers and best workmen had habits of cloth, like
" the Spaniards. The women received every year, two chemises, a
" gown, and a blanket. When the hides, tallow, grain, wine, and oil
" were sold at good prices to ships from abroad, the monks distributed
" handkerchiefs, wearing apparel, tobacco, chaplets, and glass trinkets
" among the Indians, and devoted the surplus to the embellishment of
" the churches, the purchase of musical instruments, pictures, sacerdo-
" tal ornaments, etc. Still, they were careful to keep a part of their
" harvest in the granaries, to provide for years of scarcity." 1 De Mofras, 263, 267.

DESCRIPTION OF A PRESIDIO.

§ **25.** " All the PRESIDIOS were established on the same plan:
" Choosing a favorable place, they surrounded it by a ditch, twelve
" feet wide and six deep. The earth of the ditch served for the out-

"work. The enclosure of the Presidio was formed by a quadrilateral, "about six hundred feet square. The rampart, built of brick, was "twelve to fifteen feet high, by three in thickness; small bastions "flanked the angles; the Presidio had but two gates. Its armament "generally consisted of eight bronze cannon, eight, twelve, and sixteen "pounders. Although incapable of resisting an attack of ships of war, "these fortifications were sufficient to repel the incursions of the Indi- "ans. Not far from the Presidios, according to the topography of the "land, was an open battery, (batterie découverte) pompously styled "'the castle,' (castillo). Within the enclosure of the Presidio were "the church, the quarters of the officers and soldiers, the houses of col- "onists, store-houses, work-shops, stables, wells, and cisterns. Outside "were grouped some houses, and at a little distance was the 'King's "Farm,' (el rancho del rey,) which furnished pasturage to the horses "and beasts of burden of the garrison. Four coast batteries and four "presidios defended Upper California. Those of San Diego, founded "in 1769; Monterey, in 1770; SAN FRANCISCO, in 1776; and Santa "Barbara, in 1780. After the year 1770, the infantry in all these "garrisons were replaced by dragoons, called (compañias de cuera,) "companies with leather armor. These soldiers, who formed the pre- "sidial garrisons of all New Spain, wore, besides their ordinary cloth "uniform, a sort of buckskin dress, like a coat of mail, which descen- "ded to the feet, and was impenetrable to arrows. They wore this uni- "form only when in the field, and at the moment of combat, with a "double visored helmet; a leathern buckler worn on the left arm, "served to ward off arrows and thrusts of the lance in single combat; "but, while they defended themselves with the sabre or the lance, they "could use neither their pistols nor their muskets. The horses them- "selves, like those of the old knights of chivalry, were covered with "leathern armor." 1 De Mofras, 279, 281. "The equipment of each "Presidio was a Lieutenant, with a pay of $550; a Health Officer, "$450; an Ensign, $400; a Sergeant, $265; a Corporal, $225; and "seventy soldiers at $217 each. Each soldier had seven horses and "a mule, kept on the King's Farm. Artillerymen were furnished "from the marine department of San Blas. The whole establishment "of Presidio and forts, including the pay of the Governor, at $4,000, "(he having the rank of Lieutenant Colonel,) was $55,000 per an- "num." 1 De Mofras, 287. PRESIDIUM and PRESIDIO :—we have here the vital and persistent tradition of the Roman Camp, thus plant- ing itself in the American wilderness, and perpetuating its name for a period which cannot be estimated.

THE MISSIONS HAD NO PROPERTY IN LANDS.

§ 26. "The term 'Mission' includes only the collection of houses, "vineyards and orchards in the immediate vicinity of the churches, in- "cluding the stock of cattle, and other personal property in the posses- "sion of the priests, and useful and necessary in carrying on the es- "tablishments. The 'Mission lands,' lands adjacent and appurtenant

"to the Missions, used by them for grazing purposes, were occupied
"by them only by permission, but were the property of the nation, and
"at àll times subject to grant under the Colonization Laws.," Ritchie's
Case, 17 Howard, U. S. S. C. Rep., pages 540, 561; Jones' Rep., 13.
These are the definitions and propositions of the law-Executive of the
United States Government.   But the Missionaries from the beginning
resisted the application of this principle, and denounced as a robbery
every attempt to convert any of the adjacent lands to private or secular purposes.   An intelligent Spanish traveler, quoted by Mr. Bryant,
writes, in 1822, as follows: "The Missions *extend their possession*
"*from one extremity of the territory to another, and have made the*
"*limits of one Mission form those of another.*   Though they do not
"require all this land for their *agriculture and the maintenance of their*
"*stock, they have appropriated the whole; always strongly opposing any*
"*individual who may wish to settle himself or his family on any piece*
"*between them.*   But it is to be hoped that the new system of illus-
"tration, [enlightenment?] and the necessity of augmenting private
"property, and the people of reason, (*gente de razon*, white population,)
"will cause the Government to take such adequate measures as will
"conciliate the interests of all."   Bryant's California, page 281.   These
immoderate pretensions of the monks undoubtedly hastened, if they
did not invoke, the project of secularization.   It may appear strange
that when it became inevitable that the lands adjacent to the Missions
must be granted to private settlers, the Missionaries did not then
protect themselves at once and forever, by procuring the limits of their
lands to be fixed, and formally granted to them.   The answer to this
suggestion is, that *the Missions were never intended to be permanent
establishments.*   The following from the opinion of Judge Felch, in the
California Board of Land Commissioners, in the case of the Bishop
of California's petition for the churches, etc., at the Missions which
were finally confirmed to him, clearly and concisely expresses the
theory of the Missionary colonization: "The Missions were intended,
"from the beginning, to be temporary in their character.   *It was con-*
"*templated that in ten years from their first foundation they should cease.*
"It was supposed that within that period of time the Indians would be
"sufficiently instructed in Christianity and the arts of civilized life, to
"assume the position and character of *citizens;* that these Mission
"settlements would then become PUEBLOS, and that the Mission
"churches would become parish churches, organized like the other es-
"tablishments of an ecclesiastical character, in other portions of the
"nation where no Missions had ever existed.   The whole Missionary
"establishment was widely different from the ordinary ecclesiastical
"organization of the nation.   In it the superintendence and charge
"was committed to priests who were devoted to the special work of
"Missions, and not to the ordinary clergy.   The monks of the College
"of San Fernando and Zacatecas, in whose charge they were, were to
"be succeeded by the secular clergy of the National Church, the Mis-
"sionary field was to become a DIOCESE, the President of the Mis-
"sions to give place to a BISHOP, the Mission churches to become

" CURACIES, and the faithful in the vicinity of each parish to become " the parish worshippers."

This policy of the Spanish law incorporated into the Missionary system itself, thus forbade the assignment of the ownership of lands to any Mission, inasmuch as the law of extinguishment was stamped upon the Mission itself. Mr. William Carey Jones remarks that they were always " liable to be secularized, that is, their temporalities delivered " to lay administration; their character as Missions taken away by " their conversion into secular curacies under charge of the secular " clergy, and the lands appurtenant to them to be disposed of as other " domain." Jones's Rep. 13. As early as the year 1813, the Spanish Cortez showed its impatience at what even then seemed the protracted existence of the Missions, *as such*, by passing a law indicating its purpose to enforce their secularization. Id. When, therefore, we read of lands " belonging," " heretofore belonging," or " appurtenant" to a Mission, we shall understand that lands are spoken of which are or have at some time been in the possession of a Mission, for the temporary uses of the establishments, lands in which the Mission had an easement, servitude or usufruct, until terminated by some legitimate act of a competent superior authority.

THE TERMS " RELIGIOUS," " SECULAR " AND " SECULARIZATION."

§ **27.** The terms " religious " and " secular " are strongly contra-distinguished in the Catholic Church, which distinction enter into the written law of Spain. A " Religious " *(religioso)* is one who has taken the habit and the vows of one of the " *Regular* Orders," such as the Franciscans, the Dominicans, the Capuchins, and the like; hence he is also called a " Regular," or one of the " Regular Clergy." Having taken the three vows of chastity, obedience and poverty, he has renounced the world, and therefore is held to be *civilly dead.* For this reason he cannot make a contract, nor take or hold property, either by purchase or descent; nor sue or be sued; nor make a will; nor fill any fiduciary or civil office. A " Secular " Clergyman, (also called *clerigo*) who has not taken these vows, is not subject to these disabilities; he can contract, buy and sell; take by purchase or descent; make a will; and hold fiduciary and civil offices. He therefore has still a hold upon " secular " or worldly matters; hence the term " secular." A thing is also said to be " secularized " when it is changed from an " ecclesiastical " use, purpose, or control, to a secular one. *Escriche,* Diccionario de Legislacion; *Religioso, Clerigo, Secular y Secularizacion.* A Mission is therefore secularized when its temporalities are given in charge to a secular or civil officer, when its Missionary establishment is superceded, converted into a curacy, and given into the charge of a Secular Priest. Jones's Report, p. 13.

THE RIGHTS OF PUEBLOS, AS SUCH.

§ **28.** The Hispano-American laws recognized the mode of founding towns by contract, and provided ample compensation for such *em-*

presarios—contractors or undertakers—as would agree to make such settlements under certain fixed conditions. Thus it was enacted by an ordinance of King Philip the Second, (who died in 1598,) that to every such contractor founding such a settlement, composed of at least thirty heads of families, and complying with the requisite conditions, there should be given four square leagues of land, to be measured in a square, or in a prolonged parallellogram, according to the nature of the ground. Recopilacion de Leyes de los Reynos de las Indias, Lib. IV, Tit. V, Ley 6. (Vol. II, folio 89, Madrid edit. of 1774.) See the law in full, ADDENDA, No. I. Subsequently, the same privileges and the same donation of land were extended to any number of married men, not fewer than ten. Ibid. Lib. IV, Tit. V, Ley X, (Vol. II, fol. 89.) See the law in full, ADDENDA, No. II. It has been very ingeniously suggested that this law did not apply to New Spain, but was confined to Old Spain; probably because the law is found among the laws enacted for the *Indies* only, which included Mexico and New Spain, and because it provided against encroachment upon the rights of the *Indian Pueblos!* In effect, it is suggested that these laws did not apply to the Spanish colonies, because in truth they were specially devised for those colonies, and had no application to anything else!

No Special Grant of Land was Needed.

§ **29.** It is often asked where is the GRANT of these PUEBLO lands? Who has ever seen it? If a paper title, or a document written on parchment, signed, sealed and delivered, is to be produced, or its former existence proved, it may be conceded that there was no grant. But no such paper or parchment grant ever existed. It was enough that every PUEBLO, when it reached a certain state of development, became *ipso facto* entitled to certain rights in land. It is enough that that development was attained by the PUEBLO of San Francisco, was officially conceded to exist by the Government, and its rights in its Pueblo lands also recognized. It is not by an actual printed or written deed of conveyance that the present City of San Francisco holds its Beach and Water Lots, but only by a Legislative declaration in the form of a law. Laws 1851, chap. 41, page 307. When special corporations are created by a general statute, their general powers are not enumerated, but they obtain them from the general Act. Laws of 1850, page 347, which declares that "every corporation, *as such,* shall have power,"—etc., etc. So the laws of Spain and Mexico have declared from time immemorial that "every fully organized PUEBLO, as such, shall be entitled to four square leagues of land," as we have just seen in the next preceding section.

How the Measurement of Pueblo Lands was to be made.

§ **30.** The Spanish law, with that extreme minuteness and precision which eminently characterize it, provided for the survey of all donations or appropriations of public lands in those regulations called " *Ordenanzas de Tierras y Aguas.*" Without entering into the geometrical and arithmetical details of these regulations, it is sufficient for our present purpose to observe that, in case there were no natural obstacles, such PUEBLO lands were to be surveyed in the form of a square, first establishing a central point, which in the case of a PUEBLO was the centre of the Plaza, or Public Square, from which transverse lines were drawn in the direction of the four cardinal points, and then squared ; but that if the nature of the ground did not admit of that mode of surveying, as, for example, if the sea, mountains, lakes, deserts, rocky wastes, or the like, interposed, then the requisite quantity of land was to be made up in some other convenient direction; or the survey might be made in the direction in which mountains, lakes and other wastes were found, in which case they would be included within the boundaries, but rejected from the computed area of the measurement. Ordenanza de Tierra y Aguas, chap. XI, pages 181, 185, 187. (Edition of Madrid and Paris, 1855). For the *mode* of making such and the like surveys, see the same work, Figure 11, page 170 of the same edition. It is not necessary to refer minutely to these details, as the peninsula of San Francisco is of such conformation that the tide waters of the ocean and Bay present natural obstacles in every direction, except towards the south. The four leagues of the Pueblo must therefore be determined by taking all the land embraced in the peninsula north of such a parallel of latitude, as, with its tide-water limits, shall include four square leagues. See the maps of the U. S. Coast Survey, and the map prefixed to this argument. The map prefixed to Langley's San Francisco Directory for 1862 contains the section lines of the U. S. Land Office survey for the tract embraced in the county of San Francisco, and they can easily be extended through the whole map. I shall refer to it as Langley's map.

A. D. 1769—1770.

FOUNDATION OF THE FIRST TWO PRESIDIOS IN CALIFORNIA : SAN DIEGO AND MONTEREY.

§ 31. Pursuant to the above mentioned scheme of the Civil and Religious conquest of California, two Presidios were immediately founded in Upper California, that of San Diego, Lat. 32° 39′ 30″ North, in 1769, (1 De Mofras, 328, 332,) that of Monterey, Lat. 36° 37′ 15″ North, in 1770, (1 De Mofras, 395, 403). Near those Presidios, as a part of the plan of civil and religious colonization of the country, were founded, in the same years respectively, the Mission of San Diego, near the Presidio of that name, and the Mission del Carmelo, near the Presidio of Monterey. See ADDENDA, No. LXVII, page 97.

EXPLORATION OF THE HARBOR OF SAN FRANCISCO.

§ 32. But the establishment of these two Presidios of San Diego and Monterey, with the consequent support which they gave to the pious labors of the missionaries, did not satisfy those devoted men. Father Junípero Serra, the founder and first President of the Franciscan Missions of Upper California, and the real conqueror of this region, with that pious zeal for the salvation of souls which prompted him ever to go on with the conquest (ir á la conquista!) represented to the Marquis de la Croix, the then Vice-Roy of Mexico, that it was a reproach to Catholic Christianity that there was no Mission dedicated to San Francisco de Asis, the founder and patron of the order which bore his name. There is a current and credible tradition among the old native Californians that the Vice-Roy replied: " If our Father " San Francisco wants a Mission dedicated to him, let him show us a " good port up beyond Monterey, and we will build him a Mission there !" Long before this there had existed a tradition, coming down from the early navigators, that on the North-Western Coast, about a hundred miles north of Monterey, there existed the entrance of a large bay, through which vast volumes of fresh water poured into the sea from rivers flowing from an unknown distance in the interior. But later explorers had not been able to find this entrance, probably because then, as now, a thick fog frequently obscured the entrance of the Golden Gate. Sir Francis Drake did not succeed in entering the straits, but anchored instead in the bay a few miles above to which he gave his name, designating the white cliffs which bound it as New Albion. This bay afterwards was often reached by the explorers who were seeking the *real* " Bay of San Francisco," as it has often in our time been mistaken for it by careless or eager navigators, and thus made the scene of numerous disasters ; and in the time of the Marquis de Croix, the Bay of San Francisco had come to be considered quite as apocryphal as the Island of Formosa or the Antarctic Continent of Commodore Wilkes in our day. It was therefore with a feeling of prayerful humorousness that the Vice-Roy invoked the aid of Saint Francisco in the discovery of this concealed harbor. Father Junípero, however, took the Vice-Roy at his word, and, sailing from Monterey in 1772, happily established the existence of the Bay of San Francisco, which he re-discovered, and to which he permanently affixed the name of the patron of his order. Vida del Venerable Padre Fray Junípero Serra, por Palou Cap. XXX, etc.

A. D. 1773.

INSTRUCTIONS TO COMMANDANTS OF PRESIDIOS IN CALIFORNIA IN 1773.

§ **33.** As late as 1773 only the two Presidios of San Diego and Monterey having been founded in California, as I have stated in preceding § 31, instructions were given to the Commandantes of those Presidios to assign common lands, suertes, solares, and sitios to Indians and colonists, which instructions are found at large in the California Archives, Vol. I of Missions and Colonization, page 812, etc. A few of these instructions are printed in the Addenda, No. III, pages 2 and 3. They have the value of showing that at this early date there were *pobladores*, or colonists in California, and that the object of these Instructions was to provide that these colonists should have lands distributed to them, even though they were not sufficiently numerous to form such Pueblos as were entitled to the four square leagues of land. They show, also, that these settlements were to be compact, to be made in general conformity with the laws which I have cited in the preceding § 30 of this argument; and were intended to form the cores of fully organized PUEBLOS. The Pueblo of San José, founded in the year 1777, 1 De Mofras, 413, seems to have been founded under these special regulations; and in fact the *espediente* on that subject found in the Archives seems to demonstrate that there were not ten heads of families among its colonists, and in that case the new Pueblo was not entitled to all the rights of a complete Pueblo under the laws contained in the ADDENDA, Nos. I and II. See California Archives, Vol. I, Missions and Colonization, p. 683, etc.

A. D. 1776.

FOUNDATION OF THE PRESIDIO AND MISSION OF SAN FRANCISCO.

§ **34.** The Bay of San Francisco having been re-discovered, as I have stated in § 32 of this argument, the then Vice-Roy of New Spain—the Marquis de Croix—thereupon, by an order dated November 12th, 1775, gave directions for the foundation of a Fort, Presidio and Mission upon the Bay of San Francisco. California Archives, Vol. I of Provincial State Papers, page 100, etc. The colonists with their cattle and the necessary provisions for the journey were to go by land from Monterey, while the rest of the equipment was sent from the same port by sea.

" The said overland expedition left the 'presidio' of Monterey on " the appointed day, 17th of June of said year of 1776; it was com- " posed of the said lieutenant commanding, Don José Moraga, one " sergeant and sixteen soldiers clad in leather—all married men with " large families [todos casados y con crecidas familias, de siete pobla- " dores tambien casados y con familias], of some followers and ser- " vants of the same, of herdsmen and drovers who drove the neat stock " of the Presidio, and the pack train with provisions and necessary " equipage for the road, the rest of the freight being left for the vessel " which was about to sail. And as regards the Mission, we, the two " missionaries above named, joined the party with two young men- " servants for the Mission, two neophyte Indians of old California, and "another of the Mission of San Carlos for the purpose of trying " whether he could serve as an interpreter; but as the idiom was found " to be a different one, he only served to take care of the cows that " were brought for the purpose of raising a stock of cattle. The said " expedition went on towards this port." Vide de Junípero Serra, por Palou, Cap. XLV. The Presidio was founded the 17th of September, and the Mission the 9th of October, 1776. The colony, it will be observed, consisted of eight pure colonists and sixteen soldiers, all married, that is, of twenty-four heads of families. The Presidio and Mission occupied the localities designated by those names on the accompanying map. A Fort was soon after built upon the " Fort Point " indicated on the same map.

THE NAME "SAN FRANCISCO DE ASIS."

§ 35. The new settlements having been founded in honor of the Patron saint of the "Order of *Franciscans*," his name, " San Francisco de Asis,—San Francisco of Assisi," was properly given to them. The addition of "de Asis" was necessary to prevent confusion, to give a specific designation to the title " San Francisco," which, from the number of saints of that name was hardly more than generic. For in the calendar of Saints, there were at least three thus canonized. San Francisco *de Asis*,—so called because born at *Assisi*, in Italy, A. D. 1182, the founder and patron of the Franciscans; San Francisco *de Paula*, born at *Paula*, in Italy, A. D. 1416, the founder of the Missions; San Francisco *Salano*, born at Sales, in Savoy, A. D. 1567.* So that SAN FRANCISCO *de Asis*, as applied to the Mission, the Presidio, and the Presidial-Pueblo, was then the complete, and therefore the only correct designation of each settlement respectively, and without this full designation the term " San Francisco " simply must have created confusion, except when used in the immediate vicinity of those populations. San Francisco *Solano* had a Mission in this vicinity, at Sonoma. See ADDENDA, No. LXVII, page 97. In Lippincott's Gazetteer, A. D. 1860, are *five* San Franciscos, all Hispano-American, and none of recent origin. What would the simple term " San Francisco " have suggested to a Spanish king, colonial minister or viceroy, forty years ago? There is even a port of " San Francisco " on the Western Coast of Lower California, in Lat. 30° 45′ N. Long. 113° 40′ W.† and near it an old Jesuit Mission of the same name. Cal. Archives, Vol. I, Miss. and Colon., p. 288. The Mission of San Francisco de Asis early came to be called the Mission de los *Dolores* de nuestro Padre San Francisco de Asis," [of the anguish or sufferings] probably to avoid any confusion between the designation of the Mission and the Presidio, or *Presidial-Pueblo*. Thus when we find the Presidio or Pueblo styled " San Francisco *de Asis*," we should recognize only their full designation, and not confound them with the Mission, but rather the contrary.

A. D. 1779.

FELIPE DE NEVE'S REGULATIONS OF COLONIZATION FOR CALIFORNIA.

§ 36. Prominent among the acts of legislation respecting the colonization of California, stand the celebrated " Regulations for the gov-" ernment of the Province of California by Don Felipe de Neve, Gov-" ernor of the same, dated in the Royal Presidio of San Carlos de

---

* See Butler's Lives of the Saints, and the Encyclopædias generally.

† NOTE.—There is a current and true anecdote of one of the early commanders of the Pacific Mail Steamship Company, who was sent from New York, in 1848, before the discovery of gold in California was announced there, to obtain a cargo of coal at Cardiff, Wales, and bring it to San Francisco, who, in good faith, made this port of San Francisco in Lower California, as his port of destination. *Vive Le Roy !*

"Monterey, 1st June, 1773, and approved by his Majesty in a Royal "order of the 24th October, 1781."* The first section of this Title fully expresses the purpose of these Regulations.

"1st. The object of greatest importance toward the fulfillment of "the pious intentions of the King, our master, and towards securing to "his Majesty the dominion of the extensive country which occupies a "space of more than two hundred leagues, comprehending the new "establishment of the *presidios*, and the respective ports of San Diego, "Monterey, and San Francisco, being to forward the reduction of, and "as far as possible to make this vast country (which, with the excep- "tion of seventeen hundred and forty-nine Christians of both sexes in "the eight missions on the road which leads from the first to the last "named presidio, is inhabited by innumerable heathens) useful to the "State, by erecting pueblos of white people, (*pueblos de gente de ra-* "*zon*) who, being united, may encourage agriculture, planting, the "breeding of cattle, and successively the other branches of industry; "so that some years hence their produce may be sufficient to provide "garrisons of the presidios with provisions and horses, thereby obviat- "ing the distance of transportation and the risks and losses which the "royal government suffers thereby. With this just idea, the Pueblo of "San José has been founded and peopled; and the erection of another "is determined upon, in which the colonists (pobladores) and their "families, from the provinces of Sonora and Sinaloa, will establish "themselves, the progressive augmentation of which, and of the families "of the troops, will provide for the establishment of other towns, and "furnish recruits for the presidio companies, thus freeing the royal "revenue from the indispensable expenses at present required for these "purposes."

§ **37.** The following regulations provide for the distribution of house lots and cultivable lands (solares y suertes de tierra) among the *pobladores* and *vecinos;* (poblador *conditor*, founder, settler; vecino, *municeps*, citizen; Salvá,) §§ 2, 4, 6; that moneys, rations, agricul-tural implements and domestic animals shall be furnished to the colo-nists, §§ 2, 3; that they shall be exempt from taxes for a certain period, § 9; that the lands granted to them shall be inalienable, not capable of hypothecation, and perpetually hereditary, § 6; and many other articles exhibiting a wise and beneficent spirit of legislation, curi-ous to study, but not necessary to our present purpose, inasmuch as this system was soon superseded by another. It is curious, however, to note that § 16 provided that every colonist to whom lands were granted under that law, was bound to keep himself constantly equipped with two horses, a saddle complete, a musket, besides other arms, ready to march at the order of the Governor. It was provided by § 17 that the titles to lands should be made out by the Governor or commissary whom he might appoint for that purpose, and that records of the same

---

* The fourteenth title of these Regulations, relating to the colonization and political government of California, is printed in full in the ADDENDA, No. IV, page 3, etc. DE NEVE was Governor of California. See a list of the Colonial Governors ADDENDA, No. LXXIX.

should be kept in the general book of colonization in the Government archives. The municipal expenses are called, in § 14, "*gastos de* REPUBLICA." See ADDENDA, No. IV, page 3, etc.

THE FOUR SQUARE LEAGUES RECOGNIZED.

§ 38. The principal value of this document consists in the fact that it incidentally assumes the existence of previous laws, which assigned four square leagues of land to each *Pueblo*, and that it everywhere avoids that confusion of terms which has been attempted to be introduced into this discussion. It is provided as follows by § 4 of this law: (ADDENDA, No. IV, § 4, page 4,) " the house lots to be granted to the new pobladores (colonists) are to be designated in the situations and the extent corresponding to the locality on which the new pueblos are to be established, so that a square and streets be formed agreeably to the provisions of the laws of the kingdom ; and conformably to the same there shall be designated competent *ejidos* for the Pueblo, AND *dehesas*, together with the cultivable lands which may be suitable for propios : (conforme á lo prevenido por las Leyes del Reyna, y *con su arreglo* se señalará *exido* competente para et Pueblo y dehesas con las tierras de labor que convenga para propios.* In § 8 it is provided that the new colonists shall enjoy, for the purpose of maintaining their cattle, the use in common of the water and pasturage, fire-wood and timber of the *ejido*, forest, *and dehesa*, which are to be designated according to law to each new Pueblo. Addenda, No. IV, § 8, page 5. From these references and enumerations, it is established :

First : That each new Pueblo (cada nuevo Pueblo) had a right, according to previous laws alluded to, but not specifically mentioned, to the admeasurement of certain lands, and we find no such laws except those above cited in § 28 of this argument.

Secondly : That these lands were divided into Suertes, Solares, Propios, Ejidos, Montes and Dejesas, designations perfectly distinct, and in no case to be confounded with each other: and that these terms, as thus used, completely justify the definitions we have given them in §§ 10 to 15, inclusive, of this argument.

Thirdlg : That in the ejidos, montes, and dejesas of a Pueblo all the inhabitants had a right of common.

The original of this document is to be found in the Archives, Vol. I, of Missions and Colonization, page 761.—An English translation is contained in 1 Rockwell, 445, and also in Halleck's Report, app., 2, Exec. Doc. No. 17, H. of Reps., 31st Cong., 1st Sess., p. 134, and printed in the ADDENDA, No. IV, page 3 ; but this translation is not to be always relied upon for the exact rendering of legal terms. For example, *comun* is not exactly rendered by *community*, nor is *common lands* a full translation of the term *ejidos*. See §§ 14 and 17 of this

---

* I shall show, hereafter, that although the four leagues belonging to a Pueblo were capable of being divided into ejidos and dehesas, that the right of property in these four leagues did not depend upon this division, but existed antecedent to, and irrespective of, such division, which might or might not be effected.

argument. The original rough draft and the perfected one, and the official printed copy, form one of the most valuable curiosities of the Archives, and are to be found in Volume I of Missions and Colonization, at pages 636, 507, and 733 respectively.

A. D. 1786.
A COTEMPORARY OFFICIAL CONSTRUCTION OF THE FOUR-LEAGUE GRANT TO PUEBLOS.

§ **39.** That the construction I have put upon the preceding Regulations of Felipe de Neve is correct in regard to the four square leagues to which organized Pueblos were entitled appears from the highest authority, that of the Vice-royalty of New Spain, which I am about to cite. In November, 1784, certain settlers in California petitioned the Governor of that province for grants of lands which were situated within the four square leagues belonging to the Pueblos. The Governor reported this fact to the Commandánte General, together with his recommendation that the prayer of the petition be granted. The matter was referred by the Commandánte General to Galindo Navarro, who was Asesor, an officer whose functions in this respect seem to have exactly corresponded to those of Attorney General under our laws. In his report, dated at Chihuahua, October 27th, 1785, which was approved by the Commandante General on June 21st, 1786, and returned to the Governor of California for his instruction, where it now remains in the Archives, Vol. I Missions and Colonization, page 809, and is also in evidence in the case, Exhibit V, and printed in full in the ADDENDA, No. VI, page 9, referring to the preceding Regulations of Felipe de Neve, he says:

"In title 14 of the Regulation for that Peninsula,* approved by his "Majesty in a Royal Order of the 24th of October, 1781, it is "directed by Art. 8 that the new settlers should enjoy, for the mainten-"ance of their stock, the common advantage of waters and pastures, "wood and timber of the commons, (ejidos,) forests, (montes,) and "pasture grounds, (dehesas,) which, in compliance with the laws, are "to be marked out to each Pueblo: (Se ha de señalar á cada Pueblo).
    *   *   *   *   *   *

"In allotting of tracts of land for cattle, (sitios,) which some set-"tlers in California claim, and the Governor proposes in his official "communication of the 20th November, 1784, cannot nor ought to be "made to them within the boundaries assigned to each Pueblo, which, "in conformity with the law 6, title 5, lib. 4, of the Recopilacion, must "be (deben ser) FOUR LEAGUES OF LAND in a square or oblong body, "according to the nature of the ground; because the petition of the "new settlers would tend to make them private owners of the forests, "pastures, water, timber, woods and other advantages of the lands "which may be assigned, granted and distributed to them, and to "deprive their neighbors of these benefits, it is seen at once that their "claim is entirely contrary to the directions of the aforementioned

---

* California was always called a *peninsula* by the Spaniards.

" laws and the express provision in Art. 8 of the Instructions for settle-
" ments (Poblaciones) in the Californias, according to which all the
" waters, pastures, wood and timber within the limits which, in confor-
" mity to law, may be allowed to each Pueblo, must be for the common
" advantage, so that all the new settlers may enjoy and partake of them,
" maintaining therein their cattle and participating of the other benefits
" that may be produced : [result]."

From this opinion of Navarro it follows :

FIRST : That the Regulations of Felipe de Neve did not abolish
law 6, title 5, liber 4 of the Recopilacion de los Leyes de los Indios,
which assigned four leagues of land to each organized Pueblo, but that
the said law remained in full force, as I have insisted in § 28 of this
argument.

SECONDLY : That this dedication of the four leagues of land to
each Pueblo was so absolute that even the Governor of California
could not, at that time, (1784–6,) make any grants of grazing lands
(sitios) within those four leagues.

THIRDLY : That the only object of the assignment of the four
leagues by actual measurement, was to ascertain *what particular* four
leagues were thus assigned, under such obstacles as might or might
not be presented, " according to the nature of the ground," whence we
are entitled to infer that if these natural obstacles were such that only
one particular parcel of land could by any possibility be included in
that assignment of four leagues, then that particular parcel of four
leagues necessarily belonged to the respective Pueblo, without any
admeasurement. As for instance, if the Pueblo were founded on an
island containing exactly four leagues, or less, *or if it were situated,
like the Pueblo of San Francisco, on a peninsula, less than two leagues
in average breadth, and on which the measurement could be in only one
direction, namely from the head of the peninsula southwards.* See
map prefixed, and also Langley's map, mentioned in § 30 of this
argument.

FOURTHLY : That although it was a historical and well known fact
that the allotted tract of four square leagues had never been admeas-
ured to any Pueblo in California in the years 1784, 1785, 1786, still
the Government protected the proprietary rights of the Pueblos in
those adjacent lands which it was presumed would fall within the limits
of those four leagues.

A. D. 1789.

REGULATIONS FOR COLONIZATION FOR CALIFORNIA—CALLED THE PLAN OF PITIC.

§ **40.** The first section of the regulations of Felipe de Neve recite
that the Pueblo of San José had already been founded, and that it was
in contemplation to found another. See Ante § 37, ADDENDA, No. IV,
page 3, § 1. This other Pueblo, that of Los Angeles, was accordingly founded, under these regulations, by the Governor of California,
in December of the same year, 1781. 1 De Mofras, 353. There is
no record that any other Pueblo was ever founded under these regu-

lations, which, it will be borne in mind, were purely *civil* Pueblos of the first class mentioned in § 19 of this argument, and were, on the face of the regulations, wholly disconnected from the military Presidios, except as providing supplies and recruits for them, and furnishing a place of residence for the increase of their families, and a retreat for the soldiers in their old age. Regulations, §§ 1, 5, 14, 15. ADDENDA, No. IV, page 4. The whole system was almost immediately changed, by the substitution of what is called the PLAN OF PITIC.

BY WHOM THIS PLAN OF PITIC WAS PROMULGATED.

§ **41.** As matter properly introductory to this PLAN, and absolutely necessary to the comprehension of its legal effect, I am permitted to copy the following condensed statement from the manuscript memoranda of R. C. Hopkins, Esq., Keeper of the Archives: " In the year " 1776, in order to assist the Viceroy in the discharge of the duties of " his office, and in some degree to relieve him from the onerous burden " the ' Comandancia General de Provincias Internes ' was established, " but as soon as his Excellency, Don Teodoro de Croix, who was ap-" pointed to the office of Commandante-General, had taken charge of " the same, he foresaw the difficulties he would have in properly dis-" charging the duties of the same, without subordinate assistance. He, " therefore, petitioned his Majesty for a division of the territory em-" braced in the Comandancia General, representing that it was impos-" sible for him at Arispe (his headquarters) to properly attend to mat-" ters in the distant Provinces of Coahuila and Texas. Although said " petition was taken under consideration, yet, as the government was " much occupied with the war with England, no steps were taken in " the matter, till 1786, when royal instructions were issued, authorizing " the Comandante-General to place the Provinces of Nueva-Vizcaya, " and New Mexico under the charge of the Comandante-Inspector, and " those of Texas and Coahuila under the charge of Don Juan Ugalde, " the Comandante-General himself having charge of the Provinces of " Sonora and California—and exercising general supervision of the " whole extent of territory.

" But as these instructions did not meet the wants of the case, on " the 3d of December, 1789, provisional Regulations were made by the " Viceroy, subject to the royal approbation, to take effect on the 1st of " January, 1788. Art. 1st of said Regulations provided that the then " Comandante-General, Don Jacobo Ugarte y Loyola, should remain in " command of the Provinces of the Californias, Sonora, New Mexico, " and New Vizcaya, exercising in the same all the authority delegated " to him by the King. This was styled the *Comandancia General of* " *the Four Interior Provinces of the West.* Under this Comandante-" General there was one Comandante-Inspector, and three Ayudante-" Inspectors. The Comandante-General had no fixed residence, but " went from place to place, wherever his presence might be most re-" quired. Art. 9th of said Regulation, established a second Comandan-" cia General, comprising the Provinces of Coahuila, Texas, Nueva

" Reyno de Leon and the Colony of New Santander, under the style
" of the *Comandancia of the Four Interior Provinces of the East.*
" The same being under the charge of Colonel Don Juan Ugalde."
Archives, Vol. I, of Missions and Colonization, page 378.   So that the
" Plan of Pitic " promulgated at Chihuahua, on the 14th of November,
1789, became at that time the law of colonization of the Comandancia-
" General of the Four Interior Provinces of the West," namely, CALI-
FORNIA, Sonora, New Mexico, and New Vizcaya (Biscay). The authority of the Asesor Navarro and of the Comandante General Ugarte to
construe the Regulations of Felipe de Neva, as set forth in § 39 of
this argument, also distinctly appears from the above historical sketch.

A. D. 1789.

OCCASION OF THE PLAN OF PITIC.

§ **42.**   This plan of Pitic, Exhibit ZZ, ADDENDA, No. VII, page
11, is from the Archives, Vol. I, of Missions and Colonization, page 853.
This town of Pitic which was thus founded, was, like San Francisco,
Santa Barbara, and Monterey, a PRESIDIAL-PUEBLO, for the Presidio
of San Miguel de Orcavitas was removed to the locality of Tepic in
order to protect and guard the new settlement.   Plan of Pitic, § 3,
ADDENDA, No. VII, § 3, page 11.   The pressing reasons in which this
new plan originated are not stated in any of the documents, but in a
map inserted in a curious History of Lower California, published in
German at Mannheim, in 1773, by Father Begert, a Jesuit Ex-Mis-
sionary of that Peninsula, the site of Guayamas is marked with a cross
and the inscription " Guayamas M. distr. per Apostatas Seris;" Guayamas Mission, destroyed by the apostate Seris (Indians.)   (Nachrichten
von der Amerikanischen Halb-Insel Californien ; geschrieben von einem
Priester der Gesellschaft Jesu, welcher lang darinn diese letzere Jahr
gelebet hat. Mannheim, 1773).   The Seris were a tribe of warlike and
exceedingly barbarous Indians, who fought as they still fight, with arrows doubly poisoned, by means of a most horrible fermentation.*   The
modern city of Hermosillo, with a population of 20,000, represents the
Pueblo thus founded, while of the Seris Indians, who then occupied
the country, but whose designation seems to have puzzled the translator of this " Plan." (See §§ 2 and 6 of the Plan).   ADDENDA, No.
VII, pages 11, 12.   One portion, which is Christianized, reside in their
own village near Hermoisillo (Pitic) in the town provided for them in
§ 6 of the Plan, and the other, still savage, occupy the island of Tibu-
ron, in the Gulf of California, north of Guayamas, a terror to the white
inhabitants.   Bartlett's personal narrative, Vol. I, pp. 463, 466 ; 1 De

---

* NOTE.—" They first kill a cow and take from it its liver; they then collect rattle-
" snakes, scorpions, centipedes, and tarantulas, which they confine in a hole with the
" liver.   The next process is to beat them with sticks, in order to enrage them, and being
" thus infuriated, they fasten their fangs and exhaust their venom upon each other and
" upon the liver.   When the whole mass is in a state of corruption, the women take the
" arrows and pass their points through it ; they are then allowed to dry in the shade."
Bartlett, as above.   Hardy's Travels in Mexico, London, 1829, p. 298.

Mofras, 181. In their barbarous warfare, doubtless, originated this new "Plan" of colonization.

MAIN FEATURES OF THIS PLAN OF PITIC.

§ **43.** The main features of this PLAN OF PITIC are those which generally characterize the wise, pious, and eminently practical schemes of colonization which emanated from the kings of Spain and the sagacious councellors by whom they were guided. The right of the town to four leagues is recognized in the second section of the Plan. ADDENDA, No. VII, page 11. If it be contended that the phrase "*may* be granted to the town in question four leagues," is only a permissive one, we reply that the phrase "podrá conceder" (literally "*shall can* be granted") has a force nearer to "must" than to "may," and that this is one of those cases where no discretionary power being vested in the officer, even the word "may" means "shall" and is imperative. Sedgwick on Statutory and Constitutional Law, 438, 439. The object being to found a town with reference to pre-existing and unrepealed laws. That this is the true interpretation appears from Section Six of the Plan, where the concession of the four leagues to the new town is taken for granted, and the right of commons in that tract of land is expressly declared: "the tract of four leagues granted to the new settlement being measured and marked out: demarcado y amonohado que sea el terreno concedido á la nueva poblacion." So also Section Eleventh of the Plan gives the same definition to *Ejidos* which is given in § 14 of this argument,—a place at the *exit* or immediate surroundings of the *Pueblo*, suitable for the settlers to amuse themselves, and where a few milch cows could be pastured, while sections twelve and thirteen again place the ejidos and dehesas in opposition, and fully define the latter term (dehesas): "§ 13. The laying out of the commons and of the common pasture grounds, or vast pasture of the herds being completed; evacuando et señalmiento de los ejidos y á la dehesa comun ó *Prado Boyal.*" This last phrase is hardly translatable without a periphrasis. *Prado Boyal,* which is thus used as a definition of *dehesa,* is rendered in Latin by *Pratum bovillum,* and designates the *great* pasture grounds where the vast herds roamed distant from the Pueblo. The lands granted to the settlers were to be distributed by a commission in the name of the king, and alienation, hypothecation and mortmain were carefully guarded against, §§ 17, 18; and when the settlement counted thirty heads of families, it was to have alcaldes, councilmen and an Ayuntamiento or Common Council of its own, §§ 4, 5, 17, and the Ayuntamientos were to pass "municipal ordinances" for the economical and political management of the *Pueblo.* § 24.

A. D. 1791.

ANOTHER OFFICIAL CONSTUCTION OF THE FOUR-LEAGUE LAW. THE PRESIDIOS DECLARED TO BE PUEBLOS, AND EACH ENTITLED TO FOUR LEAGUES OF LAND.

§ **44.** We have seen that a question arose in the year 1784,

3

whether *sitios*, or large tracts of grazing lands might not be granted to settlers within the four leagues belonging to the Pueblos, and that it was decided that such grants could not be made within those limits, because that would be prejudicial to the rights of the *Pueblos*. § 39 of this argument, and also ADDENDA, No. VI, page 9. Very singularly a contest of an opposite nature arose within the next seven years, and the point presented seems to have been announced in this form : Captains of Presidios cannot grant house-lots (solares) or cultivable lands (suertes) to soldiers and citizens; but granted that they have that power, then they are restricted in the exercise of it to the tract of four leagues belonging to the Presidial-Pueblos. For the government of New Spain, which included all the Hispano-American Provinces of Mexico and to the north of it, there were promulgated at Madrid, on December 4th, 1786, certain directions called familiarly the " Ordenanza de Intendentes," but whose full title was, " A Royal Ordinance for the empowering (establecimiento) and direction of the Intendentes (Vice-Governors) of the army and province of New Spain. (Real Ordenanza para et Establecimiento é Instruccion de Intendentes de Exercito y Provincia en el Reino de la Nueva-España. De órden de su Magestad. Madrid, Año de 1786). By article 81 of this " Ordenanza de Intendentes," it is provided that the INTENDENTES shall be judges of the propriety of distribution of the " Royal lands," (Realengos) and shall decide upon all grants of them. The question then arose ; " Can the Captains of the Presidios make grants of lands which " shall be valid without the consent of the Intendentes ; and if so, can " they make valid grants of lands *outside* of the PUEBLO limits of four leagues ?" The following is the decision of the then Comandante-General, Pedro de Nava, in which he decrees that the Captain of a Presidial-Pueblo had an unlimited power to grant lands within the four leagues belonging to the PUEBLO, but had no power to make grants outside of those four leagues :

　　" In conformity with the opinion of the *Asesor* of the Comandante " General, I have determined in a decree of this date, that notwith- " standing the provisions made in the 81st Article of the *Ordenanza of* " *Intendentes*, the captains of Presidios are authorized to grant and dis- " tribute house-lots and lands to the soldiers and citizens who may " solicit them to fix their residences on: (corresponde á los Capi- " tanes de Presidio mercenar y repartir solares y tierres á los Sol- " dados y *vecinos* que los pidieren para figar su residentia en ellos.) " And considering the extent of four common leagues measured from " the centre of the Presidio square, namely, two leagues in every direc- " tion, to be sufficient for the new Pueblos which are growing up under " the protection of the said Presidios, I have likewise determined, in " order to avoid doubts and disputes in future, that said captains res- " trict themselves henceforward to the house-lots and lands within the " four leagues already mentioned, without exceeding in any manner " the said limits, leaving free and open the exclusive jurisdiction belong- " ing to the *Intendentes* of the royal hacienda, respecting the sale, com- " position and distribution of the remainder of the land in the respective

" districts :) considerandose suficiente para las nuevas poblaciones que
" van formnandose, [literally ' which are going on forming themselves ']
" a su abrigo el termino de cuatro leguas communes medidas desde el
" centro de la Plaza del Presidio, dos para cada viento.   *   *   *
" que los capitanes se limiten desde ahora en la consecion de mercedes
" de solares y tierras á las que estuviesen comprehendidas en dichas
" cuatro leguas sin excedese en manera alguna.)   And that this order
" may be punctually observed and carried into effect, you will circulate
" it to the captains and comandantes of the Presidios of your province,
" informing me of having done so.   God preserve you many years.
    " Chihuahua, Oct. 22nd, 1791.
                                        " PEDRO de NERVA.
    " To Señor Don JOSE ANTONIO ROMERO."

This document is the Exhibit Z in this case.   It is found also in 1
Rockwell, 451, not translated with entire precision, and misdated
March, instead of *October*.   The original is in the Archives, Vol. I of
Missions and Colonization, page 850, and the approval of it dated Jan.
19, 1793, is found at page 814 of the same volume.   It is printed in
full in the ADDENDA, No. VIII, page 17.

From this valuable document it appears :

FIRST : That the " Intendentes " who had the right to decide upon
the propriety of grants made out of the Royal lands, had no such right
in regard to lands granted within the four leagues belonging to *Pueblos*,
BECAUSE belonging to the *Pueblos*, the king had no ownership in them,
although they were granted in his name under every system.   Regu-
ulations of 1781, 1 Rockwell 447, § 5, Addenda No. IV, § 5, page 5 ;
Plan of Pitic, § 18, ADDENDA, No. VII, page 15.

SECONDLY : That *é converso*, because the lands lying outside of the
four leagues did not belong to the *Pueblo*, but did belong to the king ;
the captains of Presidios, who could grant only the lands belonging
to PRESIDIAL-PUEBLOS, had no authority to grant those outside
lands.   Also that each Presidial-Pueblo was entitled to four leagues of
land.

DEMOCRATIC FEATURES OF THE PLAN OF PITIC.

§ **45.**   In perfect consistency with my previous argument, we find
that the Regulations of 1781, 1 Rockwell 450, § 18, ADDENDA, No. IV,
page 7, provide for the election of the *Pueblo* officers after the first two
years by the settlers themselves ; which the PLAN OF PITIC, AD-
DENDA, No. VII, page 14, Exhibit zz, in sections 17, 20, 21, 22 and
23, speak of " the Ayuntamiento of the new settlement," as an institu-
tion existing as a matter of course ; while section 24 of the same PLAN
expressly gives to such Ayuntamientos of the new Pueblos the power
to make and enforce all the ordinances and municipal regulations necessary to the political government, management, economy, and police, of
civilized towns.   This section is a perfect paraphrase of those enumerations in Anglo-American city charters, which follow the declaratory
clause : " The Mayor and Common Council shall have power," etc., etc.

A. D. 1796.

It is Decided not to Establish a "Villa of Branciforte" at San Francisco.

§ **46.** In the year 1796 it was proposed to build a villa in Upper California in honor of Don Miguel de Lagrua, Marquis de Branciforte, at that time Viceroy of New Spain. Alexander the Great was not the only chief who indulged the fancy of giving his name to a great city. Alvarado endeavored to give to San José the designation of the "Pueblo de Alvarado." 1 De Mofras, 415. And Vallejo gave to the Pueblo which he founded the title "Sonoma de Vallejo." 1 De Mofras, 446. Thus the Marquis de Branciforte had both illustrious examples and imitators in his laudable ambition. Among the localities enumerated by Don Pedro de Alberni, who was directed to examine the country and report upon several places indicated, was that of San Francisco, which he represented to be the very worst of all those mentioned for the foundation of such a villa, for the reason that there were but few cultivable or irrigable lands, and that there was a general deficiency of wood and water in and about the Presidio. See the Report in the ADDENDA, No. IX, page 18. The whole report shows that the intention was to build a rural villa depending upon agriculture and grazing for the subsistence of its inhabitants. This report has been sometimes referred to as justifying an inference that at the time it was made there was no civil settlement at the Presidio. But it expressly states that there was such a settlement there, although it was composed of only "a few families;" and a "PUEBLO of San Francisco," existing at the Presidio, would gladly have received an additional population and a higher grade of rank, with the title of "VILLA of Branciforte." This villa was afterwards founded in the same year, 1796, at the place now called Santa Cruz, (1 De Mofras, 409,) but does not seem to have figured largely in history.

A. D. 1812.

Law of the Cortes of Spain respecting the Formation of Ayuntamientos of Pueblos.

§ **47.** In the Leyes Vigentes, a collection of those decrees and orders of the Cortes of Spain, which survived the political revolution that severed the Republic from the mother country, published at Mexico in the year 1829, page 28, is found a "Decreto de 23 de Mayo de 1812," entitled "Formacion de los Ayuntamientos Constitucionales:"—"Decree of May 23d, 1812, concerning the *formation* of Constitutional Ayuntamientos, or Common Councils." This is printed in full in the ADDENDA, No. X. No repeal of this law appears to have been made; it is published as an existing law in 1853, by Rivera, in Vol. I, page 890, of his "Nueva Coleccion de Leyes y Decretos Mexicanos," and it is evident, from its continued promulgation from its enactment down to the era of the American Conquest of California in 1846, that it was a portion of the law of California long after the

Mexican Revolution of 1821, and, as will be seen hereafter in § 72 of this argument, down to and including the year 1835. This is enough for our present purpose. It related to the mode of forming Ayuntamientos, and although the *basis of population* was afterwards changed—see §§ 89, 90 of this argument—this law seems to have survived, in relation to the *modus operandi* of organizing those bodies.

§ **48.** The preamble of this law respecting Ayuntamientos recites, generally, that, in the judgment of the Cortes, the PUEBLOS, or towns, ought to be governed by Ayuntamientos, or Common Councils: [which, it is to be remembered, are *Commune* Councils]. Article I provides that *towns* and *pueblos* which have no Ayuntamientos, but which are entitled to them, may apply for them; and Articles II, VIII, and IX enact that Pueblos which are not themselves entitled to Ayuntamientos shall be aggregated together under a common Ayuntamiento. Leyes Vigentes, page 28, etc. 1 White's Recopilacion, 416, etc. ADDENDA, No. X, pp. 18, 19. Article IV provides that, in all *Pueblos* not exceeding two hundred inhabitants, there shall be one Alcalde, two Regidores, (Common Councilmen,) and one Procurador Sindico; one Alcalde, four Regidores, and one Procurador Sindico in Pueblos having more than 200 and less than 500 inhabitants; one Alcalde, six Regidores, and one Procurador Sindico in those having between 500 and 1,000 inhabitants; two Alcaldes, eight Regidores, and two Procurador Sindicos in those having between 1,000 and 4,000 inhabitants; and twelve Regidores in PUEBLOS of more than 4,000 inhabitants. These Alcaldes, Regidores and Procuradores Sindicos composed the Ayuntamiento of the Pueblo.

THE COMPLEX SYSTEM OF A DOUBLE ELECTION FOR THE OFFICERS OF AYUNTAMIENTOS.

§ **49.** The Ayuntamientos were not elected directly by the people, who chose only electors for that purpose; and the elections of these electors were to be held in local election districts at elections called *juntas de parroquia*, (parish or district elections). Article VIII. But no such junta de parroquia could be formed in a town having less than fifty inhabitants, (Article IX); and this was, therefore, probably the limit of population below which a *Pueblo* could not have its own Ayuntamiento. Compare Leyes Vigentes, page 28, Art. IV, VIII, and IX.—Translated in 1 White's New Recopilacion, 416, etc. ADDENDA, No. X, pp. 18, etc.

HOW A PUEBLO MIGHT LOSE ITS AYUNTAMIENTO.

§ **50.** Article II recognizes the fact that a town which has once had an Ayuntamiento may lose it by a diminution of its population. " Aggregandose al [Ayuntamiento] mas immediato en su provincia las " [Pueblos] que se formaran nuevamente y los despoblados con juris- " diccion." And in that case the provision just cited directs that they shall be united to the nearest Ayuntamiento in their province. There were therefore three kinds of Ayuntamientos :

1st. Ayuntamientos existing for a single Pueblo, which may therefore be styled AYUNTAMIENTOS SOLE.

2d. Ayuntamientos composed entirely of populations each of which was too small to have an Ayuntamiento of its own, and which may therefore be styled AYUNTAMIENTOS AGGREGATE.

3d. Ayuntamientos composed of the Ayuntamiento of a Pueblo, to which were joined other small populations, each too small to have an Ayuntamiento of its own, and which I shall term COMPOSITE AYUNTAMIENTOS, neither purely, sole nor aggregate.

ACTUAL DIVISION INTO DISTRICTS AND PARTIDOS.

§ **51.** The Departments of Upper and Lower California were repeatedly divided into Districts, and Partidos, as it was required by law that they should be: § 8 of this argument. Governor Alvarado, on February 26th, 1839, divided this Department into Districts, and the northern District into two Partidos, and decreed that the "second Partido should comprehend from the Point de los Llajas (below the latitude of Santa Cruz) up to the Sonoma frontier of the North ;" and that its cabecera, or official centre, to which official communications were to be addressed, should be the "Establishment of Dolores." California Archives, Vol. IV, Departmental State Papers, page 589. In 1845, California was again divided into Districts and Partidos, and Yerba Buena is indicated as the cabecera. *Ibid*, page 199. I cannot find that previous to 1839, as above mentioned, there was any formal division of the Californias into Districts and Partidos. But that division was necessary as a matter of administration : Law of the Cortes of Spain, of Oct. 9, 1812. Leyes Vigentes, 35. San Francisco was recognized as cabecera of the frontier of the North on January 17th, 1839, by Governor Alvarado, previous to his division of Districts and Partidos made as above, in February of that year. See ADDENDA, No. XXXVIII, page 57, § 4 ; and even earlier, on November 4th, 1834, Governor Figueroa recognizes a Partido of San Francisco as already in existence, and as having theretofore been, and still being under the jurisdiction of the military commandánte of San Francisco. See ADDENDA, No. XXI, page 35. From the absence of any evidence in the Archives showing that there was an actual, formal division into Partidos previous to February, 1839, Mr. R. C. Hopkins, the Keeper of the Archives, is of opinion that the jurisdiction of the Presidios, respectively, was regarded as a practical division of the Department into Partidos, and treated as such, and I fully concur in this opinion. The Presidio of San Francisco included San José, Santa Clara, Santa Cruz and the Villa of Branciforte in its jurisdiction, from A. D. 1800 to 1830. California Archives, Vol. III of Missions, p. 278 ; *Ib.*, Vol. V, p. 165 ; *Ib.*, Vol. V, p. 297. But in 1836, at least, the Partido of San Francisco did not include that portion of California lying west of the Bays of San Francisco and San Pablo, the Straits of Carquinez, and the Sacramento River, and this explains the language then used by Governor Alvarado in defining the limits of the Partido : " The second Partido shall comprise from the Point de las Llayas up to (hasta) the Sonoma frontier of the North." For the tract west of the Bay of San Francisco and its tributaries, as above mentioned, belonged to the independent jurisdiction of the military commandánte, and was known as the " Sonoma Frontier of the North," as decided by the Departmental Junta, on July 7th, 1836. See Exhibit 2 to testimony of R. C. Hopkins in the case. Also, California Archives, Legislative Proceedings, Vol. III, page 141.

A. D. 1813.

THE CORTES OF SPAIN ORDER ALL THE PROPERTY OF THE PUEBLOS, EXCEPT THE VACANT SUBURBS, (EJIDOS,) TO BE GRANTED IN PRIVATE OWNERSHIP.

§ 52. One of the desperate necessities resulting to the Spanish Government from the attempt of Napoleon to place his brother upon the throne of Spain, and from the civil war to which it gave rise, was an enactment made by the Cortes on the 4th of January, 1813, that all the property of the Pueblos, not only in Spain but in the provinces beyond the seas, should be sold or granted to private owners. This law is published in the Leyes Vigentes, at pages 56, etc., as one which survived the Mexican Revolution of 1821: it is printed in full in the ADDENDA, No. XI, at page 20, etc. The avowed object in the preamble is the welfare of the PUEBLOS and the improvement of agriculture and industry ; the real object clearly appears, from Articles 6, 7, 8, 9 to 15, to have been to reward soldiers for services in the war against Napoleon, and to raise a fund wherewith to pay a portion of the National Debt. Article 3 provides that " in the transfer of the " said lands the residents of the Pueblos within the limits of which " said lands may be shall be preferred, and the commoners of said " Pueblos in the enjoyment of said vacant lands." See ADDENDA, No. XI, page 21. These enactments will become very important in a subsequent part of this argument.

A. D. 1813.

THE CORTES OF SPAIN DECLARE THAT THE MISSIONS OUGHT TO BE SECULARIZED.

§ 53. In the same year, 1813, the Cortes of Spain, not by an absolute enactment, but by an authentic act, expressed their opinion that the Missionary establishments ought to be discontinued, and converted into curacies, in other words, that the Indian Missions ought to be secularized. But as this declaration went no farther, and never attained the form or force of a law, it is not deemed necessary to make any further reference to it, than to allude to it as one of the landmarks in the progress of opinion. See Jones' Report.

A. D. 1821.

The Mexican Revolution.

§ 54. Next in the order of time, among political events, is the Mexican Revolution of 1821. How far this Revolution affected the political powers of the military governors, it is not now necessary to inquire. It is a well established principle of law that a change in the sovereignty of a country changes the political law, but leaves all the laws respecting private property in full force. American Insurance Co. vs. Canter, 1 Peters, 542 ; Fleming vs. Page, 9 Howard U. S. S. C. R. Rep., 603 ; Cross vs. Harrison, 16 Howard U. S. S. C. Rep., 164. This is well stated in Governor Riley's Proclamation of June 5, 1849. Addenda, No. LXXV, 3d ¶. Thus, when Louisiana was acquired from France, it was understood that lands held by the former citizens or municipalities of that territory were to be held and enjoyed as before; but that the public lands were not to be granted by the Governors, as theretofore, under the laws of Spain and France, but were subject only to the laws regulating the public lands of the United States. So when California was acquired, it was generally and correctly understood that all municipal corporations retained their landed property, while the new Governors of California could not grant a foot of land, though their Mexican predecessors could grant it eleven leagues at a time. That the laws relating to the landed property of the Pueblos of California were not changed by the Mexican Revolution will appear from the whole course of this argument, and by consulting the Addendas, Nos. X and XI, pages 18 to 23, which are taken from the Leyes Vigentes—that collection of the laws of Spain which *did* survive the Mexican Revolution. The same principles are admirably stated in the preface to the Leyes Vigentes, pages i to iv.

A. D. 1825.

Progress of the Pueblo of San Francisco.

§ 55. Meanwhile the Pueblo of San Francisco had attained but a small growth, with a sluggish, indolent population. Captain Benjamin Morrell, who visited San Francisco in May, 1825, thus describes the town: " The town of San Francisco stands on a table land, elevated "about three hundred and fifty feet above the sea on a peninsula five "miles in width, on the south side of the entrance to the bay, about "two miles to the east of the outer entrance, and one-fourth of a mile "from the shore.* It is built in the same manner as Monterey, but

---

* Note.—It is hardly necessary to remark that this is a description of the Pueblo as it then existed at the Presidio. It seems to be inaccurate in the estimated elevation of three hundred and fifty feet above the sea; but very singularly in "California," by Alexander Forbes, published in London, in 1839, facing page 127 is an engraving of the Golden Gate, in which the Presidio is represented at about the same height above tide water. Probably both Capt. Morrell and Forbes were deceived in their estimates, as most early Californians were, by the exceeding clearness of the atmosphere. Looking at the settlement from afar, knowing how many miles they were distant, and perceiving objects with great distinctness, they judged of heights as they would have done in an obscure atmosphere, and so both the nautical observer and the artist were deceived.

" much smaller, comprising only about one hundred and twenty houses
" and a church, with perhaps five hundred inhabitants. * * * The
" inhabitants of this place are generally Mexicans and Spaniards, who
" are very indolent, and consequently very filthy. They cultivate
" barely sufficient land to support nature; consequently, nothing can
" be obtained by way of refreshments for ships. * * * The table
" land before mentioned would produce abundantly with proper culti-
" vation; but its surface is scarcely ever disturbed by plow or spade,
" and the garrison depends entirely upon the Mission for all its sup-
" plies." Morrell's Narratives of four voyages to the Pacific, etc., New
York, 1853, page 211.   This account I shall concede to be inexact as
to the number of the population, houses, and other matters of mere
estimate, because such statements almost always exaggerate the numbers involved in the calculation.   But one thing remains as a conclusive result of Captain Morrell's observation, namely: that there was an
actual PUEBLO at San Francisco, so large that a disinterested observer
estimated it at five hundred inhabitants and one hundred and twenty
houses.   The population probably never reached 400.   See post § 73
and ADDENDA, No. LXXVI.   Mr. Richard H. Dana, in his " Two
Years before the Mast," speaks of San Francisco " as a newly-begun
" settlement, mostly of Yankee-Californians, called Yerba Buena,
" which promises well."   Page 280.   Mr. Dana arrived in San Francisco on December 4th, 1835.   Compare the dates in his book at pages
66 and 280.   It thus appears that the inhabitants of the town were
already shifted or shifting from the Presidio to Yerba Buena, both
localities being within the four leagues belonging to this Pueblo.   See
the map prefixed, and Langley's map, in § 30.

MEXICAN COLONIZATION LAWS OF 1824 AND 1828.

§ 56.   No sooner, however, had the Mexican Revolution become
an accomplished fact, than the Sovereign General Constituent Congress, by a decree bearing date August 18th, 1824, enacted a general
law of Colonization, commonly styled the " Colonization Law of 1824."
This will be found printed at large in the ADDENDA, No XII, page
23.   This wise and liberal plan is worthy of the attention of the historian and of the political economist, but our present purpose leads us to
cite only the 2d Article of the decree, which is in these words:
     " 2d. The object of this law are those national lands which are
" neither private property nor belonging to any corporation or PUEBLO,
" and can therefore be colonized—Son objeto de esta ley aquellos ter-
" renos de la nacion, que no siendo de propiedad particular, ni per-
" tenecientes á corporacion alguna ó PUEBLO, pueden ser colonizados."
     This decree of Colonization, therefore, embraces all lands which
were neither of private ownership nor belonged to any corporation or
Pueblo.   This decree was soon followed by " General Rules and
Regulations for the Colonization of the Territories of the Republic,"
adopted at Mexico, November 21, 1828, and commonly styled the
" Regulations of 1828."   These are to be found in the ADDENDA, No.

XIV, page 25. We need not pay any particular attention to these Regulations, any further than to observe: that all applications for grants of lands were to be made to the Governor; that *he* was to cause the necessary information to be obtained; and that, if satisfied, *he* was to make the grant, and that there is no provision authorizing him to *delegate* his power to any person or officer. Articles 1, 2, 3, and 4. If, therefore, on comparing this decree of 1824 with the Regulations of 1828, we find a class of lands granted by the public authorities, not of private ownership, nor belonging to the nation, we shall be tempted to adopt the only remaining alternative and ask: "To what corporation or Pueblo did these lands belong?" See § 2 of the Law of 1824, cited in this section.

A. D. 1828. NOVEMBER 6TH.

It is decided that Comandantes of Presidios have no power to grant Public Lands outside of their Pueblos. Was the power to grant Public Lands in Abeyance?

§ **57.** After the enactment of the Mexican Colonization laws of 1824, and before the adoption of the Regulations of 1828, both of which are referred to in the preceding § 56 of this argument, an incident occurred which is curiously illustrative of the Colonization laws of California, and confirms the propositions I have heretofore maintained. A person named Willis, a resident of San José, some time in 1828, petitioned the Governor for a grant of public lands, lying outside of the lands of that Pueblo. The Governor refused the petition, because there were sufficient lands upon which to maintain his flocks and herds, in the Pueblo of San José to which he belonged. Willis thereupon presented himself to the Comandante of the Presidio of San Francisco, and having persuaded him that he had the power to grant, obtained a concession of the lands. The Governor repudiated the grant as being beyond the powers of the Comandante, and directed the latter to summon Willis before him and fine him fifty dollars for his fraudulent conduct. See Addenda, No. XIII, page 24, Exhibit C in the case. This is strongly confirmatory of the position I have assumed to demonstrate in § 44 of this argument, namely, that captains (comandantes) of Presidios could not grant lands *outside* of their Presidial-Pueblos (see Addenda, No. VIII), while it decides nothing on the question whether the power remained to them to grant lands *within* such Pueblos. If the power to grant within Pueblos was a part of their *political* authority, it is very certain that they lost it by the happening of the Mexican Revolution of 1821. Leyes Vigentes, Preface; see also § 54 of this argument. That there was an *interregnum* between the laws of August 11th, 1824, *directing* colonization, ante § 56, Addenda, No. XII, page 23, and the Regulations of November 21, 1828, which prescribed the *mode* of colonization, can easily be imagined. See § 56, also Addenda, No. XIV, page 25. Thus grants of lands were interdicted, unless made by certain authorities, and in a prescribed form, but at the same time the authorities were not named nor the form indicated, and so no grants could be made for the time being. A singular confirmation of this view is furnished by Capt. Beechy, who visited the Presidio of San Francisco, in November, 1826: "A further grievance has arisen by the "refusal of the Government to continue certain privileges which were "enjoyed under *the old system.* At that time soldiers entered for a "term of ten years, at the expiration of which they were allowed to "retire to the Pueblos,—villages erected for this purpose, and attached "to the Missions, where the men have a portion of ground allotted to "them for the support of their families. This afforded a competence to "many; and while it benefitted them, it was of service to the Govern-"ment, as the country by that means became settled, and its security "increased. But this privilege has been latterly withheld and the "applicants have been allowed only to possess the land and feed *their* "*cattle* upon it, until it should please the Government to turn them "off." Narrative of a voyage to the Pacific Beering Straits, in the year 1825–1828, by Capt. F. W. Beechy, R. N., F. R. S.: London, Colburn & Bentley, 1831; Vol. II, pages 10, 11. This account is full of errors, such as a stranger would naturally fall into, but it contains enough of truth to confirm my proposition. Between the adoption of the Law of Colonization in 1824 (next preceding § 56) and the Regulation of Colonization, prescribing the *mode*, (see next § 56) it is not improbable that the power to grant lands outside of the Pueblos was wholly in abeyance. Certainly Comandantes of Presidios could not then grant such lands, nor could they have done so before that time. See ADDENDA, No. VIII, page 17. See § 44 of this argument.

A. D. 1833.

THE MEXICAN GOVERNMENT ORDERS THE MISSIONS OF CALIFORNIA TO BE SECULARIZED.

§ **58.** I have shown ante §§ 26, 53, that the Missionary system was tended to be succeeded by a purely civil colonization; that the Missions were to be secularized; and that the Cortes of Spain, in 1813, had shown their impatience that secularization had not been already accomplished. But in August, 1828, the Congress of Mexico decreed that the secularization of the Missions should be "proceeded with." ADDENDA, No. XV, page 26. Pursuant to that decree, Governor Figueroa, in August 1833, enacted certain "Provisional Rules for the Secularization of the Missions," which were to go into effect in August, 1834, "commencing with ten Missions, and afterwards with the remainder." ADDENDA, No. XIX, page 31, Art. I, Id. No. XX, page 34. But the execution of the whole scheme was suspended by a decree of the President of Mexico, of November 7th, 1835. ADDENDA, No. XXVIII, page 43. There is not a shadow of pretence that up to January, 1835, the Mission of Dolores had been *secularized*, although nothing is more certain than the fact that the Majordomos mentioned in Article 8 of these "Provisional Rules" had taken possession of the property of the Missions.

THE SUCCESS OF THE MISSION SYSTEM.

§ **59.** The results of the Mission scheme of Christianization and Colonization were such as to justify the plans of the wise statesmen who hitherto devised it, and to gladden the hearts of the pious men who devoted their lives to its execution. At the end of sixty years, (in 1834) the missionaries of Upper California found themselves in possession of twenty-one prosperous Missions, planted upon a line of about seven hundred miles, running from San Diego north to the latitude of Sonoma. More than thirty thousand Indian converts were lodged in the Mission buildings, receiving religious culture, assisting at divine worship, and cheerfully performing their easy tasks. Over four hundred thousand horned cattle pastured upon the plains, as well as sixty thousand horses, and more than three hundred thousand sheep, goats and swine. Seventy thousand bushels of wheat were raised annually, which, with maize, beans and the like, made up an annual crop of one hundred and twenty thousand bushels; while, according to the climate, the different Missions rivalled each other in the production of wine, brandy, soap, leather, hides, wool, oil, cotton, hemp, linen, tobacco, salt and soda. 1 De Mofras, 320, 321, 338, 348, 366, 486, 488. Of two hundred thousand horned cattle annually slaughtered, the Missions furnished about one half, whose hides and tallow were sold at a net result of about ten dollars each, making a million of dollars from that source alone. 1 De Mofras, 320, 480, 484. While the other articles, of which no definite statistics can be obtained, doubtless reached an equal value, making a total production by the Missions themselves, of two millions of dollars. Gardens, vineyards and orchards surrounded all the Missions, except the three northernmost, Dolores, San Rafael, and San Francisco Solano, the climate of the first being too inhospitable for that purpose; and the two latter, born near the advent of the Mexican Revolution, being stifled in their infancy. The other Missions, according to their latitude, were ornamented and enriched with plantations of palm trees, bananas, oranges, olives, and figs; with orchards of European fruits; and with vast and fertile vineyards, whose products were equally valuable for sale and exchange, and for the diet and comfort of the inhabitants of the Missions. 1 De Mofras, 350, 351, 366, 420, etc. Aside from these valuable properties, and from the Mission buildings, the self-moving or live stock of the Missions, valued at their current rates, amounted to three millions of dollars of the most active capital, bringing enormous annual returns upon its aggregate amount, and, owing to the great fertility of animals in California, more than repairing its annual waste by slaughter. 1 De Mofras, 320, 472, 476. Such was the great religious success of the Catholic Missions in Upper California; such their material prosperity in the year 1834, even after many depredations had been committed upon them by the first Governors of the regime of "Independence." See ADDENDA, No. LXVII.

THE "PIOUS FUND" OF THE MISSIONS OF CALIFORNIA.

§ **60.** "What is remarkable in the establishment of these Missions, *they cost the government nothing.* When the Missions of Lower California were first founded, the Viceroys furnished some assistance. Philip V, gave them in the first years of his reign an annual pension of $13,000 ; but in the year 1735, the Jesuits, having received some large donations, administered them so well, that they not only supplied all the wants of their Missions, but added to the capital of their funds by the purchase of productive real estate, *(mais encore acheter de nouveaux terrains.)* In 1767, a lady of Guadalajara, Dona Josefa de Miranda, left by will to the College of the Society of Jesus, of that city, a legacy of more than $100,000, which the Jesuits, who were already the objects of the slanders of all Europe, had the delicacy to refuse." 1 De Mofras, 266 ; Clavigaro.

WHAT CONSTITUTED THE " PIOUS FUND."

§ **61.** " The property belonging to the 'Pious Fund of California,' with its successive additions, comprised the following : The landed estates, *(haciendas)* of San Pedro, Torreon, Rincon, and the Golondrinas, including several mines, manufactories, and immense flocks, with more than five hundred square leagues of land, all situated in the new kingdom of Léon, or province of Tamaulipas. These properties were given voluntarily to the Society by the Marquis de Villa Puente, Grand-Chancellor of New Spain, and by his wife, the Marchioness de Las Torres, on June 8th, 1735. Other legacies enriched the Society of Jesus with considerable estates, situated near San Luis de Potosi, Guanajuato and Guadalajara. The property known under the name of 'la Ciénega del Pastor,' near the last named city, and which, notwithstanding its dilapidated condition, and its mal-administration, is still rented annually for more than twenty thousand dollars. Another estate of the Society, the Hacienda of Chalco, belongs to the Pious fund, which possesses besides, a very great number of houses, and other real estate, situate in the cities, particularly in Mexico." 1 De Mofras, 267.

SPOLIATION OF THE " PIOUS FUND."

§ **62.** " In 1827, the government forcibly seized $78,000 in specie, deposited at the mint in Mexico, and which was the produce of the sale of the Arroyo Zarco, an estate of the Society. The ' Pious Fund' was also despoiled of immense tracts of land by the Congress of Jalisco." 1 De Mofras, 268.

ANNUAL PRODUCE OF THE " PIOUS FUND."

§ **63.** " Under the Spanish Government the revenues amounted to about $50,000 a year, which paid the stipends (sinodos) of the monks, namely, fifteen Dominicans, at $600 each ; and forty Franciscans at $400 each ; and, this total of $24,000 being deducted, the balance was used in the purchase of cloths, implements, tools, (étoffes, machines, outils,) church utensils and ornaments for the service of religion. The royal government reimbursed to the agent of the Missions at Mexico, the value of all supplies furnished by the Missions to the Presidios; and the agent converted that money into merchandize, which he sent, at his own charge, to the port of San Blas, whence, twice a year, frigates transported it gratuitously to the various ports of California." De Mofras, Vol. I, pp. 266 to 268.

The Stipends Fail: $1,000,000 due the Missions.

§ **64.** "From 1811 to 1818, and from 1828 to January, 1831, the Missionaries ceased to receive their stipends regularly, on account of the political troubles which, at those epochs, agitated Spain and Mexico. Thus, adding together the sums due to the Franciscans of Upper California only, amounting to $192,000; the $78,000 taken by force; the $272,000 for which the Missions of Upper California were out of pocket for supplies furnished to the Presidios; and the revenues of the ' Pious Fund' for more than ten years, we obtain a total of *more than a million of dollars*, of which the Mexican Government had already despoiled the Missionary Association." De Mofras, Vol. I, pp. 269, 270. This, it will be observed, does not include the *capital* of the Pious Fund, except the $78,000 which was, as above stated, the proceeds of the sale of an estate belonging to that fund.

The "Pious Fund" diverted into the Public Treasury.

§ **65.** "On May 25th, 1832, the Mexican Congress passed a decree by which the executive power was directed to rent out for a gross sum for seven years, (or farm out: *affermer,*) the property of the ' Pious Fund,' and pay the proceeds into the national treasury." 1 De Mofras, 270. Arrillaga, Colleccion de Decretos, 1832–1833, page 114.

The "Pious Fund" Restored to the Bishop of California. *

§ **66.** A second decree of Congress, of the 19th September, 1836, directed that the ' Pious Fund' should be placed at the disposal of the new Bishop of California and his successors, to the end that these prelates, to whom its administration was thus confided, might employ it in the development of the Missions, or in similar enterprises, according to the wish of its founders. 1 De Mofras, 270. Arrillaga, Colleccion de Decretos, July to Dec. 1836, page 107.

---

* NOTE.—This is the first time that the designation "BISHOP OF CALIFORNIA" occurs. Previous to 1840, California was not a Diocese of any church, but the Popes had, by various Bulls, granted Episcopal powers to the Apostolical Prefect [President of the Missions] of California, for the time being. Bull of Leo X, April 25th, 1521; of Adrian VI, May 9th, 1522; of Clement XIV, June 16th, 1774. But in 1840 the then Pope, Gregory XVI, erected California into a Bishopric, and named to that See the Rev. GARCIA DIEGO, a Mexican Franciscan, who had been for some time a Missionary in California, designating San Diego as his residence. 1 De Mofras, 275. The title "BISHOP OF CALIFORNIA" was thus appropriated by the Catholic Church at least twenty years before any other person claiming episcopal functions appeared on this coast, and has been so used with uninterrupted succession since.

SANTA ANNA "ADMINISTERS" THE "PIOUS FUND."

§ **67.** "On February 8th, 1842, General Santa Anna, Provisional President, by virtue of his discretionary power, deprived the Bishop of California, notwithstanding his protest, of the administration of the 'Pious Fund;' and, by a decree of the 21st of the same month, entrusted it to General Valencia, chief of the Army Staff. To any one who is acquainted with Mexico, the word 'administer' has an unmistakable sense. This was the last blow which the organization created by the Jesuits received before the final sale. Let us add, however, in justice, that hitherto the few Franciscans who remain in California have received an annual relief of $400 in merchandise, marked at exorbitant prices." De Mofras, Vol. I, pages 270–271. This decree of Santa Anna is to be found in El Observador Judicial y de Legislacion, 1842, Vol. I, p. 351.

THE "PIOUS FUND" IS SOLD AND THE PROCEEDS ABSORBED.

§ **68.** Finally, President Santa Anna sold the 'Pious Fund' in a mass, to the house of Barrio, and to Rubio brothers.

The final sale above alluded to, namely, "that President Santa Anna sold the 'Pious Fund' in a mass to the house of Barrio, and to Rubio brothers," De Mofras, Vol. I, page 268, is thus mentioned at pages 65–66 of the same volume: "Bold by the very excess of weakness, the Mexican Government recoils from no arbitrary measure to supply its financial deficits. Thus it has not hesitated to seize the property belonging to the Missions of California, whose value is not less than *two millions of dollars*, and sell it to the house of Barrio." The date is not given, but is stated at page 271 to have been after the fund was entrusted to Valencia, which was on Feb. 21, 1842, and the decree, the first section of which incorporates into the national treasury (erario nacional) the entire "Pious Fund," and the second section of which provides for the sale of the property, is dated Oct. 24, 1842, and may be presumed to have had a sufficiently rapid execution. See the original decree: El Observador Judicial y de Legislacion, 1842, Vol. 2, page 340.

A. D. 1834.

MEANWHILE THERE WAS NO AYUNTAMIENTO AT SAN FRANCISCO. AYUNTAMIENTOS DIVIDED INTO THREE CLASSES.

§ **69.** During all this period, and up to the autumn of 1834, there had been no Ayuntamiento, or Common Council, at San Francisco. This clearly appears from the ADDENDA, No. XVI, page 27, No. XVII, page 28, and No. XVIII, page 29, all of which belong to the documentary testimony in the case. The population of San Francisco was ruled by a Military Comandánte of the Presidio, who was also a Judge of First Instance, while the Governor generously imposed license fees and taxes on a liberal scale. *Ibid.* It is necessary to recur here, for a moment, to three different classes into which we have divided Ayuntamientos, namely :

1st. AYUNTAMIENTOS SOLE, existing for a single Pueblo.

2d. AYUNTAMIENTOS AGGREGATE, composed of small populations, each too small to have an Ayuntamiento of its own.

3d. COMPOSITE AYUNTAMIENTOS, formed of the Ayuntamiento of a PUEBLO, to which were joined other small populations. See § 50 of this argument.

A. D. 1834.

AN AYUNTAMIENTO AGGREGATE ORDERED FOR THE PARTIDO OF SAN FRANCISCO.

§ **70.** On the 14th day of November, 1834, Governor Figueroa communicated to the Military Comandante of San Francisco, that the Territorial Deputation, exercising the powers conferred upon it by the law of June 23d, 1813, had directed the election of a Constitutional Ayuntamiento for the *Partido* of San Francisco. See Exhibit No. 1, to Vallejo's deposition. ADDENDA, No. XXI, page 35. What these powers were which were conferred by the law of June 23d, 1813, appears from Chap. II, Art. I, as set forth in the Leyes Vigentes, page 91, where the Provincial Deputations are empowered to aggregate populations for the purpose of forming Ayuntamientos, in cases where the population of a Pueblo is insufficient for that purpose. The Ayuntamientos thus ordered to be formed, was, therefore, for the purpose of giving a municipal government to those small populations of the Partido which could not otherwise have an *Ayuntamiento.* It is evident that it did not include San José, and the reason for this exception was that San José had had immemorially an Ayuntamiento of its own. ADDENDA, No. XXIX. And yet San José was within the Partido of San Francisco. The Ayuntamiento of the Partido of San Francisco was an aggregated Ayuntamiento, constituted under the laws above cited from Leyes Vigentes, page 91, Chap. II, Art. I, *Id,* page 28, Arts. II, VIII and IX, 1 White's New Recapitulacion, 416, etc. ADDENDA, No. X. This order for the election of an Ayuntamiento, as will be seen by consulting it, ADDENDA, No. XXI, page 35, directed the election of an Ayuntamiento for the Partido, to reside at the Presidio of San Francisco, and to consist of an Alcalde, two Councilmen, and one Syndic Procurador.

THIS PARTIDO AYUNTAMIENTO WAS ORGANIZED.

§ **71.** Was this Ayuntamiento of the Partido ever elected and constituted? Messrs. J. H. McKune and Horace Hawes, in their joint printed brief, entitled, "Documents, Depositions and Brief of Law "Points raised thereon in behalf of the United States, in Case No. 280, "(this same case) before the U. S. Board of Land Commissioners," at page 10, after reciting that by Exhibit Nos. 1 and 2, annexed to the deposition of M. G. Vallejo, in this case, ADDENDA, No. XXI, pages 35 and 36, after stating that electors were chosen on Dec. 7th 1834, "who were to elect the municipal officers," add : "but whether the elec- "tion of Ayuntamiento took place, does not appear from any docu-

" ment on file." But we are prepared to prove that this Ayuntamiento of the Partido was elected, was duly installed, and entered upon its functions. For in the inventory of the Documents on file in the Juzgado of San Francisco de Asis, which appears twice in the documentary testimony, first as Exhibit Hopkins, No. 1, offered by the claimants, and as Exhibit Hopkins, M, offered by the United States, under date of January 1835, appears the record of an *oficio*,—an official communication,—from the government, approving the appointment of a Secretary of the Ayuntamiento, and of an Assistant Alcalde for Contra Costa—the Counter-Coast, *the other side of the Bay.* The importance of this latter *oficio* will be shown hereafter; we shall meanwhile bear in mind that this Ayuntamiento of the PARTIDO *had authority for appointing Alcaldes for the other side of the Bay.*

A. D. 1835. JANUARY.

A COMPOSITE AYUNTAMIENTO ORDERED TO BE ELECTED FOR THE PUEBLO OF SAN FRANCISCO.

§ **72.** But it is equally evident that this *aggregate* Ayuntamiento for the PARTIDO of San Francisco, was immediately superseded by a *composite* Ayuntamiento for the Pueblo of San Francisco. For in the same document marked " Exhibit Hopkins, No. 1 " and also M, under the date of November, 1834, is a synopsis of an *oficio* from the Governor directing a census of the population of San Francisco to be taken and returned to him. This *oficio* is lost, existing neither in the Archives of the Pueblo nor of those of the Department in any form. See testimony of Hopkins and Dwinelle. But the direction was executed, for the Governor, under date of January 31st, 1835, announces to the same Military Comandante that he had received the census of the PUEBLO OF SAN FRANCISCO, by which it appeared that it was entitled to an Ayuntamiento of its own, composed of one Alcalde, two Regidores, and one Sindico Procurador, and directing him to proceed to their election accordingly. See Exhibit No. 14 to R. C. Hopkins's deposition, printed in the ADDENDA, No. XXIII, page 37. The census of San Francisco disclosed therefore between 50 and 200 inhabitants. Leyes Vigentes, page 29, Arts. IV and IX. ADDENDA, No. X, Arts. 4 and 9, pages 18, etc., because " one Alcalde, two Regidores, and one Procurador Syndic " were the officers prescribed for those PUEBLOS whose population was less than fifty and did not exceed two hundred inhabitants.

WHAT WAS THE ACTUAL POPULATION OF THE PUEBLO OF SAN FRANCISCO IN 1834–1835?

§ **73.** We have seen in the preceding § 72, that the population of the PUEBLO of San Francisco in 1834–1835 could not have exceeded 200 inhabitants. This was established as matter of law, by the census returns and the act of the Governor founded on them, as detailed in that section. The same result would have been reached proximately by statistical data, and calculations founded on them. From the data contained in the ADDENDA, No. LXXVI, we obtain the following data as to the

POPULATION OF THE PRESIDIAL–PUEBLO OF SAN FRANCISCO.

A. D.	Men.	Women.	Boys.	Girls.	Total.
1794	46	33	38	26	143
1800	79	49	46	49	223
1815	125	92	74	82	373
1830	59	46	13	13	131

See ADDENDA, No. XXLVI, page 110.

These returns in a perfect or aggregate form come no lower than 1830. In 1842, the aggregate white population of the *political* jurisdiction of San Francisco did not exceed 160. See ADDENDA, No. LV, page 78, etc. This strongly confirms the official data of the census and order of the Governor, and taking the two together, it shows that the population of the Pueblo was less than 200. Moreover, these same official returns in the Archives, show that at the same dates above mentioned there was the following

POPULATION (INDIAN) OF THE MISSION OF DOLORES.

A. D.	Men.	Women.	Boys.	Girls.	Total.
1794	355	369	110	79	913
1800	315	260	32	37	644
1815	542	391	90	92	1115
1830	140	53	13	13	219

From all of which we are compelled to infer:

FIRST: That the whole white population of the PUEBLO of San Francisco in 1834–1835 did not exceed 200 inhabitants. For, taking the whole population of the Pueblo and Mission at 350 in 1830, as above, and at 196 in 1842 (ADDENDA, No. LV), I know of no law of estimation which would not give the aggregate population of both Pueblo and Mission at more than 200 in 1836, especially as the population of the Pueblo did not begin to diminish until 1833. See §§ 90, 91 of this argument. But the PUEBLO proper must have had less than 200 inhabitants in 1834–5, or *four* Regidores would have been ordered to be elected instead of only *two*. Law of 1812, ADDENDA, No. X, page 19, § 4.

SECONDLY: That the population of the Indian neophytes of the Mission of Dolores, although within the political jurisdiction of the PUEBLO of San Francisco, yet being in a state of pupilage, and not exercising the rights of citizenship, were not counted in the electoral basis of a Pueblo. They were like a sandy, marshy, mountainous or rocky tract included in a survey of lands, embraced within its boundaries but not counted in acres as a part of it. See Ordenanzas de Tierras y Aguas, ante § 30, ut supra. If any one is inclined to believe in the perfectness of these California Archives, let him try to reproduce the census of California from the materials there found. Each Presidio and Mission was bound to report every three months, and yet I have not been able to find any civil reports of the Presidios later than 1832, and that one incomplete (Vol. V Missions, page 344), and none for the Missions separately later than 1817 (Vol. IV Missions and Colonization, page 532.) I have searched myself, and employed the most competent assistance of gentlemen familiar with the Archives. Still such data may be in the Archives and not yet be discovered, such is the confusion which has been introduced there under the so-called " arrangement " made by a late special Attorney of the United States.

This New Ayuntamiento was Elected and Organized.

§ **74.** That this Ayuntamiento for the PUEBLO of San Francisco was elected and organized, appears from the acts of election. ADDENDA, Nos. XXX, page 47, and XXXV, page 53, being Exhibits 3, 8, and 9, to the deposition of Vallejo, in the case. It was also recognized as the Ayuntamiento of the PUEBLO by the General and Departmental Junta or Legislature. ADDENDA, No. XXVI, page 42, etc.; No. XXIX, pages 44, etc., and in various other proceedings to which reference will be made in the course of the argument. It is never styled the Ayuntamiento of the PARTIDO, but always called the Ayuntamiento of the PUEBLO. It therefore superseded the Ayuntamiento of the Partido. Instead of being an *aggregated* Ayuntamiento *composed* of small populations in the PARTIDO, it was an Ayuntamiento of the PUEBLO, *to which* various small populations of the Partido were *aggregated*, or, as I have styled it, ante § 30, a *composite Ayuntamiento*.

§ **75.** If it be asked, where is the official act, the *espediente* of the formation of this Ayuntamiento of the Pueblo of San Francisco, we ask in reply, where did we find the *expediente* of the formation of the Ayuntamiento of the Pueblo of Santa Barbara, which is in evidence in this cause? Was it found in the Archives, where it ought to have been found? It was found in private hands, and if the Archives alone had been relied upon, that document would never have been forthcoming. But we do find fragmentary records of the existence and continuance of this Ayuntamiento of the Pueblo of San Francisco in Exhibits Nos. 3 and 6, annexed to the deposition of M. G. Vallejo, ADDENDA, No. XXVI, page 42, No. XXX, page 47; and Exhibits 8 and 9, annexed to the same deposition, ADDENDA, No. XXXV, page 53, § 54 show the formation of the electoral college of the same Ayuntamiento of the Pueblo, on December 3d, 1837, and the election of the Ayuntamiento by that college, on January 8th, 1838. Are we asked to call Vallejo? The *expediente* could never have been properly in his custody, for it belonged to the Archives of the Government; he could therefore depose only orally to a disputed fact, and in so doing, must contradict his testimony already given in the case. We know of no rule which compels us to call a witness whom our adversaries insist on discrediting, or to consume the time of the Court in demonstrations which must be utterly fruitless. The book of elections mentioned in Exhibit No. 1, to the testimony of R. C. Hopkins is unfortunately " lost." See testimony of R. C. Hopkins, and J. W. Dwinelle.

THIS WAS AN AYUNTAMIENTO FOR THE PUEBLO.

§ **76.** I have said that the only Ayuntamiento of whose actual formation and continued existence we have any record, was always spoken of as that of the PUEBLO of San Francisco. In Exhibit No. 3 to the deposition of Vallejo, ADDENDA, No. XXX, page 47, San Francisco is twice spoken of as a Pueblo; in Exhibit No. 6 to the deposition of Vallejo, ADDENDA, No. XXVI, page 42, on October 26, 1835, it is spoken of in a letter to the Alcalde of San Francisco, as the "Ayuntamiento of that PUEBLO"—" el Ayuntamiento de ese PUEBLO," and the Alcalde is directed to inform the "inhabitants of that PUEBLO" that the Ayuntamiento could grant solares at Yerba Buena, showing that the Ayuntamiento of the PARTIDO was not then in existence, but that the Ayuntamiento of the PUEBLO was. The acts of election of this Ayuntamiento again appear in 1835, 1837 and 1838, in Exhibits Nos. 3, 8 and 9 to Vallejo's depositions, ADDENDA, No. XXX, page 47, No. XXXV, page 53, always held in the PUEBLO of San Francisco. On the 30th of May, 1835, certain petitioners, describing themselves as residents of the Ranchos of the North, San Antonio, San Pablo and those adjoining, petition the Governor, representing that they are *attached* to the jurisdiction of the port of San Francisco, and asking to be *detached* therefrom, and *attached* to the jurisdiction of San José. Document C, P. L. in the case. ADDENDA, No. XXIX, page 44. The Governor directs *informes* (reports) to be-made by the *Ayuntamientos* of the PUEBLOS of SAN JOSE and SAN FRANCISCO and the *expediente* is returned to those Ayuntamientos accordingly. *Id.* When completed, it was to be accompanied with a list of the inhabitants of the "PUEBLO of San Francisco." The Ayuntamiento of San José in their report state that the petitioners had formerly belonged to that jurisdiction. See the same document. From this one *expediente*, several facts are apparent:

FIRST: That the inhabitants of these ranchos were not a constituent or essential part of the Ayuntamiento of San Francisco, but were only *attached*, or *aggregated* to it under Article IX of the decree of May 23d, 1813, Leyes Vigentes, page 29, 1 White's Recopilacion, 418, §§ 2 and 9. ADDENDA, No. X, pages 19, 20, §§ 2, 9. See § 50 ante.

SECONDLY: That it was the *Ayuntamiento of the* PUEBLO of San Francisco, from which they wished to be *detached* and *annexed* to the Ayuntamiento of the PUEBLO of San José.

THIRDLY: That although the PUEBLO of San José and the Pueblo of San Francisco were both in the same PARTIDO, yet each PUEBLO had its own AYUNTAMIENTO.

FOURTHLY: That there was no longer any Ayuntamiento for the PARTIDO of which San Francisco was the *cabecera*, or capital.

A. D. 1835.

A COMPLETE PUEBLO EXISTED AT SAN FRANCISCO.

§ **77.** We see, therefore, that there was a complete PUEBLO of San Francisco, with its own Ayuntamiento, and thus possessing the highest political organization known to the laws of Spain and Mexico. For, a Pueblo thus organized under Article IV of the Law of May 23, 1812, with one Alcalde, two Regidores, and one Sindico Procurator, Leyes Vigentes, page 28, ante §§ 47–51, ADDENDA, No. X, page 18, etc., had as high a political capacity as those Pueblos with ·two Alcaldes, and eight, twelve, or even sixteen Regidores, as provided in that and the succeeding article. In each and every case, the Ayuntamiento of a Pueblo possessed the general functions and powers usually belonging to Spanish, French and English Common Councils (Councils of the *Commune*) and which are defined at great length in the Leyes Vigentes, page 85, etc. Decretos de 23 de Junio de 1813, Instruccion para el gobierno economico politico de las *provincias*. Capitulo I, De las obligaciones de los Ayuntamientos; Decree of June 23d, 1813. Directions for the politico-economical government of the provinces (California was a *Department* after the Revolution of 1821); Chapter I, concerning the duties of Ayuntamientos, Leyes Vigentes, 50, ut supra. See also Decreto de 9 de Octobre de 1812; Reglamento de las audiencas y juzgados de primera instancia; Capitulo III. De los Alcaldes constitutionales de los Pueblos—Concerning the constitutional Alcaldes of the Pueblos; showing that these Alcaldes belonged to the same constitutional system as the Ayuntamientos of Pueblos, Leyes Vigentes, pp. 35, 50; 1 White's Recopilacion, 419, etc. See by comparison, Merlin, Repertoire de Jurisprudence, Vol. 5, p. 191, title Commune. The title of Villa, which some Pueblos had, was only one of dignity, as that of Ciudad, city, was of nobility; neither conferred any increase of political or municipal power or consideration.

A. D. 1835. JUNE.

THE AYUNTAMIENTO OF SAN FRANCISCO ASK FOR THEIR EJIDOS AND PROPIOS TO BE ASSIGNED.

§ **78.** Among the papers mentioned in the list of PUEBLO Archives contained in the document Exhibit No. 1 to testimony of R. C. Hopkins, is the following: "1835, June. A reply to the petition made "by the Ayuntamiento in relation to the assigning of *ejidos* and lands "for *propios*." This document is one of the lost documents; the original is not to be found in the Archives, nor is its duplicate among the PUEBLO papers. It seems, therefore, that the Ayuntamiento of San Francisco, in 1835, thought that that PUEBLO was entitled to *Ejidos*, and *Propios*, respecting which see §§ 11 and 14 of this argument. The Departmental Junta was not in session from Nov. 3d,

1834, to August 5th, 1835. California Archives, Legislative Records, Vol. II, pages 247–250. September, 1835, Don Lorenzo Quijas, the missionary monk at the Mission of Dolores, petitioned to have *ejidos* assigned for that Mission ; but this petition was rejected by the Departmental Junta. *Ibid,* pages 600, 282. It thus appears that the Pueblo of San Francisco and the Mission of Dolores were not at that date confounded with each other.

A. D. 1835.

THE POLITICAL AUTHORITIES PREPARE TO SECULARIZE THE MISSIONS. THE REAL OBJECT OF SECULARIZATION. IT IS ATTEMPTED AND SUSPENDED, BUT THE MISSIONS RUINED MEANWHILE.

§ **79.** The theory of secularization was a plausible one. It was : that the country having been colonized, and the Indians converted, the Missionary system had thus become spent by accomplishing its object ; that the system of Secular curacies—a normal one in the church—should now be substituted in their stead, and the population around them established in villages ; that the Monks, who were mostly Spaniards, and, as such, nationally unpopular, and supposed to be hostile to the newly acquired " Independence," should be got out of the country ; leaving California fully colonized, with uniform and homogeneous institutions, united, prosperous and contented. Ante, §§ 26, etc. But, beneath these specious pretences, was undoubtedly a perfect understanding between the Government at Mexico and the leading men in California, that such a condition of things should be created that the Supreme Government might absorb the " Pious Fund " under the pretence that it was no longer needed for missionary purposes, and thus had reverted to the State as a *quasi* escheat; while the co-actors in California should appropriate the local wealth of the Missions, by the rapid and sure process of "administering" their temporalities. The history of the " Pious Fund " already given (ante, §§ 60 to 68 of this argument), and that of " Secularization," hereafter sketched in this argument, leave no doubt of the truth of this proposition. Already on August 17th, 1833, the Mexican Congress had ordered the Missions to be secularized, the object being to convert the Missions into villages, the Indians into citizens, and the Mission chapels into parochial churches, under the charge of secular Priests. See ADDENDA, No. XV, page 26. This scheme was attempted to be carried into effect by Governor Figueroa, who adopted certain " Provisional Rules for the Secularization of the Missions," bearing date August 9th, 1834, and which were to be put in force in August, 1835. See ADDENDA, No. XIX, page 31, Art. I. These regulations were approved by the California Legislature on Nov. 3d, 1834, and further steps taken by them to provide for the payment of the parochial priests. See ADDENDA, No. XX, page 34. It will be seen by examining the provisions of these three laws that they contemplated the gradual change of these *religious communities* into *civil municipalities,* that their property, (flocks, etc.) should pass at once into civil administration, and that secular priests should take the place of the missionaries. That administrators did at once assume the charge of the temporalities of the Missions is very evident, for in September, 1835, we find Flores acting as Administrator of the Mission of Dolores. ADDENDA, No. XXV, page 39. But greedy and ready as the Administrators were, the parochial priests were not forthcoming, and consequently the President of Mexico, by decree of November 7th, 1835, suspended the execution of the law of secularization until the parochial curates should appear and take possession of the Missions; that is, suspended the law for the time being. See ADDENDA, No. XXVIII, page 43. Governor Alvarado, in his "Regulations respecting Missions," of January, 1839, states explicitly that the secularization of the Missions had not yet at that late date been effected, while they had been plundered by persons acting as administrators. ADDENDA, No. XXXVII, page 55, preamble and Art. I. We shall bear in mind, then, that during the period from 1833 to 1839, the secularization of the Missions of California had been decreed by law and regulated by "Provisions," all of which were suspended, and not carried into effect any further than to place the Missions in the charge of administrators who "administered" them much as Santa Anna administered the "Pious Fund of California," ante, §§ 67, 68. Meanwhile there was no Indian Pueblo at Dolores, but the Indians still lived in *community* there. See all the documents cited in this section.

A. D. 1835.

THE GOVERNOR OF CALIFORNIA BEGINS TO GRANT SITIOS, OR RANCHOS FROM THE PUEBLO LANDS.

§ **80.** Meanwhile, it having been determined that the Missions should be plundered, private individuals began to petition for grants of grazing lands, which, when obtained, were for the most part stocked with the spoils of these religious establishments. 1 De Mofras, 301, 303, 390. Among such grants were many from the lands of various Pueblos, and in the number of these is that of San Francisco. It is necessary now to inquire by what right the Governor could make such grants of Pueblo lands?

AUTHORITY OF THE GOVERNOR TO MAKE GRANTS OF PUEBLO LANDS.

§ **81.** There are several principles enunciated in the case of Brown against the City of San Francisco, 16 California Reports, 451, upon any of which the authority of the Governors of California to make grants of lands situate within the limits of Pueblos, may be sustained; and that they had such authority, that case decides expressly in point. Independently of any express authority being shown, such authority will be presumed. United States vs. Perchman, 7 Peter, 95. But the true source of that power seems to be in that enactment made by the Cortes of Spain on the 4th of January, A. D. 1813, to which I have before referred, ante § 52, which is one of the laws that survived the Mexican Revolution, and is contained in the Leyes Vigentes, at page 56. It is printed in full in the ADDENDA, No. XI, at pages 20, etc. Section 1 of this decree provides that all the lands and property of the Pueblos, both in Spain and beyond the seas, except the *ejidos*, or commons, (vacant suburbs) should be reduced to private ownership; while Article 3d enacts that, in the distribution of the lands, prefer- ence should be given to the residents of the respective Pueblos—"Los vecinos de los Pueblos en cuyo termino existen." No other authority was needed.

A. D. 1835.

GALINDO'S ESPEDIENTE FOR THE LAGUNA DE LA MERCED.

§ 82. Several *espedientes* of grants of lands in the vicinity of San Francisco have been introduced in evidence, and they all illustrate the views which I have endeavored to enforce, and shed a strong light upon the progressive growth of the PUEBLO of San Francisco. The first in order of date is the "Espediente sobre el Parage nombrado " 'Laguna de la Merced,' solicitado por José Antonio Galindo." " *Es-* "*pediente* for the place called 'Laguna de la Merced,' (Lake of Mercy,) "petitioned for by José Antonio Galindo." This is the *espediente* No. 10, in Wm. Carey Jones' list, U. S. Senate Documents, 1850–1851, Vol. 3, Doc. 18, p. 95, etc., and set forth in Exhibit Hopkins, No. 12, duplicated in Exhibit Hopkins, R, and printed in the ADDENDA, No. XXV, at page 38. The *espediente* commences with a petition of Galindo to the Superior Political Chief (Governor) for the Rancho known as "La Laguna de Merced," dated at San Francisco, Aug. 15, 1835. The land is described in the petition as "vacant, lying near " San Francisco *and* Dolores." The Governor, in the marginal *informe*, dated Sept. 5, 1835, directs the "Ayuntamiento of San Fran- " cisco to report whether the interested party has the requisite qualifi- " cations. Whether the land * * * is the property of any "individual, Mission, corporation or Pueblo," (corporacion ó Pueblo,) and after they had made their report to "transmit the espediente to "the superintendent of the Mission, that he may report also :"—" al " Señor mayor domo de la misma Mission para que esponga lo que le " ocurra sobre el particular." The Ayuntamiento of San Francisco, by a report dated at *San Francisco*, Sept. 10th, 1835, (el Ayuntamiento de esta demarcacion) state " that the land formerly belonged to the "Mission of San Francisco, from which it is one league distant, to the " west, that the land is almost worthless, which is all that *this corpo-* "*racion* (esta corporacion) has to say in the matter." This report is signed by Francisco De Haro as President of the Ayuntamiento, and by Francisco Sanchez as Secretary. The *espediente* next contains the report of Guermecindo Flores, Superintendent of the Mission, dated at *Dolores*, Sept. 13th, 1835, which states " that the lands belong to this Community," (Comunidad,) [see ante § 17] that " it is at the " distance of a little more than a league from it and not occupied by " it, but, as the *ejidos* and *propios* which, it seems to me, will remain

" to this (place) when *it shall be* erected into a *Pueblo* are not yet
" designated. I do not know whether or not they will embrace this
" land, or whether or not they can be granted without injury to this
" *community*. (Pero con motivo que no estan aun señalados los ejidos
" ó propros que me parece quedaran á esta cuando se erija en Pueblo,
" etc)." The *espediente* was carried forward to its conclusion, and the
land granted to the petitioner, being approximately the tracts marked
" Merced " and De Haro on the accompanying map.

From this *espediente* several important facts appear :

FIRST : That although the term San Francisco was often applied
to the Mission of Dolores, because it was the Mission " de los Dolores
de San Francisco de Asis," yet when official acts or proprietary rights
were concerned, the two were kept perfectly distinct. Here, in the
same petition, these two places are spoken of as " San Francisco *and*
Dolores," and while all documents relating to San Francisco are dated
at that place, yet those relating to the Mission are dated at Dolores.

SECONDLY : That there was at that early date an " Ayuntamiento
of San Francisco," which had a President and Secretary, and which
styled itself a " corporation."

THIRDLY : That although there was at that early date a " PUEBLO
of San Francisco," (see §§ 72 to 77,) yet that this PUEBLO was not
at the Mission of Dolores, for we find the mayor domo of that Mission
expressing his hopes that the Mission would yet be erected into a
PUEBLO : hopes which he may be pardoned for entertaining in the
second year of the secularization of the Missions.

FOURTHLY : That the Mission is always spoken of as a *community*,
(comunidad,) the Missions and the Indian Pueblos always enjoying
their property in that form. See ante § 17.

FIFTHLY ; That the lands petitioned for being within or near the
four leagues claimed for the PUEBLO of San Francisco the Ayuntamiento of that " corporation" were consulted on the subject. The
Administrator of the Mission was consulted because that establishment
had still an existing servitude in the lands : the Ayuntamiento of
San Francisco was consulted because that PUEBLO might have the
ultimate right to the lands themselves. The lands are spoken of by
the Administrator of the Mission as " belonging to it," a thing which
was impossible. Ante, § 26. Doubtless they had formerly been in
the possession of the Mission, though Flores reports that they were
not now in its possession. The Ayuntamiento of San Francisco report
that the lands are worthless, and so beneath their concern.

1835.

THE AYUNTAMIENTO OF THE PUEBLO OF SAN FRANCISCO HAD THE
POWER TO GRANT SOLARES, OR BUILDING LOTS, AND SUERTES,
OR LOTS FOR CULTIVATION.

§ **83.** In 1835, after the establishment of the Ayuntamiento of the
Pueblo of San Francisco, Don José Joaquin de Estudillo petitioned
De Haro, the Judge of First Instance, at San Francisco, for a grant of

a building lot and of a suerte for cultivation. The Judge of First Instance referred the matter to Governor Figueroa, who, on August 6th, 1835, replied that the Ayuntamiento had not the power to grant such lands. See ADDENDA, No. XXIV, page 37. But this reply does not seem to have been either right or acceptable, for the matter was afterwards brought before the Territorial Deputation of Upper California, who, on the 22d of September, approved that the "Ayuntamiento of that PUEBLO" might make such grants, and Governor Castro in his order of October 27th, 1835, directs the Alcalde of San Francisco to make the decision of the Territorial Deputation known to "the inhabitants of that PUEBLO." See ADDENDA, No. XXVI, page 42. From this document last cited, three things are evident:

FIRST: That in September, 1835, the Territorial Legislature of Upper California were of opinion that there was a "PUEBLO of San Francisco," and an "AYUNTAMIENTO OF THAT PUEBLO," which, consequently, was not the Ayuntamiento originally established for the PARTIDO.

SECONDLY: That in October, 1835, Governor Castro was of the same opinion.

THIRDLY: That in 1835, the "AYUNTAMIENTO OF THE PUEBLO OF SAN FRANCISCO" HAD THE POWER TO GRANT LANDS FOR BUILDING LOTS.

THE LAST PROPOSITION ABOVE STATED IS DECISIVE OF THE QUESTION.

§ 84. For, if the Ayuntamiento of the Pueblo of San Francisco had the power to grant lands, IT COULD BE ONLY BECAUSE SUCH LANDS BELONGED TO THAT PUEBLO.

I have before shown that the law passed by the Cortes of Spain, on January 4th, 1813, directing all the lands and other property of the PUEBLOS to be sold or granted in private ownership, was held by the Mexican jurisconsults to have survived the Mexican Revolution of 1821. See § 52 of this argument. Also, Leyes Vigentes, Preface, pages i to iv. Also, ADDENDA, No. XI, page 20. But in the recent case of the United States vs. Vallejo, 1 Black, St. S. S. C. Reports, page 541, decided in 1862, the Supreme Court of the United States decided that this enactment by the Cortes of Spain, in 1813, so far forth as the Crown Lands [or *public* lands], was repealed by the Colonization Laws of Mexico, enacted in 1824 and 1828. See § 81 of this argument. See these laws of Colonization, ADDENDA, No. XII, page 23, Id. No. XIV, page 25. But as these laws of Colonization thus repealed all former laws relating to public lands; and as by their terms these public lands could be granted only by the Governor, who had no power to *delegate* this authority, Law of 1824, ADDENDA, No. XIV, page 25, §§ 1, 2, 3, 4; and as lands belonging to private persons, corporations or PUEBLOS were excepted from the provisions of these Colonization laws, Law of 1824, ADDENDA, No. XII, page 23, § 2; and as the Ayuntamiento of San Francisco had the power to grant these lands, see preceding § 83; it therefore follows: that the Pueblo of San Francisco, not being a private person, but still owning lands not subject to the Colonization Laws, and which it had the power to grant, was either "a corporation or a PUEBLO," § 2 above: in other words, was an organized PUEBLO, and, as such, was a CORPORATION, or, at least, a *quasi* CORPORATION. The established fact that the Ayuntamiento of the Pueblo of San Francisco could thus grant lands, becomes decisive of the ownership of lands by that Pueblo. And this also shows that whereas the lands belonging to Pueblos were excepted from the operation of the Colonization Law of 1824, see ADDENDA, No. XII, page 23, § 2, that law survived as to the lands owned by such Pueblos, and consequently the source of the power of Ayuntamientos of Pueblos to grant such lands is to be found in that act of the Cortes of Jan. 4, 1813, which expressly gives it to them. See the act of the Cortes, ADDENDA, No. XI, page 22, §§ 15 to 17 inclusive. So that Governor Castro and the Departmental Legislature proved themselves better lawyers in this point than Governor Figueroa. See ante § 83.

§ **85.** It thus appears that the Ayuntamiento of San Francisco had the power to grant *solares* to the *vecinos* of the *Pueblo*. By what right? Not from the colonization law, for this gave no such right to towns; nor was any power of granting lands under that law capable of being delegated by the Governor or Departmental Junta to an Ayuntamiento, and yet the power was by the Governor and Departmental Junta declared to exist in the Ayuntamientos of the Pueblos, and was exercised by them for years without question, in face of the colonization laws of 1828. The right, then, was superior to the colonization laws, and anterior to them; founded on the laws of Old Spain, and therefore expressly excepted from the operation of the colonization laws. In the decree of August 18, 1824, respecting colonization, 1 Rockwell, 451, ADDENDA, No. XII, page 23, Sec. 2, it is declared: "The objects of this law are those national lands which are neither "private property nor belong to any corporation or pueblo, and can, "therefore, be colonized." The *Pueblos*, therefore, by their constituted agents, the Ayuntamientos, had an original power to make grants of these lands; and the validity of an execution of this power was not in any degree impaired by the fact that the Governor, representing the Sovereign as the supreme visitor of all corporations, could also make a beneficial disposition of such of these lands as had not been granted by the *Pueblo*, by conceding them to *vecinos* of the Pueblo.

1835–1836.

SURVEY OF THE BURI-BURI RANCHO.

§ **86.** In 1835 a grant was made to Don José Sanchez, of the Rancho Buri-Buri, see Jones's list, No. 20, and juridical possession was to be given to him. See the accompanying map: "BURI-BURI." This matter was intrusted to De Haro, who was Judge of First Instance in San Francisco. The Pueblo of San Francisco was thus represented in the person of its first officer. He therefore gave notice to the Mayordomo of the Mission of Dolores, to appoint his surveyor, and appear in court for the purpose of making the survey and finishing the proceeding. See ADDENDA, No. XXVII, page 43. The survey appears to have been had, and to have been wrong, as interfering with the private rights of certain Indians to whom tracts of land had been previously granted in private ownership; for which reason the then Governor, Gutierrez, ordered a new survey. See ADDENDA, No. XXXII. It has been attempted from these proceedings to draw the conclusion that the Mayordomo of the Mission of Dolores [de San Francisco] having been summoned to take part in these proceedings as the only coterminous neighbor (unico colindante) of the grantee of the Rancho of Buri-Buri, therefore the Pueblo of San Francisco could have no ownership or interest in the lands. But in reply it is to be remarked:

First. That by the previous laws the Catholic Missions in California, although not recognized as the owners of lands, were recognized as possessing an easement or servitude in the lands actually occupied by them, until that easement or servitude should be terminated by some legal official act. Ante § 26.

SECONDLY: That by § 17 of the Regulations of colonization of 1828, the lands occupied by the Missions could not be granted in colonization until some proceeding in the nature of an inquest of office had been had in regard to them. See the Law, ADDENDA, No. XIV, page 26, § 17. How, then, *could* lands adjoining a mission be granted without summoning the officer representing the Mission as the only coterminous neighbor in possession? In our Anglo-American law, when a railroad or other corporation wishes to condemn lands, is a tenant in possession of the lands to be regarded at all, or is he entitled to be summoned and heard? But in the case in hand we see that the Pueblo of San Francisco was represented by the very officer who was to superintend the proceedings, and that the Mayordomo of the Mission, representing only an easement or servitude, was duly summoned.

THIRDLY: That on consulting the maps it is doubtful whether any of the lands in question were within the four leagues of the PUEBLO, but its authorities were notified, as the lands *might* be within those four leagues.

A. D. 1836.

THE AYUNTAMIENTO OF THE PUEBLO OF SAN FRANCISCO GRANT
BUILDING LOTS TO RICHARDSON AND OTHERS.

§ **87.** The Territorial Legislature having decided that the Ayuntamiento of the Pueblo of San Francisco had the power to make grants of building lots, (see ante, § 83, ADDENDA, No. XXVI, page 43,) that Ayuntamiento immediately began to exercise this right. Among other grants was one made to William Richardson, bearing date June 1st, 1836, which is printed in full in the ADDENDA, No. XXIV. Other grants of the same kind are in evidence in the case, but this will serve as a sufficient specimen of the whole. From this one it appears not only that the Ayuntamiento exercised this right of granting lands, but that it considered and styled itself a "corporation."

DE HARO'S ESPEDIENTE FOR THE RANCHO SAN PEDRO.

§ **88.** The next *espediente* in order of date, of a grant of sitios near the Pueblo lands, is that of Francisco De Haro for the Rancho San Pedro, (see "SAN PEDRO" on the accompanying map of the petition,) being dated at the port of San Francisco, Nov. 22d, 1835, and the grant made on March 14, 1836. Exhibit Hopkins, S. ADDENDA, No. XXXI, page 48. De Haro states that the land has formerly been occupied "by the Indians of the Pueblo of Dolores," but is not now occupied by them. Perhaps he thought that the secularization of the Mission had converted it at once into an Indian Pueblo. But the Governor did not think so, for in his informe dated Feb. 26, 1836, he directs "the Administrator of the Ex-Mission of San Fran- "cisco de Asis to report upon the petition," and Flores, the Administrator, reporting upon it on March 9th, 1836, styles it the Ex-Mission, (esta Ex-Mision,) and says that the lands are more than four leagues distant from it; but he states that, in his opinion, the tract "should "remain to this ' COMMUNITY,' when it *shall be erected* into a Pueblo; " (Pero con motivo de no estar señalados les ejidos ó proprios que me "*parece deben quedar* à este *cuando* se erije en Pueblo.") In fact the Mexican Government, by a decree of November 7th, 1835, had suspended for the time being the further execution of the secularization laws, so that no Indian Pueblos could for the present be formed, and doubtless both the Governor and Administrator knew that fact. See the decree, 1 Rockwell, 462. Halleck's Report, Appendix, No. 16. Jones' Rep., 63. ADDENDA, No. XXVIII, page 48. From this last expediente also it is apparent:

FIRST: That although there was a PUEBLO OF SAN FRANCISCO, with an Ayuntamiento, Alcaldes and Rejidores, (§§ 72 to 77,) there was no PUEBLO at the Mission of Dolores, which still lived only in the expectation of being erected into an *Indian Pueblo* at some future time.

SECONDLY: That this Indian *Pueblo* HOPED to have *ejidos* assigned to it at a place called San Pedro, which was four leagues from the Mission of Dolores, and consequently nearly five leagues from the PUEBLO of San Francisco, and therefore far beyond the lands claimed by it.

THIRDLY: That the reason why the municipal authorities of the Pueblo of San Francisco were not consulted upon this *espediente* was, because the lands were far beyond the limits of its own property, that is to say, beyond the limits of the four square leagues belonging to the PUEBLO of San Francisco.

FOURTHLY. That this *espediente* fully justifies the definition I have given of the word PUEBLO in § 9 of this argument: that is, in a general sense, a hamlet, a village or any other settlement; but in an exalted and specific sense, an organized town,—a body politic and corporate.   Here, in this same *expediente* we find the petitioner styling the Mission of Dolores the PUEBLO of Dolores, and the administrator of the Mission declining to recommend the prayer of the petition, because the Indians who then lived in COMMUNITY, (see § 17 of this argument,) hoped thereafter to become a Pueblo, or as the Spanish has it "to be erected into a Pueblo." How, then, is this to be explained ? Dolores a PUEBLO, and still expecting to be *erected into a* PUEBLO ? The explanation is simple : the Mission of Dolores was a PUEBLO in the generic sense of hamlet, village or settlement : it hoped to be *erected into a* PUEBLO an *organized* town, or PUEBLO politic and corporate. See § 9 of this argument.   That the Mission of Dolores had not been erected into an organized PUEBLO, politic and corporate as late as April 8th, 1844, will appear hereafter in § 114 of this argument ; that it was *never* erected into such a PUEBLO will appear in § 118 of this argument.

A. D. 1838.

SUSPENSION OF THE AYUNTAMIENTO OF SAN FRANCISCO : JUS-
TICES OF THE PEACE SUCCEED THE AYUNTAMIENTO.

§ **89.**   How long did this Ayuntamiento continue ?   We find evidence of its existence down to the year 1838, as above referred to, in Exhibit No. 9, annexed to the deposition of M. G. Vallejo.   We find in Exhibit No. 1, and duplicated M, annexed to the deposition of R. C. Hopkins, under date of December, 1835, and January, 1836, mention made of Joaquin Castro, who was then *Regidor*, and also, in January and July, 1836, of Gregorio Briones and José de la Cruz Sanchez, who were then *Regidores;* and in December, 1837, of the then *Síndico*, Blas Angelino.   But it is probable that the Ayuntamiento elected in January, 1838, ut supra, was the last Ayuntamiento of the Pueblo. We have already adverted to the fact stated in the Decreto de 23 de Mayo de 1812—Leyes Vigentes, p. 28, Art. II, ante § 47, ADDENDA, No. X, page 19, Art. II—that Pueblos might lose their Ayuntamientos by diminution of their population.   We find in the Message of the Governor to the Departmental Junta, delivered on February 16th, 1840, the following passage :   "There is no Ayuntamiento whatever " in the Department, for there being no *competent number of inhabit-* " *ants* in any of the towns, as provided by the Constitution, *those then* " *existing had to be dissolved;* and only in the capital there ought to " be one of such bodies."   Document D.P.L. in the case.   See AD-DENDA, No. L, page 70, title Ayuntamientos.   It is thus evident that between the election of the Ayuntamiento of the Pueblo in January, 1838, and February, 1840, that body had ceased to exist, because its electoral basis of population required a numerical figure higher than that represented by the actual population.

WHY THE AYUNTAMIENTO CEASED TO EXIST.

§ **90.**   The reason of this failure of the requisite basis of population was two fold.   For by the Mexican Constitution of 1836, the population requisite to sustain an Ayuntamiento was raised to *four thousand* in sea ports, and to *eight thousand* in other Pueblos, and in those Pueblos not thus qualified in point of population, Justices of the Peace were to be appointed with the powers of Ayuntamientos. Sixth Constitutional Law of 1836. ADDENDA, No. LXIX, page 100, Art. 22. De Mofras states, Vol. 1, page 222, that official despatches were often a year in the passage between California and Mexico. Governor Alvarado in a proclamation dated January 17th, 1839, states that he has just received in the last mail a Law of Elections passed on November 30th, 1836 from the Supreme Government to be put in force in California. Exhibit No. 10, to testimony of Vallejo. ADDENDA, No. XXXVIII, page 57. Meanwhile the primary and secondary elections for the Ayuntamiento of 1838 had taken place. Exhibits 8 and 9 to Vallejo's deposition. ADDENDA, No. XXV, page 53. This was the last Ayuntamiento of the PUEBLO under the Mexican dominion.

SCATTERING OF THE POPULATION.

§ **91.** It is easy to indicate the causes of an actual diminution of population in the Pueblos. The first law for the secularization of the Missions was passed in 1833. These laws, whose ostensible purpose was to covert the Missionary establishments into Indian Pueblos, their churches into parish churches, and to elevate the christianized Indians to the rank of citizens, were, after all, executed in such a manner that the so-called secularization of the Missions resulted only in their plunder and complete ruin, and in the demoralization and dispersion of the christianized Indians. So complete was this ruin that the number of Mission Indians which was 30,650 in 1834, had diminished to 4,450 in 1842; and the number of horses, mules, cattle and sheep which was 808,000 in 1834. had sunk to 63,020 in 1842. See the Statistical Tables, 1 De Mofras, 320 ; and ADDENDA, No. LXVII, page 97. Only a single grant of land was made under the colonization laws before the year 1833, but with that new era of secularization and plunder commenced the granting to private persons, under the colonization laws, of lands which were afterwards stocked with horses, cattle and sheep from the spoils of the Missions. During the period above indicated from 1833 to 1842, inclusive, more than three hundred grants were made in colonization, as appears from the *espedientes* preserved in the archives. See the list in Wm. Carey Jones's Report. The grantees of these lands became for the greater part rancheros upon the domains thus conceded to them, and this immense drain upon the population of the *Pueblos*, in a department whose whole white population did not exceed 5,000 as late as the year 1842 (1 De Mofras, 318, 319,) must have greatly weakened all the PUEBLOS, while it certainly nearly depopulated Branciforte, and perhaps others. The process of the " scattering of the inhabitants from the fact that each one has his " agricultural and stock interests at a great distance from this place," (San Francisco) is described in so many words by De Haro, Alcalde in 1839 in Exhibit Hopkins **K,** ADDENDA, No. XLI, page 61.

THE PUEBLO OF SAN FRANCISCO STILL EXISTED.

§ **92.** But the Pueblo did not therefore cease to be a PUEBLO— did not lose its political or quasi-corporate character. The only result was that under a law of March 20, 1837, which is recited in the proclamation of Micheltorena of November 14th, 1843, Exhibit 11 to Vallejo's Deposition, ADDENDA, No. LVII, page 84, the government of the PUEBLO fell into the hands of the Justices of the Peace, who formed a Municipal Junta for that purpose. See ante § 90 and Constitutional Law of Mexico of 1836. ADDENDA, No. LXIX, page 100, Arts. 22, 29, etc. But the Ayuntamiento itself was not abolished. It was only suspended. The moment that the population should reach the requisite number of 4,000, the Pueblo would again be entitled to its Ayuntamiento. Const. 1836. ADDENDA, No. LXIX, Art. 22, page 100. Accordingly we shall find that when the Pueblo of San Francisco, after the American conquest of California, attained the requisite population, it again elected its Ayuntamiento, not under any provision of the laws of the conquerors, but under these very provisions in the Mexican Constitution of 1836, under which the Ayuntamiento of the Pueblo was suspended in 1839. See ADDENDA, No. LXXV, page 108, and No. LXXVII, page 111.

A. D. 1839. JANUARY AND MARCH.
ALVARADO'S REGULATIONS RESPECTING MISSIONS.

§ **93.** In January, 1839, Governor Alvarado promulgated certain regulations respecting Missions. See ADDENDA, No. XXXVII, page 55. This document is of importance only because it shows that hitherto the secularization of the Missions had not taken effect, but had only been attempted, and that the Missions, including Dolores, had not yet been converted into Indian Pueblos, but that the Indians were still living in them in COMMUNITY. See ante § 17. These regulations were followed by others promulgated in March of the same year, which have the same, but no further importance in the case. See ADDENDA, No. XXXIX, page 57. It will be observed that all these regulations contemplate the secularization of the Missions as a thing still to be accomplished, whereas I have shown that the PUEBLO OF SAN FRANCISCO was already in existence. Ante §§ 74 to 78. The effect of these regulations was to complete the ruin of the Missions.

1839. FEBRUARY.
No JAIL IN SAN FRANCISCO.

§ **94.** The causes which had weakened the Pueblo of San Francisco, as before related, had been so [effective that in February, 1839, José Antonio Galindo, who, in his expediente of 1835, for the Laguna de Merced, see ADDENDA, No. XXV, page 39, is described by Justice De Haro as "an honest man," seems now to have lapsed into the position of a criminal, and the same Justice De Haro reports to the Governor that the population having become rancheros, there are few remaining at San Francisco to guard him, and as there is no jail, the justice asks that Galindo be sent to San José for security. See ADDENDA, No. XLI, page 61. This document is curious, but not important. It illustrates the primitive simplicity of the golden age in Upper California, in which the cause came always before the effect, and no necessity was found for jails, until criminals existed to be restrained of their liberty. Happy was San Francisco, to whom the "fact" criminal had not yet suggested the word "jail:" less happy, but more wise San José, whose experience had already advanced to the word and fact of "prison."

A. D. 1839.

CONSTITUTIONAL ELECTIONS FOR 1839–1840.

§ **95.** By a law promulgated November 30th, 1836, under the Mexican Constitution of that year, definite rules were established for the election of deputies to the General Congress, and of members to the Juntas of the Departments, [or Departmental Legislatures.] The terms of this law are of no importance to the present discussion; the law provided for a Primary election of Electors, and a Secondary election, in which the Electors were to choose the Deputies to Congress and the members of the Departmental Junta. See the law at large: " Bases y Leyes Constitucionales de la Republica Mejicana, decretadas "por el Congreso General de la Nacion en el año de 1836. Mejico, "imprenta del Aguila, dirigida por José Ximeno, 1837," page 106, etc. Elections were ordered under this law in California by Governor Alvarado, by a proclamation dated January 17, 1839. See this proclamation in the ADDENDA, No. XXXVIII, page 57.

From this document it appears:

FIRST: That this law, which had been in force more than two years, had been received by the Governor of California by the "last mail" only.

SECONDLY: That San Francisco is by it classed as a PUEBLO with San José, Los Angeles, the Villa of Branciforte etc., which were undeniably fully organized Pueblos, bodies politic and corporate.

THIRDLY: That the Port of San Francisco was recognized as the capital [cabecera] of the Northern Partido.

1839. MAY 20.

GUERRERO, JUSTICE OF THE PEACE, PROMULGATES CERTAIN ORDINANCES FOR THE GOVERNMENT OF THE PUEBLO OF SAN FRANCISCO.

§ **96.** On May 20th, 1839, Francisco Guerrero, "Justice of the Peace of this section of San Francisco," publishes certain municipal regulations for the "Pueblo under his charge." See ADDENDA, No. XLIII, page 62. The "section" was doubtless the district comprised within the limits to which the jurisdiction of the Judge of the Pueblo extended, otherwise called the "termino Jurisdicional," ante § 9,

5

ADDENDA, No. XXXIII, page 51. Guerrero promulgates these ordinances "in conformity with Article 29th of the law of November 30th, 1836." This is the law above cited, § 90, contained in the ADDENDA, No. LXIX, page 100, *adopted* Dec. 29th, 1836, and *published December* 30, 1836, wrongly cited by Guerrero as *November*, and the article cited by him is that which gave him as Justice of the Peace, the powers of an Ayuntamiento of the Pueblo in respect to police. The ordinances are declared to be for the "order and good management of the Pueblo." Preamble. The Pueblo had its demarcation. § 7th. The proclamation was given in "the Pueblo of San Francisco." And yet it is contended that there was no organized political or *quasi* corporate Pueblo of San Francisco!

A. D. 1839.
ESPEDIENTE OF LEESE FOR THE RANCHO LA VISITACION.

§ 97. The *espediente* of Jacob P. Leese for the Rancho La Visitacion, Exhibit V to deposition of R. C. Hopkins, began in November, 1839, and concluded in July, 1841, is of little value, except as showing how completely the Mission of San Francisco had passed out of existence as a living organization. It is mentioned only once in the *espediente*, and then only as a locality, while the Justice of the Peace of the Port of San Francisco is the officer who executes the *informe*. These lands are those marked in the lower right hand portion of the accompanying map as "LA VISITACION." See ADDENDA, No. XLVII, page 67.

1839. NOVEMBER 3.
BUILDING LOTS ARE GRANTED TO SETTLERS AT THE ESTABLISHMENT OF THE MISSION OF DOLORES.

§ 98. On April 20th, 1839, De Haro, Justice of the Peace, represents to the Governor that a house-lot [solar] had been petitioned for by one Gomez. See the document, ADDENDA, No. XLII, page 61. He dates from the Establishment of Dolores; while he calls it an Ex-Mission, he pleads that it has "a character of Pueblo" because it had been named the head of the Partido. From this document it is evident that the Indian village at Dolores was not *that* PUEBLO OF SAN FRANCISCO which we have seen had already been in existence for four years. Who ever heard of a PUEBLO, recognized and existing with its Ayuntamiento, pleading for a *character* of Pueblo? Who ever dreamed of a PUEBLO existing for four years in which not a single house-lot had ever been granted? That building lots were granted in Dolores, appears from the ADDENDA, No. LXXVIII, page 113.

§ 99. This communication seems, however, to have been without effect, for on July 15th, 1839, Guerrero, Justice of the Peace of San Francisco, writes to the Prefect Castro, stating that some residents of the MUNICIPALITY of San Francisco, wished to settle themselves in the ESTABLISHMENT of Dolores, and asked to have house-lots granted to them. Guerrero was a native of Tepic, a laborer by occupation, and in 1839, twenty-eight years of age. ADDENDA, No. LV, page 79. His official documents are unique, full of new idioms, newly conceived words, and replete with involved sentences and confused ideas. In the above cited communication to the Prefect, see ADDENDA, No. XLIV, page 63, Guerrero, discharging the office of Justice of the Peace at San Francisco, and going home at night to his house at Dolores, 1 De Mofrás, 426, 427, where he wrote his communication as it seems, knowing that he was writing in *behalf* of the PUEBLO of San Francisco, and still being conscious that he was *at* the Mission, apparently confounds "the MUNICIPALITY of San Francisco" with "the ESTABLISHMENT of Dolores." But the Prefect, Castro, forwarding this request to the Governor, under date of Nov. 25, 1839, while he adopts the plan of Guerrero's communication, carefully removes all confusion and obscurity. See the Prefect's letter, ADDENDA, No. XLVIII, page 68. "The residents of the MUNICIPALITY of San "Francisco have made various verbal representations through the "Justice of the Peace, to the end that through this Prefectura, they "may receive the necessary license to establish themselves in the "ESTABLISHMENT of Dolores, where they wish to form a settlement." * * * "All are now dispersed." The Governor grants the Justice the power to concede building-lots at the Establishment of Dolores, under several conditions, one of which is that they shall not "disturb the Indians so long as the COMMUNITY exists." *Ib.*

From these documents it is evident :

FIRST : That the MUNICIPALITY of San Francisco was perfectly distinct from the Establishment of Dolores.

SECONDLY : That although house-lots had been granted for years in the PUEBLO of San Francisco, ante § 83, ADDENDA, No. XXVI, page 42; XXXIV, page 53; yet that down to November 3d, 1839, no building-lots had been granted at the ESTABLISHMENT of Dolores.

THIRDLY : That most of the neophytes of the Mission were dispersed, for the phrase "all are now dispersed," can be applied only to them, and not to the *residents* of San Francisco, who wished to establish themselves at the Ex-Mission.

FOURTHLY : That Dolores had not yet been converted into an INDIAN PUEBLO, for the few Indians there were living "in community," and it was intended to transfer them to San Mateo. See COMUNIDAD, ante § 17. ADDENDA, No. XLVIII, page 69, Governor's order, § 2.

A. D. 1839, ETC.

OTHER GRANTS OF PUEBLO LANDS.

§ **100.** Various other grants of lands within the PUEBLO of San Francisco appear in the testimony, made by Justices of the Peace and others.* These grants I regard as of but little importance in the case. We have already established, ante § 83, that the lands in the imme-

---

* A list of these grants, supposed to be perfect, will be found in the ADDENDA, No. LXXVIII, pages 113 and 114, but whether complete or not matters little to the principle of our argument. There were also Alcaldes in San Francisco for a time under a law of March 20th, 1837, but our present purpose requires no further notice of them. Justices were generally *ex officio* Alcaldes. See the same law last cited.

diate vicinity of San Francisco were subject to be granted by the AYUNTAMIENTO OF THAT PUEBLO. Consequently they were exempted from the Colonization laws of 1824—1828; consequently they BELONGED TO THE PUEBLO OF SAN FRANCISCO. Ante §§ 83, 84. But we have also seen that when the AYUNTAMIENTO of San Francisco ceased to exist, the PUEBLO did not lose its corporate character, which still survived under JUSTICES OF THE PEACE who discharged the functions of the Ayuntamiento. Ante § 92. We also know, as matter of well adjudicated law, that the Legislature of a country has visitatorial and legislative power, which can always inspect, direct, control and dispose of the property of Municipal Corporations, so far as that property is derived from the sovereign and not bound by *private* contracts or conditions of dedication or endowment. City of New Orleans *vs.* The United States, 10 Peters, 662, 736, 737; 4 Wheat. 660; 20 Howard, S. C. Rep. U. S. 534; Hart *vs.* Burnett, 15 Cal. 612. Therefore, having shown these to be town lands, (Bienes Concejiles, ante § 13,) subject to grant by the Ayuntamiento of San Francisco, (ante § 83,) and the Justices of the Peace not *supplanting* the PUEBLO, but merely *succeeding* the Ayuntamiento as the TOWN COUNCIL, ante § 89; when we find Justices of the Peace, Governors, or other officers granting these PUEBLO lands, ante §§ 92, 100, we shall conclude that such grants are made by them either as officers of the PUEBLO or as acting under that superior authority which as inspector, visitor, or legislature can dispose of *all* the property of municipal corporations, with the exceptions above stated.

A. D. 1840. MAY 20.

LIST OF FOREIGNERS IN SAN FRANCISCO IN 1840.

§ **101.** A curious document has been introduced in evidence in this case, being a List of Foreigners established in the "Sixth Section of San Francisco de Asis in 1840." See ADDENDA, No. LI, page 72. This "Sixth Section" was undoubtedly the Judicial District included within the Jurisdiction of the Judges of the Pueblo. Ante §§ 9, 16, ADDENDA, No. XXXIII, page 51. The value of this document consists in this, that it shows that San Francisquito creek at that time divided the judicial jurisdiction of the Pueblo of San Francisco from that of San José, (Pueblo of Alvarado,) 1 De Mofras, 415, and that Saucelito on the north-west of the straits and Bay was not within the jurisdiction of San Francisco. The fact that all the region north-west of the straits and Bay, and west of the Sacramento river, including the Pueblo of Sonoma, were without the jurisdiction of San Francisco, appears from a document produced in evidence in the case in connection with the testimony of R. C. Hopkins, and marked "Exhibit Hopkins No. 3." It appears from the first part of this *espediente*, dated January 1st, 1836, that the Ayuntamiento of San Francisco had appointed an auxiliary Alcalde "for the other side of the Bay of San Francisco, by which a dispute has arisen in relation to jurisdiction between the Alcalde of said Pueblo and the Military Commandante of the Frontier of the North," meaning that side lying west of the Bay and of the Sacramento river. The matter was referred to the Departmental Junta [Legislature] who decided on July 7th, 1836, "that the Illustrious Ayuntamiento of San Francisco should not extend its authority as far as the FRONTIER, as was done by the appointment of an auxiliary Alcalde; * * * * the appointment of an auxiliary Alcalde of the FRONTIER, made by the Ayuntamiento of San Francisco, is rejected as being beyond the limits of its jurisdiction." This document is very long, and not of sufficient importance to be printed, but is of some value as defining the territorial limits of the judicial jurisdiction of the Pueblo of San Francisco,—its "termino jurisdiccional." See ADDENDA, No. XXXIII, page 51, ¶ 3d from the foot.

A. D. 1840.

BERNAL'S ESPEDIENTE FOR THE RANCHO LAS SALINAS.

§ **102.** The *espediente* promoted by José Cornelio Bernal for the place called Las Salinas, commenced in 1835 and concluded in 1840, is the *espediente* numbered 2 and 177 in Jones's List, and duplicated in Exhibits No. 13 and T, to the testimony of R. C. Hopkins. ADDENDA, No. XLVI, page 64. See the place marked BERNAL RANCHO on the accompanying map. The first document in this *espediente*, whose papers are deranged in the order of date, is the decision of Governor Figueroa, misplaced from its order of date, but dated at Monterey, January 2d, 1835, which refers to *preceding reports, which are not contained in the* ESPEDIENTE, and which must themselves have been based upon a petition and *informé* which are also lost. The Governor decrees as follows: "As from *the preceding reports* it appears that the "tract of land petitioned for by José Cornelio Bernal is the property "of the PUEBLO of San Francisco de Asis, to which it serves as *ejidos*, "for the cattle of the *Public*, (es de la propiedad del pueblo de San "Francisco de Asis a quien sirve de ejidos para las ganados del *comun*,) "[not comunidad, as translated, see § 17, ante,] his application is not "admissible, as it cannot be granted in full property; but the party "may retain his cattle there in the same way as the other citizens do, "(lo mismo como los demas ciudadanos,) or apply for some other place "which is not appropriated."

Afterwards, on October 3d, 1839, as appears from the same *espediente*, Bernal again petitions for the same Rancho, and the matter is referred to the "Justice of the Peace of *San Francisco*," who is to transmit the *espediente* with his report to the "Administrator of the *Establishment of Dolores*." The Justice of the Peace, dating from the Justice Court of *San Francisco*, October 8, 1839," reports in favor of granting the concession, adding that "the said Bernal is recommendable for the "services which he has rendered and is rendering in this *municipality*," "(en esta municipalidad.)" The administrador of the Ex-Mission, dating from "Dolores" on the same day, reports that "this establish-"ment is not in need of the tract of land petitioned for, because the "most of the cattle belonging to the ESTABLISHMENT are on the place "called the Pilarcitos on the coast." This place "Las Pilarcitos" on the coast, is the same place otherwise called "San Pedro," where the

Mission of Dolores always pastured its cattle. See § 88, of this argument. From this *espediente* the following facts appear:

FIRST :   That there was a PUEBLO called San Francisco de Asis, which was composed of citizens who possessed cattle, and that for the cattle of the public of said PUEBLO the lands called "Las Salinas" were used and appropriated. We submit that there is no instance, before or after the total ruin of the Missions, where a Mission Indian was ever called citizen (cuidadano.)   He was always called Indian, Native or Neophyte, (Indio, Indigena, ó Neofito.)   Although his ultimate equality in the sight of the law was declared, he was always a pupil, and even the laws of secularization contemplated that he should ever remain such.

SECONDLY : That the cattle of the neophyte Indians did not occupy the same *ejidos* as those of the citizens of the Pueblo of San Francisco, either in 1835 or in 1839.

THIRDLY : That there was no confusion between the PUEBLO of San Francisco and the ESTABLISHMENT of Dolores ; but each stands out distinctly in its own individuality whenever there is a question respecting the possible rights of either, the Superintendent of the Establishment of Dolores representing every existing interest of the neophytes, and the Municipal Authorities of San Francisco those of the PUEBLO.

A. D. 1840.   FEBRUARY 16.
GOVERNOR'S MESSAGE RESPECTING AYUNTAMIENTOS, PROPIOS, EJIDOS, JUSTICES, ETC.

§ **103.** On February 16th, 1840, the Governor of Upper California, at the opening of the Departmental Assembly, delivered his Annual Message, extracts from which will be found in the ADDENDA, No. L, page 70, etc.   From this it appears that no PUEBLO, except Monterey, had ever had its *Propios* or *Ejidos* measured and set apart ; that all the Pueblos had lost their Ayuntamientos because the basis of population had been so greatly increased by the Constitution, (see ante §§ 89, 90) ; and that Justices of the Peace had succeeded the Ayuntamientos in the politico-economical government of the Pueblos, also exercising the judicial functions of Judges of First Instance. These facts have all been stated before in this argument.   The inexactness of some translator appears in this translation, where " propios y ejidos " is translated " common and landed property," English terms which would include the dehesas, or large pastures ; and " fundo legal " is rendered simply " legal property," instead of " propios " and the like landed property from which municipal funds were raised by way of rent.

A. D. 1841.   AUGUST 8.
MIRAMONTES, VICE-JUSTICE OF THE PEACE AT DOLORES, RESIGNS HIS OFFICE.

§ **104.** On August 8th, 1841, Vicente Miramontes, Vice-Justice of the Peace "in the Pueblo of Dolores, in the jurisdiction of the

Port of San Francisco," addresses the Prefect, and pleads ignorance and poverty as reasons why he should nôt be reappointed. ADDENDA, No. LIII, page 74. This document is dated at the Pueblo of Dolores. This word *Pueblo* is here evidently used in the sense of "village or hamlet," as I have before shown. Ante, § 9. That there never was an organized politic or corporate Pueblo there is clearly apparent from all the documents in evidence. See §§ 88, 102, 114.

A. D. 1842. JANUARY.

THE PUEBLO OF SAN FRANCISCO HAD A COMPLETE FISCAL OR-
GANIZATION—FULLER, SYNDIC.

§ **105.** On July 20th, 1839, Guerrero, Justice of the Peace, asked the Prefect to appoint a Sindico Procurador for San Francisco, and nominated Juan Fuller for the office. ADDENDA, No. XLV, page 63. It will be observed that although Sindico Procuradores were offi-cers of Ayuntamientos, (ante, §§ 12, 47, ADDENDA, No. X, page 19, § 4,) yet the Constitution of 1836 did not supply such officers to the Pueblos which were not entitled to have Ayuntamientos. See AD-DENDA, No. LXIX, page 100. Fuller seems, however, to have been appointed Syndic, for in the ADDENDA, No. LIV, page 75, etc., we find the "Account made out by Don Juan Fuller as Sindico of the Munici-pality of San Francisco," extending from August, 1839, to January 10th, 1842. This document is curious and important, showing the receipt of moneys from all the ordinary sources of municipal revenue, and from the sale of solares, in addition. The office of Syndic con-tinued to exist down to the last year of the Mexican dominion, for on February 7th, 1846, we find Francisco Guerrero, Sub-Prefect, dating from Yerba Buena, invoking "the Judge of First Instance of the "PUEBLO of San Francisco to follow Don Pedro Sherreback, the "defaulting Syndic, to attach his property, imprison him, or send him "to the public works, in case he refuses to present his accounts, produce "his vouchers, and make payment." ADDENDA, No. LXV, page 95.

A. D. 1842. OCTOBER 31.

CENSUS OF SAN FRANCISCO IN 1842.

§ **106.** We have in the ADDENDA, No. LV, page 78, etc., a full cen-sus of all the inhabitants in the *jurisdiction* of San Francisco, for the year 1842. This word "jurisdiction," of course, signifies the "judicial jurisdiction" extending far beyond the Pueblo, as before noticed, ante § 9, ¶ 2d. We here find that all the inhabitants, of both sexes, men, women and children, amounted to only 196. We can recognize at least 18 families of married persons with children. The whole num-ber of Indians in the population was 37 : all of these were *neophytes*, or Mission Indians, except one boy, Carlos, who seems to have been an unconverted Indian, from Sacramento ; and all of these Indians, both neophyte and pagan, were domestic servants, except three, who are classed as "laborers." How well this justifies De Mofras, who estimated the number of neophytes at Dolores in 1842 at 50, (ADD-

ENDA, No. LXVII, page 97) ; and how completely fades away the phantasm of a political and *quasi*-corporate Indian Pueblo, composed of three Indian laborers and thirty-four Indian domestics ! Where are the *Indian* Alcaldes and *Indian* Councilmen spoken of in § 17 of this argument?

CONDITION OF THE MISSIONS AT THAT TIME.

§ **107.** But already, even as early as the year 1842, before the termination of De Mofras' visit to California, the pillage and ruin of the Missions was almost entirely completed. That accurate and intelligent observer has given the fullest details of the results to which eight years of civil "administration" had brought the Missions of California. As a general fact, the cattle had been given away, stolen and slaughtered ; the Mission buildings appropriated or suffered to fall into ruin ; the Indians dispersed ; the vineyards and orchards suffered to grow wild ; and in some cases the vines were uprooted and taken away. Of the twenty-one Missions, the following were in that year (1842) reported to be in a fair condition, having some valuable live stock remaining, Indians still under instruction and performing labor, and the Mission establishment in operation : Santa Barbara, 1 De Mofras, 371 ; San Gabriel, *Ib.*, 351 ; Santa Inez, *Ib.*, 377 ; San Antonio, *Ib.*, 387 ; Santa Clara, *Ib.*, 416 ; San José, *Ib.*, 418. Those nearly ruined were San Fernando, *Ib.*, 360 ; San Diego, *Ib.*, 338 ; San Luis Rey, *Ib.*, 342 ; San Buenaventura, *Ib.*, 365 ; La Purisima, *Ib.*, 376 ; San Luis Obispo, *Ib.*, 378 ; and San Miguel, *Ib.*, 383. Those that were entirely ruined, were San Juan Capistrano, *Ib.*, 348 ; La Soledad, *Ib.*, 390 ; El Carmelo, *Ib.*, 391 ; San Juan Bautista, *Ib.*, 407 ; Santa Cruz, *Ib.*, 410 ; DOLORES DE SAN FRANCISCO, *Ib.*, 424 ; San Rafael, *Ib.*, 444 ; San Francisco Solano, *Ib.*, 446. The results in comparative figures (round numbers,) is thus stated :

In 1834, when the Missions went into civil "administration," the Missions had *thirty thousand Indian neophytes* sustained and instructed by them, living at the Mission establishments : in 1842, *four thousand.*

In 1834, the Missions had *four hundred and twenty thousand* horned cattle ; in 1842, *twenty-eight thousand.*

In 1834, *sixty thousand* horses ; in 1842, *four thousand.*

In 1834, *three hundred and twenty thousand* sheep, goats and swine ; in 1842, *thirty thousand.*

In 1834, they produced *one hundred and twenty thousand* bushels of wheat, maize, etc. ; in 1842, *seven thousand.* In a tabular form the result is thus presented :

	Religious Administration. 1834.	Civil Administrations. 1842.
Indians	30,000	4,000
Horned Cattle	400,000	28,000
Horses and Mules	62,000	3,000
Sheep, etc.	321,000	31,000
Grain	122,000	7,000

The table from De Mofras, Vol. I, p. 320, printed in the ADDENDA, No. LXVII, gives these data more specifically, except that the crops of grains for 1842 are not there given, but the amount 7,000 bushels

(4,000 hectares,) is given by him at page 421 of the same volume. The grain crops are measured by the Spanish *fanega*, which is rather more than the English bushel, but may be rendered by it for general purposes.

A. D. 1843.   MARCH 29.

AN ATTEMPT MADE TO RESTORE THE MISSIONS.

§ **108.** In 1848 Micheltorena, who came from Mexico with an army as a counter revolutionary Governor, 1 De Mofras, 311, 312–17, and replaced Alvarado as Governor, among other reactionary measures conceived or accepted the scheme of restoring the Missionary system. In his proclamation of March 29th, 1843, he recites : "that the pious and charitable institutions of social order for the con-" version of the savages to catholicism and to an agricultural and " peaceful life, are reduced to the gardens and inclosures of the churches " and buildings. * * That the Indians, who are naturally lazy, now, " from additional labor and scarcity of nourishment, being in a state of "·nudity, having no fixed employment or appointed Mission, prefer to " keep out of the way, and die impenitent in desert woods, in order to " escape a life of slavery, filled with all privations, and destitute of " social enjoyment. * * That there is no other method of *reani-*" *mating* the skeleton of a giant like the remains of the ancient Mis-" sions except to fall back upon experience, and to fortify it with the " appliances of Civil and Ecclesiastical power." He then directs that twelve of the Missions, which he names, shall be restored to the Missionary Franciscan Monks, to be governed by them in the same manner as before, they taking charge of the natives. ADDENDA, No. LVI, page 83. The Mission of Dolores was not among the Missions thus restored ; but the Government pledges itself in regard to the lands formerly appurtenant to the Missions " to make no new " grants without the information of the respective authorities of the " most Reverend Fathers, notorious non-occupation, non-cultivation, or " necessity." See Micheltorena's Proclamation, 1 Rockwell, 469; Halleck's Report, App. No. 19 ; Jones's Report, page 71 ; ADDENDA, No. LVI, page 83. This therefore interrupted further grants being made from the lands adjacent to or occupied by the Missions, until it should be definitely ascertained by official acts of great formality, that such lands would not be needed by those establishments, either as Missions, or as possible future INDIAN PUEBLOS.

A. D. 1843.   JUNE.

MEXICAN CONSTITUTION OF 1843.

§ **109.** A new Constitution was adopted this year, on June 12th, and promulgated on June 13th. It does not seem to contain any provisions bearing upon the present discussion. The title of the Departmental Junta was changed to that of Asamblea—Assembly. See "Bases de organizacion politica de la Republica," published in the "Decretos del Gobierno provisional for 1842," July 1842 to June 1843, Title VII, § 131, at page 466.

A. D. 1843. NOVEMBER.

ALCALDES ORDERED TO BE ELECTED FOR THE PUEBLO OF SAN
FRANCISCO.

§ **110.** On November 14, 1843, Governor Micheltorena, by proclamation, directed Ayuntamientos to be elected in Monterey and Los
Angeles. Exhibit 11, annexed to Vallejo's deposition, Addenda No.
LVII, page 84, Art. 1st; directing, also, that in the *Pueblos* of San
Diego, Santa Barbara, San Juan, Villa de Branciforte, San José, *San
Francisco* and Sonoma, elections should be held to appoint two Alcaldes of first and second nomination, *Id.* Article 2; that said first Alcaldes
should perform the duties of Judges of First Instance, and take charge
of the prefectures of the respective districts, *Id.* Article 4; that the
newly elected officers should go into office on the first day of January
next ensuing, and "receive from those going out an exact inventory of
"all the espedientes, books, and whatever there may be belonging to
"the said *corporations*—un inventario exacto de todos los espedientes,
"libros y cuanto halla pertineciente a dichas *Corporaciones.*" *Id.* Article 5. Accordingly we find *oficios* addressed to the Alcalde of San
Francisco by the government, dated July 7th, 1844, March 7th, 1844,
January 20th, 1844, March 5th, 1845, and the Act of election of Padilla as First Alcalde on December 22d, 1844, Exhibits No. 12, 13,
14, 15, and 16, annexed to Vallejo's deposition. See ADDENDA, Nos.
LVIII, LIX, LXI.

A. D. 1844.

SAN FRANCISCO, THE PORT OF SAN FRANCISCO, AND YERBA BUENA
WERE ALL THE SAME.

§ **111.** This appears from two documents in evidence in the case.
See ADDENDA, Nos. LVIII and LIX, pages 85, 86, where the same
officer is described as "First Alcalde of the Port of San Francisco,"
"Alcalde of San Francisco," and "Alcalde of first nomination of Yerba
Buena." This, however, only confirms what appears so often else-
where. See §§ 102, 120, etc.

A. D. 1844. APRIL.

DE HARO'S ESPEDIENTE FOR THE POTRERO NUEVO. GOVERNOR
MICHELTORENA'S PARTIAL RESTORATION OF THE MISSIONS
IN 1843.

§ **112.** The espediente of Francisco De Haro for the Potrero of
San Francisco, is found duplicate among the documentary testimony in
this cause. See Exhibit Hopkins, No 11 and V; ADDENDA, No.
LX, page 86. This *espediente* shows that this Potrero (cattle enclosure) was formerly used by the Ex-Mission of San Francisco de Asis.
It included that portion represented on the accompagnying map as
lying between the Mission, the Mission Bay, and the "WALL," the wall
designated being a part of the enclosure of the Potrero. Jimeno, the
Secretary of the Government, over date of April 29th, 1844, reports,

that "the Mission of San Francisco has no longer any cattle, and con-
" sequently the Potrero petitioned for is lying unoccupied ;   *   * and
" inasmuch as the common lands (ejidos) of the said *establishment*
" are to be assigned to it, (debe señalarsele sus ejidos)"—he recom-
mends that the petitioner be allowed to occupy the lands provisionally.
A provisional licence was accordingly issued, "subject to the measure-
" ment which may be made of the ejidos of the *Establishment* of San
" Francisco; (sugetandose a la medicion que se haya de los ejidos del
" Establiento de San Franco." There is little in this *espediente* which
is pertinent to the present case, except the patent fact that the executive
officers of the Departmental Government were exceedingly anxious
not to prejudge against the possibility of an *Indian Pueblo* being
erected out of the ruins of this Mission, which, indeed, they had no
power to do, and therefore refused to grant away in absolute proprietorship the Potrero formerly enclosed and used by it, until the future
fate of the Mission should have been decided by an inquest of office.
It will be remembered that Micheltorena, the Governor who made this
provisional grant, had early conceived the project of restoring the
Missionary system, and placing the Missions again in the hands of the
Franciscans. See ante § 108, ADDENDA, No. LVI, page 83. But,
although this step did not revivify the Missions, nor even retard their
final ruin, still it contained a pledge that ˙from the lands occupied
by the Missions, the Government would " make no new grants without
" the information of the respective authorities of the most Reverend
" Ministers, notorious non-occupation, non-cultivation, or necessity."
ADDENDA, No. LVI, page 84, § 5. This Potrero, enclosed by the
Mission, which might again need it if it recovered its prosperity, and
would probably require it for its *ejidos* if it was erected into an INDIAN
PUEBLO, could not therefore be granted by the Government until the
ruin of the Mission was established officially, and therefore beyond all
hope. These were the reasons assigned by the Governor for refusing
the grant, and issuing only a provisional licence to occupy. ADDENDA,
No. LX, pages, 86, 87.

MAPS OF YERBA BUENA APPROVED BY THE GOVERNOR.

§ **113.** It appears by the testimony of Richardson and others that
two or more maps were made of the settlement of Yerba Buena, and
approved by the Governor. These maps are the nucleus upon which
the existing plat or survey of the present city has been adjusted.
They are of little or no value to the present argument. In any event
they would tend to show only what is indisputable, that the Ayunta-
mento of San Francisco had the power to make grants of lands, and
that therefore there was a political *quasi*-corporate PUEBLO of San
Francisco to which such lands belonged. See §§ 83, 84 of this argument. These maps show only that the Governor continued to recognize
the PUEBLO of San Francisco, as having an organized political and
corporate or *quasi*-corporate existence.

A. D. 1844. APRIL.

THE INHABITANTS OF THE MISSION OF DOLORES [OF SAN FRAN-
CISCO] COMPLAIN THAT THEIR SETTLEMENT HAS NEVER BEEN
RECOGNIZED AS A PUEBLO, AND ASK THE GOVERNOR TO EX-
TINGUISH THE NAME OF MISSION AND DECLARE IT A PUEBLO
FOR THE FUTURE. THE GOVERNOR DECLINES TO ACT.

§ **114.** The inhabitants of the Mission of Dolores of San Francisco, "resident in the jurisdiction of San Francisco de Asis and
established in the *Ex-Mission* of that name," on the 8th day of April,
1844, petition the Governor, stating that that Mission had never yet
been recognized as a PUEBLO ; that it ought to have that title ; and
praying that it may be recognized as a PUEBLO in future. They
recognize the fact that Indians are still living there in COMMUNITY,
(see ante § 17,) with a mayordomo, or official administrator, and thus it
appears that the Mission had not as yet been secularized. The Secretary
of State reports that the request cannot be granted until the debts of
the Mission are paid—it was, then, still a Mission—and the Governor
defers all further action on the petition. See ADDENDA, No. LXXI,
page 102. This one document effectually establishes the fact, that
the Mission of Dolores was not *that* "PUEBLO of San Francisco,"
which was established in 1835, ante § 74, and which was so often
recognized by the Governor and Departmental Legislature. See §§
77, 78, 82, 83, 87, etc.

A. D. 1845. MAY AND OCTOBER.

THE GOVERNMENT OFFICIALLY EXTINGUISH THE MISSION OF
DOLORES AND OFFER IT FOR SALE, BUT DO NOT ERECT IT
INTO A PUEBLO.

§ **115.** I have already presented my views of the objects contemplated in the foundation of the Mission, ante, § 26. The official maps
of the United States show that the Mission of Dolores existed within
the limits of the four leagues claimed by the City of San Francisco.
See map prefixed, and Langley's map. But it is well established that
this Mission had no rights in land. The so-called lands of all the
Missions were all subject to colonization. See § 26 of this argument.
They were exempted from colonization "for the present" by the regulations of colonization of Nov. 21, 1828, 1 Rockwell, 453 ; ADDENDA,
No. XIV, page 26, § 17 ; but it is notorious that that restriction was
almost immediately removed, for most of the Mission lands were soon
afterwards granted to various persons. The Missions had no landed
property. "The church edifices, cemeteries, and priests' houses,
"with the curtilages and appurtenances at the several missions, and
"the gardens and vineyards, at or near the same, planted and
"reared by the care and labor of the priests and neophytes, belonged
"to the Catholic church to which they were dedicated from the begin-
"ning." See Opinion of Commissioner Felch, in the case of Joseph
Alemany, Bishop of California, vs. The United States, claiming the

Mission churches, cemeteries, orchards and vineyards. The lands commonly treated as belonging to the Mission of Dolores, but really belonging to the PUEBLO of San Francisco, were, therefore, at most only subject to an usufruct by the Indians of the Mission, and when that usufruct determined by the dissolution of the Mission establishment, the rights of the PUEBLO became emancipated and complete. Perhaps, as was contemplated by the Plan of Pitic, the Indians and pobladores were to enjoy these lands in common. See ADDENDA, No. VII, page 12, §§ 6, 7. But even conceding that the lands were subject to a servitude, there can be no doubt that when that servitude ceased, the lands became free. The evidence is conclusive that all hopes of converting the Mission of Dolores into an *Indian Pueblo* had been abandoned for many years before its final dissolution. The Mission had never been a prosperous one. It was founded in the midst of barren surroundings, in a climate which was severe to the Indians (1 De Mofras, 424, 444), and still more rigorous to the natives of Mexico and Spain. 1 De Mofras, 274. But it was necessary that a Mission should be founded within the protection of the Presidio of San Francisco, and so the Mission of Dolores was founded on the only unappropriated spot within many miles where there was a perennial stream of fresh water; the issue of Lobos Creek being within the curtilage of the Fort. See map of the Coast Survey; Mitchell vs. The United States, 15 Peters, 52; 9 do. 711. The north-west winds were always severe; the farming lands of the Mission small in extent and not propitious to cultivation; the sowings were made at San Pablo, on the other side of the Bay (1 De Mofras, 424, 425; and at San Mateo, De Haro's espediente for Rancho San Pedro, ADDENDA, No. XXXI, page 48), and they were compelled to use the Mission of San Rafael as a hospital for their Indians, who could not endure the climate of San Francisco. 1 De Mofras, 444. Their cattle, while they had any, were pastured at San Pedro beyond the mountains. Wm. Carey Jones' Report, 115; De Haro's *espediente* ut supra. In 1815 there was an Indian population of 1,115 at the Mission, and in 1830 a population of 219, (see ADDENDA, No. LXXVI, page 110, but in 1834, at the culminating period of the prosperity of the missions, the Mission of Dolores had not exceeding 500 Indians, while San Luis Rey had 3,500, San Gabriel 2,700, San José 2,300, Santa Clara 1,800, and even San Rafael, founded in 1817, had 1,250, and San Francisco Solano (Sonoma) founded in 1823, had 1,300. 1 De Mofras, 320; ADDENDA, No. LXVIII, page 97.

§ **116.** The gradual, but complete extinction of this feeble existence of the Mission of Dolores is perfectly demonstrated by a few patent facts. The *padron* (return) of the Mission, made in 1830, the last that appears ever to have been made, shows only 219 neophytes. See ADDENDA, No. XXVI, page 110. The *padron* of San Francisco made by Guerrero, in 1842, in which the Indians are confounded with the mass of the population existing throughout the whole *termino* of San Francisco, including Yerba Buena, shows only 36 neophytes.

ADDENDA, No. LV, page 78. Deposition of H. F. Teschemacher in the case. The Ranchos of San Pablo and San Pedro, where the Indians sowed their crops, and pastured their cattle, were granted to the Castros and to De Haro respectively in 1835 and 1836. 1 De Mofras, 425. See the *Espedientes* in the Archives, Nos. 3 and 18, Also the same numbers in the list in Jones' Report, Senate Doc. Vol. 3, Doc. 18, p. 95, 1850–1851. De Mofras writes in 1842: "The inhabitants "have pillaged everything; at present there remain scarcely 60 cattle, "50 horses and 100 sheep. Some Indians inhabit a few ruined hovels "(quelques masures) around the Mission, or cultivate some small "patches of good soil sheltered from the wind. * * * The Mission "buildings are large, but dilapidated; there is no missionary." Vol. 1, page 424. The Exploring Expedition of Com. Wilkes visited the Mission of Dolores twice in 1841, but he gives it no further notice than to misname it the Mission of "*Nostra* Señora de Dolores," showing that it had ceased to attract notice as an existing establishment. Exploring Expedition, Vol. V, 249. JIMENO, Secretary of State, in his report on the Espediente of De Haro for the Protrero of San Francisco, ADDENDA, No. LX, page 86, April 29th, 1844, states that "the Mission of San Francisco has no longer any cattle." And it is not unimportant to note that it is the word "bienes, property," which is translated "cattle."

§ **117.** These facts sufficiently show the *de facto* expiration of the Mission of Dolores; but happily we are furnished an authentic record of an inquest of office by which the extinction of the Mission was declared in all legal form. By a decree of May 28th, 1845, the the Departmental Junta enacted as follows:

"Article I. The Departmental Government shall call together the "neophytes* of the Missions of San Rafael, DOLORES, Solidad, San "Miguel, and La Purisima *which are abandoned by them*, by means of "a proclamation which it will publish, allowing them the term of one "month from the day of its publication in their respective missions, or "in those nearest to them, for them to re-unite for the purpose of culti- "vating them; and they are informed that if they fail to do so, they "will be declared to be without owners (mostrencas), and the Assem- "bly and Departmental Government will dispose of them as may best "suit the general good of the Department." 1 Rockwell, 471, Halleck's Rep. Ap. 20; Jones' Rep. 72; ADDENDA, No. LXII, page 88. Here is a legislative declaration that the Mission of Dolores is abandoned by its neophytes; here is a law day given to them to come in and redeem a forfeiture; here is a forfeiture specifically and officially pronounced in case of non-redemption. The second article of this enactment decrees: "The Carmelo, San Juan Baptista, San Juan "Capistrana, and San Francisco Solano, shall be considered as PUEB- "LOS, which is the character they have at present." ADDENDA, No.

---

* "*Los neofitos*" in the original, and not Indian as generally translated, *neofito* being a christianized Indian belonging to the Mission.

LXII, page 89, Art. 2. This is a most pregnant declaration. Four Missions are excepted from the operations of the law which denounced a forfeiture against other Missions, because these four had become PUEBLOS. But there is not a hint that the other Missions had become, or could become PUEBLOS, but on the contrary a declaration they were abandoned by their neophytes, and a decree that if the neophytes did not return, the property of the Missions would be considered without owners. This is conclusive on the point that in May, 1845, there was no PUEBLO at the Mission of Dolores, as we have already seen (ante, § 114) that there was not in April of the preceding year. The Mission property of course consisted only of the buildings, orchards, cemeteries, and stock of the Establishment. Ante, § 26. The Proclamation required in the first article of the preceding law appears to have been made, from the following act of the Departmental Government of Oct. 28th, 1845: "Article I. There will be sold at this capital, to the "highest bidder, the Missions of San Rafael, DOLORES, Soledad, San "Miguel, and La Purisima, which are abandoned by their neophytes. "Art. IV. * * * What belongs to San Rafael, DOLORES, San Juan "Bautista, Carmelo, and San Miguel will be sold on the second, third, "and fourth of January next." 1 Rockwell, 472; Halleck's Report, Ap. 21; Jones' Report, 75; ADDENDA, No. LXIII, page 90. The original is, "los dias 2, 3, y 4 del mes de Enero del año entrante," instead of "23d and 24th of January," as commonly translated. This then was an official determination by actual inquest of the fact that the Mission of Dolores had ceased to exist. A few months afterwards, Mr. Edwin Bryant, a very observant and intelligent traveler, who was afterwards First Alcalde of San Francisco, visiting the Mission of Dolores and passing there the night of Sept 20–21, 1846, could hardly find shelter there, and found the main buildings contiguous to the church occupied by Mormon families, and "the Indian quarters crum-"bling into shapeless heaps of mud." Bryant's California, 320, 321. These were not ruins made since the American conquest, for no rain had fallen since the preceding spring, and the conquest was made in July of that same year.

ATTEMPT TO REVIVE THE MISSION OF DOLORES FOR THE PUR-
POSES OF THIS SUIT.

§ 118. It is out of the grave of this extinct Mission which was thus blighted in its conception, almost abortive in its birth, dwarfed in its growth, finally dying of inanition, officially declared dead, and officially buried, that the United States now attempt to evoke the ghost of an *Indian Pueblo*, not for the purpose of galvanizing it into existence, but solely with the object of depriving the city of San Francisco of its patrimony. Between the chimera of a Partido on the one side, and of a non-existent *Indian Pueblo of Dolores* on the other, it is expected that the property of San Francisco shall be converted into public lands, while other Pueblos like Santa Barbara and Monterey shall enjoy their four leagues, which have been formally confirmed to them. Even

the *Indian Pueblos* of New Mexico have had their four square leagues
allotted them—and some of them more than this. See ADDENDA,
No. LXVIII, page 98. But to San Francisco, illustrious for her
enterprise and her misfortunes, this common justice has been denied ;
and now in the twenty-eight year of her distinct political and corporate
existence she stands, as she has stood for the last eleven years in Court,
as a humble petitioner for the lands to which she became entitled in the
year 1835, and her claim is denied by the law-executive of a powerful Government which bound itself to respect the rights of a conquered
people. It seems that it is only valuable lands which are deemed
worthy of the dignity of confiscation.

A. D. 1845. MAY.

ESPEDIENTE OF BENITO DIAZ FOR THE POINT OF LOBOS.

§ **119.** This *espediente* was upon a petition for a tract of land
including the ruined Fort at Fort Point, and the Presidio, at the place
marked " Diaz " on the accompanying map. ¦This *espediente* was
not concluded before the conquest of California by the Americans, and
so never became operative." Palmer *v.* The United States, 24 Howard
Rep. S. C., U. States, 125. But the *espediente*, so far as above set
forth, is undoubtedly genuine. See report of J. De la Cruz Sanchez,
ADDENDA, No. LXIV, page 93. I cite it here to show the tenacity
with which the tradition of a legal fact retains its place, even among an
illiterate people who are destitute of law books. The *espediente*,
ADDENDA, No. LXX, page 102, contains the report of José De la
Cruz Sanchez, the judge to whom the petition was in the first instance
referred, who certifies that he cannot give information respecting the
place occupied by the military point, because he knows nothing of its
commons, or *ejidos*. It thus appears that the rude, illiterate people of
California knew that there were certain commons attached to the Fort ;
but Sanchez, the " respective Judge " to whom the matter was referred
by the Governor, ADDENDA, No. LXX, page 101, who was also
" Justice of San Francisco," which was the same as " 2d Constitutional
Justice of Yerba Buena," ADDENDA, No. LXIV, page 93, had no
means of determining what were the commons or ejidos of a Hispano-
Mexican Fort. .Those commons were equal to a square of 3,000
Spanish varas, or yards ; that is, 1,500 varas measured in the direction
of each cardinal point from the center of the Fort, and squared upon
this base. Mitchell *v.* The United States, 15 Peters, 52 ; Same *v.*
The Same, 9 Peters, 711. This is, however, to be measured in the
manner described in § 30 of this argument ; namely : if there were
obstacles interposed so that the measurement could not be made in the
form of a square, the required quantity was to be made up by measure-
ments in other directions. These commons or *ejidos* of this Fort
constitute the " Government Reserve " as laid down on the current maps.
In like manner the tradition of the " Four square leagues of a PUEBLO,"
of its *ejidos, propios* and *arbitrios,* and of its being an " Illustrious Corporation " was firmly planted in the popular mind and popular faith.

notwithstanding that there were no law books to justify these notions or to render them exact.

A. D. 1845. DECEMBER.
NOE'S EXPEDIENTE FOR THE RANCHO SAN MIGUEL.

§ **120.** The *expediente* of José Jesus Noé for a portion of land formerly appurtenant to the Ex-Mission of Dolores, Exhibit Hopkins W, ADDENDA, No. LXIV, page 92, designated "Noé Rancho" on the accompanying map, sheds no light on the subject, except that it shows that the Ex-Mission of Dolores had become completely extinct under the inquest of office made under the law of May 28th, 1845, ADDENDA, No. LXII, page 88, Art. 1, as set forth in §§ 115–117 of this brief. For the *informe* does not, as heretefore, §§ 82, 88, and 102, send the *espediente* to the administrator of the Establishment of Dolores, but only to the "Justice and Judge of San Francisco." The Judge, in his report, calls himself "Justice of the 2d Constitutional Court of YERBA BUENA," while the Governor in his *vista* styles the same Judge "2d Alcalde of SAN FRANCISCO," thus showing that Yerba Buena and San Francisco were designations indifferently used for the same PUEBLO. Noé, the petitioner, lived at Yerba Buena in 1842. See Teschmacher's deposition. He was Secretary of the Electoral College there in 1844. Exhibit 12 to Vallejo's deposition, ADDENDA, No. XLI, page 88. He was Judge of First Instance there in 1845. Exhibit 16 to Vallejo's deposition. Noé, in his deposition in the case of Bolton v. The United States, in this Court, testifies that he lived in San Francisco in 1845 and 1846; that he was Judge of First Instance there in 1846; and that during all that time he was a frequent visitor at the Mission Dolores. That Dolores was in his jurisdiction, but that he could not grant *solares* there, but only in San Francisco.* That his jurisdiction as Judge of First Instance extended over a large district, being the *jurisdiccion contenciosa* alluded to in Micheltorena's proclamation of Nov. 14, 1853, Art. 4, Document No. 11, Vallejo's deposition, ADDENDA, No. LVII, page 84. And yet it is gravely insisted that Yerba Buena was a mere hamlet near the anchorage, and that the ruined, deserted Indian hovels at the Mission Dolores constituted the PUEBLO of San Francisco!

A. D. 1846. MAY.
ANDRADE'S ESPEDIENTE FOR THE ORCHARD AND TANNERY OF THE MISSION DOLORES.

§ **121.** The *espediente* of José Andradé is introduced in evidence by the United States. Exhibit Hopkins X. It purports to be an

---

* NOTE.—Building lots had already been granted at the Mission of Dolores, but in 1843 Governor Micheltorena interdicted further grants at that locality; see § 108 of this argument, and ADDENDA No. LVI: and after this only one lot appears to have been granted at Dolores during the existence of the Mission, namely on Aug. 20, 1843, by Sanchez, Justice of the Peace, to Domingo Felis. See ADDENDA, No. LXXVIII, page 113. This grant has been rejected by the U. S. Land Commission, and the rejection has become final. See 1 Hoffman's Reports, Appendix, page 2, No. 5, and page 7, No. 46.

espediente and grant of the orchard of the Mission of Dolores, bearing date May 6th, 1846. It contains no *informe*, map or report; the claim based upon it has been rejected by the Land Commission, and the United States are now resisting it in this Court on the ground that it is forged and antedated. The same United States now introduce it in this case as a genuine grant, evidently for the purpose of basing upon it an argument to the effect that if there had been a PUEBLO of San Francisco entitled to four leagues of land, this orchard would have been included within those four leagues, and so the Governor would not have granted it to Andradé. But besides the general answer to this position, (see §§ 80, 81, of this argument,) there is another, namely : that the orchard of the Mission did not belong to the PUEBLO of San Francisco, but belonged to the Catholic Bishop of California, as a sole corporation representing the Catholic Church in that behalf, and so was not grantable to any private person, and certainly the Pueblo of San Francisco had no interest in it. Larkin *vs.* The United States, 1 Hoffman's Reports, 313 ; Den *vs.* Hill, 1 McAllister's Rep. 485. See also Judge Felch's decision in the case of Alemany, Bishop of California *vs.* The United States, Claim for the Mission Churches, Cemeteries and Orchards, confirming to the Bishop, among other property, this very orchard. If the grant be genuine, then it shows only that the establishment of Dolores had fallen so completely into decay and non-existence that its very orchard was granted away, so far as the Governor had the power to grant it. If, on the other hand, the grant be a forgery, it has no possible bearing upon the present case.

A. D. 1846. MAY.

GUERRERO AND FITCH'S ESPEDIENTE FOR THE MOUNTAIN LAKE AND LOBOS CREEK TRACT.

§ 122. The last *espediente* to which attention is called, is that numbered 578 in Jones's list, and which, although not concluded before the American conquest, is undoubtedly genuine, and is contained in Exhibit Hopkins, No. 8, ADDENDA, No. LXVI, page 95. It is that of Henry Fitch and Francisco Guerrero for a piece of land embracing an arroyo (water-course) suitable for a mill which they proposed to erect, and may be described generally as that tract of land west of the settlement at Yerba Buena, and lying along the sea-shore between the Laguna de Merced (see § 82,) and the Presidio, and embracing the Laguna called Mountain Lake and the stream of water now commonly called Lobos Creek. The petition is dated at Yerba Buena, May 13th, 1846. It is approved by "José de Jesus Noé, Just-"ice of the Peace of the Jurisdiction of Yerba Buena" on the same day. The petitioners "solicit the favor they ask without prejudice to "the *ejidos* of the settlement of Yerba Buena although they have not "yet been designated : dejando en salvo hasta los ejidos de la poblacion "de Yerba Buena aunque no estan nombrados." Guerrero, it has already been seen, had been Sub-Prefect and Justice of the Peace, ADDENDA, No. XLIII, page 62, No. LXV, page 95, and yet we find him in the month of May, 1846, and within less than two months before the conquest by the United States, thus asserting, as against his own wishes, the rights of the PUEBLO of San Francisco to its *ejidos*, its commons or vacant suburbs. This closes the record on that point.

THE PRECEDING GRANTS OF FARMING LANDS EFFECTUALLY DEFINED THE LIMITS OF THE PUEBLO LANDS.

§ **123.** I have now discussed all the *espedientes* of grants of farming lands actually made within or near the limits of the four square leagues of land belonging to the PUEBLO of San Francisco, namely: the grant of the Buri-Buri rancho to the Sanchez, § 86, of this argument; of the Laguna de la Merced to Galindo, § 82; of San Pedro to De Haro, § 88; of La Visitacion to Leese, § 97; of Las Salinas to Bernal, § 102; and of San Miguel to Noé, § 120. If we now look at the annexed map, bearing in mind that the peninsula of San Francisco is less than six miles in average breadth until we reach the Buri-Buri, and compare this map with any of the official maps of the United States, or more conveniently with Langley's sectionized map prefixed to the San Francisco Directory, as stated in § 30 of this argument, it will be found that the lands belonging to the Pueblo of San Francisco and not included in those grants, all lie northward of those grants, and include a less area than four square leagues; but if we reject the vast sandy and other wastes which occupy so many square miles of this area, as the Spanish law rejects them from the computed measurement, while they are still included within the boundaries of the grant (see § 30 of this argument) and also reject the large tract included in the *ejidos* or Government Reservation of the Presidio (§119 of this argument; see Langley's map, ut supra), we shall find the patrimony of San Francisco dwindling down to about one square league of land. But taking this area at its actual superficial measurement, and we find all the Pueblo lands not granted to the Sanchez, Galindo, De Haro, Leese, Bernal and Noé, as just mentioned, lie north of those grants, and that the northern lines of those grants, extending from the Pacific to the Bay, together with the water-lines of the Ocean, the straits and the Bay, include a less area than four square leagues. I have before said (§§ 30 and 39 of this argument) that as San Francisco was situated on a peninsula, and the PUEBLO lying at the upper end of it, the measurement must necessarily be made between the tide-water limits and extending towards the south. Again, in § 39, I remarked that if the PUEBLO were situated on an island containing exactly four leagues or less, then there could be no necessity for any measurement at all, for the *whole of it must belong to the* PUEBLO. Now the late Mexican Government itself segregated the PUEBLO lands from the public domain, by granting so much of the adjoining public lands and of the Pueblo lands themselves, that less than the patrimonial four leagues were left to the Pueblo. The surrounding natural limits of the tide waters on the west, north and east have been united by a mathematical line defining land-grants of the Mexican Government, the whole containing less than four leagues. And since then the American Government has traced its lines of survey over the whole tract, so that a child can see upon the map that there is less than four leagues left of the Pueblo lands, *Id certum est quod certum reddi potest.* When a fact is patent, what need of demonstration?

REVIEW OF THE GENERAL RESULTS OF THE MISSION SCHEME.

§ **124.** Before dismissing this subject, and passing on to the great fact of the conquest of California by the Americans, it may not be inappropriate to a discussion which has assumed a synthetic, and therefore a popular form,—as it certainly will be refreshing by way of diversion,—to contemplate for a moment the results which the pious kings of Spain and the devoted missionaries had attained under their plans of missionary colonization. Looking from a merely philosophical stand-point, let us contemplate for a moment the actual results attained by the Catholic church militant. We have already seen the wonderful material success which crowned their efforts ; § 59 of this argument. But it has been a popular theme among travellers and even foreign residents, to depreciate the results attained in point of civilization and of religious instruction ; and of these critics Capt. Beechy of the Royal Navy, and Alexander Forbes, who published a work on California in 1839, are the most prominent. It was something, surely, that over 30,000 wild, barbarous and naked Indians had been brought in from their savage haunts, persuaded to wear clothes, accustomed to a regular life, inured to such light labor as they could endure, taught to read and write, instructed in music, accustomed to the service of the church, partaking of its sacraments, and indoctrinated in the Christian Religion. And this system had become self-sustaining under the mildest and gentlest of tutilage : for the Franciscan monks who superintended these establishments, most of whom were from Spain, and many of whom were highly cultivated men—soldiers, engineers, artists, lawyers and physicians, before they became Franciscans, always treated the neophyte Indians with the most paternal kindness, and did not scorn to labor with them in the field, the brickyard, the forge, and the mill. 1 De Mofras, 263, 273, 353. When we view the vast constructions of the Mission buildings, including the churches, the refectories, the dormitories, the workshops, the granaries, and the rancherias, sometimes constructed with huge timbers brought many miles on the shoulders of the Indians, and look at the beautiful stone sculptures and ribbed stone arches of the church of the Carmelo, we cannot deny that the Franciscan missionary monks had the wisdom, sagacity, and patience to bring their neophyte pupils far forward on the road from barbarism to civilization, and that these Indians were not destitute of taste and capacity. But it is said that the Indians did not " understand the mysteries of religion ?" It is not denied that they received them as children receive them, with full and undoubting faith, and this mode of reception has been given by the author of that faith as the highest test of its purity and completeness. But who does comprehend the "mysteries of religion?" Would they not cease to be mysteries the moment they were comprehended? Does not "the untutored mind" of the "poor Indian" comprehend them as well as the highest capacity of the most enlightened intellect? It is enough that the Franciscan monks succeeded in all that they undertook to accomplish. It matters not that the Spanish theory of the available capacity of the Americo-Indian races for final self-government and independent citizenship was a false one; after having shown that these people could be christianized and civilized by the attraction of kindness, and the imposition of systematic, regular, and easy tasks while in a state of pupilage, the destruction of the Missions of California seems to have demonstrated the converse proposition that these are the only conditions of the proximate christianization of these races.

EFFECT OF THE RUIN OF THE MISSIONS. GENERAL DEMORAL-
IZATION AND RUIN. INDIAN DEPREDATIONS. MEXICO-CALI-
FORNIAN VIGILANCE COMMITTEES.

§ **125.** But the result of the good effected by the Missions can also be determined by contemplating the effects produced by their downfall. The Franciscan Monks were generally driven out, but the parish Priests did not arrive, so that the neophytes were generally left without teachers or protectors, and the services of the church for the most part ceased. 1 De Mofras, 273. The Mayor-Domos, appointed to take charge of the Missions, were often brutal and illiterate persons,—sometimes those who had been menial servants, so that frequently the missionary was at the mercy of one of his former herdsmen. *Ib.* 342, 388. The few missionaries who remained were insulted, thwarted, stinted in their allowance, and, in some instances, died of starvation while ministering at the altar. *Ib.* 303, 380, 390, 421. Meanwhile, the blight of demoralization fell upon the authors of this ruin, if we can believe the account of judicious travellers and observers. "At the same time "with a change of rulers, the country was deprived of the religious "establishments upon which its society and good order were founded. "Anarchy and confusion began to reign, and the want of authority was "everywhere felt; some of the Missions were deserted, the property "which had been amassed in them was dissipated, and the Indians "turned out to seek their native wilds." Wilkes' Exploring Expedition, vol. V., page 162. "This act (Alvarado's regulations of secular-"ization), brought about the ruin of the Missions, and the property that "was still left became a prey to the rapacity of the Governor, the needy "officers, and the administrador, who have well nigh consumed all."— Ib. 168. "The administradors have made themselves and those by "whom they were appointed, rich upon the spoils of these Missions."— Ib. 173; Bryant's California, p. 444. "Nothing can be in a worse "state than the lower offices, such as the alcaldes, etc. They are now "held by ignorant men, who have no ideas of justice, which is generally "administered according to the alcalde's individual notions, as his feel-"ings may be enlisted, or the standing of the parties. To recover a

"debt by legal means, is considered as beyond possibility, and creditors
"must wait until the debtor is disposed to pay. Until lately the
"word of a Californian was sufficient to insure the payment of claims
"upon him, but such has been the moral degradation which has fallen
"upon the people since the Missions have been robbed by the author-
"ities, and the old priests driven out, that no reliance can now be placed
"upon their promises, and all those who have lately trusted them com-
"plain that engagements are not regarded, and that it is next to impos-
"sible for any one to obtain any returns for goods that have been
"delivered."—Wilkes' Exploring Expedition, V., page 161. "Unfor-
"tunately, a great number of circumstances have latterly contributed
"to corrupt the Californians; contact with strangers, introducing among
"them habits of luxury, has multiplied their necessities, and excited
"them to the pillage of the Missions ; the disorganization of the Span-
"ish military system has rendered them less brave, and their natural
"proclivity for gambling and drunkenness has increased to such a point,
"that hardly a Californian is to be found who has not a bottle of brandy
"in his saddle-bags, with his fire-arms. They have a proverb : "Weap-
"ons for your enemy, and a bottle for your friend."—2 De Mofras, 22.
"They are excessively indolent and learn no trades."—Wilkes, Vol. V.
176. "Unfortunately, also, the inhabitants do not profit wisely by the spoils
"of the Missions. The most of them, instead of preserving the cattle, kill
"them in order to sell their hides and tallow to trading ships ; the soil
"rests untilled, for hardly any one but the Indians cultivate it."—1 De
Mofras, 321. "Agriculture, and the rearing of cattle, form the princi-
"pal wealth of California ; but these sources of prosperity are dimin-
"ishing every day, on account of the revolutionary condition of the
"country, and the dispersion of the Indians of the Missions."—Ib. 469.
"The Indians told me of the outrages they endured from the whites,
"who deprived them of the few cattle which had been given to them,
"and pastured their own flocks upon the small patches of ground
"which had been assigned to the neophytes for cultivation. ' You see,'
"said they, ' how miserable we are ; the Fathers can no longer protect
"us, and the civil authorities themselves pillage us. Is it not pitiable
"to see them tear from us those Missions which we have built, those
"immense herds gathered by our care, and to be ourselves and our
"families, exposed to the worst of treatment ? Shall we then be guilty
"if we defend ourselves, and if, when we return to our tribes in the
"Tulares, we take all the cattle that follow us ?' "—Ib. 345. This
plan of specific vengeance was soon put into execution. The neophytes, outraged in every form, generally returned to their native tribes
among the Tulares, a vast valley at the head of the river San Joaquin.*
Hardly a night passed in which a raid did not take place from these
Indians, who, knowing the country intimately, speaking both Spanish

---

* NOTE.—The natives when first seen by Father Junipero were naked, and knew
nothing of clothes. Vida de Junipero Serra, Chap. XLIV. When a neophyte deserted
a Mission and went back to his native tribe, he signified his apostacy by taking off and
throwing away his shirt, and so returned to his people in the same nude condition in
which he left them.

and their own native dialect, and being expert horsemen, descended upon the Missions and settlements, sweeping off herds of horses and cattle, and sometimes carrying into captivity the wives and daughters of the whites. These latter often retaliated by excursions into the Indian country, in which whole villages were devoted to slaughter, rapine and burning, by the wild and indiscriminate fury of revenge.— 1 De Mofras, 347, 414; Wilkes' Exploring Expedition, Vol. V., 173, 174. One of the last acts of the Departmental Assembly of California in 1846, was, on April 29th, to receive a memorial from the inhabitants of San José complaining that their lives and property were in jeopardy from the attacks of the savages, and to provide ways and means for a campaign against the Indians. California Archives, Legislative Records, Vol. IV p. 672. To crown these calamities, Governor Micheltorena, who had come up from Mexico as a counter-revolutionary governor, had brought with him an army of three hundred soldiers, which army was formed by taking that number of convicts from the prisons of Mexico. 1 De Mofras, 311, 312. See Santa Anna's order for this enlistment, El Observador Judicial y de Legislacion, A. D. 1842, Vol. I p. 372. A large number of these convict soldiers were left in California, from desertion and other causes, and began to commit acts of rape, rapine, robbery, mutilation and murder, upon the inhabitants, who often organized parties of horsemen, hunted these outlaws with lassos, and put them to death like wild beasts. Vigilance Committees in California are therefore a tradition of the Mexico-Californian *regime* —a scion grafted on a more vigorous stock. But even this did not avert the ruin of the Province, which resulted from the destruction of the Missions, and this was the deplorable condition of California on the eve of its conquest by the Americans. If we ask, where are now the 30,000 christianized Indians who once enjoyed the beneficence and created the wealth of the twenty-one Catholic Missions of California, and then contemplate the most wretched of all want of systems which has succeeded them under our own Government, we shall not withhold our admiration from those good and devoted men who with such wisdom, sagacity, and self-sacrifice, reared these wonderful institutions in the wilderness of California. *They*, at least, would have preserved these Indian races, if they had been left to pursue unmolested their work of pious beneficence.

A. D. 1846, 1849.

THE UNITED STATES CONQUER CALIFORNIA, BUT CONTINUE ITS CIVIL ORGANIZATION.

§ **126.** The conquest of that portion of California which includes San Francisco took place on July 8th, 1846, and following the principle heretofore alluded to, ante § 54, that the civil institutions of a country are not overturned by the change of sovereign or political authority, Alcaldes were at once appointed for the PUEBLO of San Francisco,— those then in office having *retired*, it is presumed. See ADDENDA, No. LXXVII, page 111; Executive Doc. No. 17, House of Reps. 1st Sess. 31st Con. pp. 452, 494, 499. So a Prefect and Judges of First

Instance were appointed for the District; *Ibid.* 797, 832; and a Superior Tribunal of Justice appointed on the Mexico-Californian basis. *Ibid.* 807, 808, 820, 821, 827. Everything proceeded as if the civil institutions of California had not lapsed, but still existed complete in form and vigor.

A. D. 1847. MARCH.

GENERAL KEARNY, MILITARY GOVERNOR OF CALIFORNIA, RECOGNIZES THE CORPORATE TOWN OF SAN FRANCISCO, AND GRANTS IT BEACH AND WATER LOTS.

§ **127.** California had not been a year in the possession of the Americans, when General Kearny, the Military Governor of the Department, on the tenth day of March, A. D. 1847, made a grant to the Town of San Francisco of all the Beach and Water Lots lying on the east front of the town, between the points known as the "Rincon" and "Fort Montgomery," being the "Rincon Point" and a Point opposite the dotted line running east from the Presidio, as both are indicated on the accompanying map. Those who came to San Francisco as late as the Fall of 1849 will remember an open battery on a high terrace cut down in the face of the cliff at the latter point, which gave its name to "Battery Street" whose lines passed through it. "Beach and Water Lots,"—lands overflowed by the ordinary tides—belong to the Sovereign of a country. Pollard *v.* Hagan, 3 Howard, U. S. Rep. Formerly these lots in question belonged to Mexico; when they were conquered from Mexico, they belonged to the United States; when California was erected into a Sovereign State they belonged to her as appurtenant to her sovereignty, and she granted them to the City of San Francisco. California Statutes of 1851, page 307, Chap. 41. But on March 10th, 1847, these Beach and Water Lots in question undoubtedly belonged to the United States, and General Kearny, being the Governor of California, and either having the right, or supposing that he had the right to grant them, did assume to grant them to the "Town of San Francisco." See the grant, ADDENDA, No. LXXII, page 104. It is remarkable that Governor Kearny uses every form of description which could be conveniently employed to designate the grantees with the greatest certainty: "Do hereby grant, convey and release to the Town of San Francisco, the people or corporate authorities thereof all the right," etc., etc. Governor Kearny was no lawyer, but he may have been told that Mexican PUEBLOS were not full corporations but only quasi-corporations, as was probably true, and so may have feared that a grant to the "*corporate* authorities" would not have been effectual. But his own good sense doubtless suggested to him that the "people" of the town really constituted the corporation, [5 Abbott Pr. Rep. 325,] and that if he used every significant term of description some of them must work effectually to vest the lands granted to the "Town." Be this as it may, this grant or attempted grant shows conclusively that the then Governor of California recognized a Town or Pueblo of San Francisco, and that this town was not the miserable ruined Indian hamlet at the Mission of Dolores, but was the Mexico-·

Californian PUEBLO theretofore known as San Francisco or Yerba Buena.

A. D. 1849. MARCH.

THE CITIZENS OF SAN FRANCISCO INSTITUTE A DISTRICT LEGIS-
LATURE.

§ 128. Nearly two years had elapsed since the conquest of California by the Americans, the gold mines had been discovered, the
Pueblo of San Francisco had attained a population of 10,000 to 15,000,
and still had no Municipal government except that of Alcaldes. There
was no Town-Council, no representative or deliberative local legislature, and meanwhile no modern city ever stood in greater need of a
strong and efficient local government, based directly upon public opinion,
responsible to it, and controlled by it. The inhabitants of San Francisco, with that executive instinct of self-government and self-preserva-
tion which first challenged the wonder of the civilized world and
afterwards won its approbation, determined that they would have a
responsible and representative government. Accordingly they organized a " District Legislature " or " Legislative Assembly," an elective
body, with a Speaker and Clerk, proceeding according to the Anglo-
Saxon Legislative and Parliamentary Law, assuming to supersede all
other local officers. See ADDENDA, No. LXXIII, pages 104, 105,
106, 107. That the citizens of San Francisco who thus undertook to
supersede the established local authorities, acted in good faith, cannot
be doubted, for on the 10th March immediately ensuing, they reported
all that they had done to Major General Persifer F. Smith, Commanding the Pacific Division U. S. Army. Executive Doc. 1st Sess. 31st
Cong. House of Reps. No. 17, pages 732, etc. General Smith, (now
long deceased,) who had been a lawyer before he entered the Military
service of the United States, instead of assenting to the projects of the
Legislative Assembly, mildly suggested to them that the municipal (or
civil) laws of California had not been changed by the conquest, and
that the " Legislative Assembly " was a body wholly unknown to the
law. Executive Doc. No. 17, 1st Sess. 31st Congress, House, pages
735, etc. See § 54 of this argument.

GOVERNOR RILEY, MILITARY GOVERNOR, REPUDIATES THE "LEG-
ISLATIVE ASSEMBLY OF SAN FRANCISCO."

§ 129. Governor Riley, the Military Governor of California, having higher powers than Major General Smith, who only remonstrated
against the creation of the " District Legislature of San Francisco " as
stated in the next preceding § 128 of this argument, and probably
being fully advised on the points of law involved in the discussion, did
not hesitate at once to repudiate the action of the citizens of San Francisco in constituting a " District Legislature." On June 4th, 1849, he
issued his proclamation in that regard. See ADDENDA, No. LXXIV,
page 107. I have entitled that ADDENDA as follows: " Governor
Riley, Military Governor of California, DENOUNCES ' the Legislative

Assembly of San Francisco.'" But here the *"facilitas utriusque linguae"* for a moment misled me. For the Spanish word *denunciar* has not the strong force of our English word "to denounce," but rather the milder sense, "to indicate, to publish, to make known." Thus Salvá, Diccionario Español, in verbo: *"Denunciar*: Noticiar; avisar alguna cosa; prognosticar algo; promulgar; publicar solemnente alguna cosa. PROMULGARE." So that when it was said that Governor Riley "DENOUNCED" the Legislative Assembly of San Francisco, it was simply meant that he DISAPPROVED of it; for, instead of threatening to hang or shoot the members of the Legislative Assembly as malefactors, he merely notified them that they had mistaken their remedy or means of relief. See ADDENDA, No. LXXIV, page 107, over date of June 4th, 1849.

GOVERNOR RILEY, UNITED STATES MILITARY GOVERNOR OF CALIFORNIA, RESTORES THE AYUNTAMIENTO OF THE PUEBLO OF SAN FRANCISCO.

§ **130.** But on the very next day, June 5th, 1849, (and perhaps accompanying it in the same envelope, with that admirable consideration which is *la politesse des supérieurs*) the Governor transmitted to some of these same gentlemen of the Legislative Assembly together with others, an order for the election of an Ayuntamiento of the Pueblo or Town of San Francisco, indicating that that was the legal and perfectly adequate mode of relieving the existing pressure upon the inhabitants of that Pueblo. See ADDENDA, No. LXXV, page 108. This admirable document sets forth in the most condensed, and yet in the clearest manner, the rights of the PUEBLO to a representative and deliberative local legislature, (ADDENDA, No. LXXV, page 109, and §§ 47, 90, 92, of this argument,) and also: ¶ 1st, the police, administrative and fiscal powers of the Ayuntamiento; *Ibid*, ¶ 2: 2dly, the right of the Ayuntamiento to grant building lots; *Ibid*, ¶ 3: ante § 83 of this argument; 3dly, the inviolability and inalienability of the *ejidos; Ibid*, ¶ 3: ante § 14 of this argument, and 4thly, that all elections should be duly certified, transmitted to the Governor, and receive his approval. *Ibid*, ¶ 4. Thus the familiar principle of the law of nations, and of all Public Law, was formally and properly recognized, and well expressed, namely, that when a country is conquered, the laws regulating the rights and relations of citizens towards each other, and the rights of property, remain unchanged. See §§ 54, 84, of this argument. And here again we see that in June, 1849, the Military American Governor of California, was fully impressed with the notion that the PUEBLO of San Francisco existed, and that it had a proprietary right to grant lands, which it could not have had unless they belonged to it. How remarkable it is, that all the Mexico-Californian Governors and Legislatures, and after them the Americo-Californian Governors and Secretaries of State should have been mistaken in this respect,—IF IT WAS A MISTAKE! That this Ayuntamiento thus ordered by Governor Riley to be instituted was elected, organized, and went into operation is very evident from public history, a condensed *résumé* of which is found in No. LXXVII, pages 111, 112, of the ADDENDA, prepared by the present very efficient City Clerk, who anticipated me in compiling that list; and also from the more convincing fact, that the present citizens of San Francisco are now submitting to annual taxation for the purpose of paying the debts created by that same Ayuntamiento or Town Council, under the pressing necessity of providing instantly for the Town Halls, Court-rooms, jails, streets, and sewers required by a WHOLE NATION of civilized people, set down bodily and at once on the sandy slopes of the old PUEBLO of San Francisco. The United States kindly concedes that we may pay the debts of the ancient PUEBLO OF SAN FRANCISCO, but endeavors to confiscate the lands of that PUEBLO. Is this the definition of a paternal government? The old caducous government of Mexico would at least have let us alone. This Ayuntamiento thus ordered to be elected by Governor Riley, and thus elected and organized, was on January 11th, succeeded by another Ayuntamiento, elected on the same Hispano-Californian basis, which held office from January 11th to May 8th, 1850. See ADDENDA, No. LXXVII, page 112.

A. D. 1850. APRIL.

THE LEGISLATURE OF CALIFORNIA RECOGNIZES THE PUEBLO OF SAN FRANCISCO.

§ **131.** On the 15th of April, 1850, the legislature of California raised San Francisco to the dignity of a City. See An Act to incorporate the City of San Francisco, Laws 1850, chap. 98, page 223. If the inhabitants had theretofore been only a *quasi*-corporation, they then became a full corporation, with all the powers belonging to such institutions. By the same act, page 229, § 11, the Legislature declare that on the day when that City Charter should go into effect, "all the "powers and functions of Prefect, Sub-Prefect, Alcaldes, Second Al- "caldes, the Ayuntamiento, and all other officers whatsoever, hereto- "fore exercising authority in the MUNICIPAL GOVERNMENT OF THE "PUEBLO OF YERBA BUENA OR SAN FRANCISCO, or City of San "Francisco, shall cease and determine." This demonstrates the fact that in less than three years after the conquest by the Americans, the Legislature of California believed that there was an organized PUEBLO of Yerba Buena or San Francisco. In § 1, page 223, of the same act, the Legislature fix the corporate limits of the City, which, on consulting the map, we find did not include the whole of the MISSION OF DOLORES. In the same section is a provision that the fixing of these boundaries shall not "be construed to divest or in any manner preju- dice any right or "privilege to which the City of San Francisco may be entitled beyond "the limits above described." These declarations establish two facts:

FIRST: That although the Legislature recognized the PUEBLO OF SAN FRANCISCO, they did not imagine that it was located at the MIS- SION OF DOLORES, for when they raised the PUEBLO to the rank of a

City, they did not include all of the Mission of Dolores within its boundaries.

SECONDLY: That the Legislature "had heard" of some claim of the PUEBLO of San Francisco to lands situate beyond the limits prescribed for the new incorporation. It was only years afterwards that counsel were found bold enough to assert that "nobody had ever heard of such a claim."

THE AUTHORITIES, THE CITIZENS, AND THE LEGISLATURE HAVE FAITH IN A PUEBLO OF SAN FRANCISCO.

§ **132.** Meanwhile the Ayuntamiento of San Francisco, supposing that they had the ownership in trust of the Pueblo lands, proceeded to execute the Legislative enactment of the Cortes of Spain of January 4th, 1813, ordering the Pueblo lands to be sold, (see ante § 52 of this argument, ADDENDA, No. XI, page 21,) and at various dates in the years 1849 and 1850 a large portion of those lands was exposed for sale at public auction by the authorities of the Pueblo, and publicly sold, the proceeds of which were paid into the treasury of the Municipality. See Wheeler's Land Titles, which are in evidence in the case by stipulation. And afterwards, when the new city found itself in debt, and was struggling to regain its credit, its Common Council created a "Board of Commissioners of the Sinking Fund of the City of San Francisco," to whom the most valuable of these lands were conveyed, in the hope that on the credit of their hypothecation a fund might be created, upon which the debt of the city might be funded for a period of years, and thus delayed until it could be gradually liquidated from the resources created by these lands and the annual revenue of the city. See the history of this plan, Smith v. Morse, 2 California Reports, 524. When this plan proved ineffectual, another device was successfully adopted, namely : to fund the existing city debt on a credit of twenty years, pledging to the payment of its annual interest and of $50,000 annually to its Sinking Fund a first lien on all the revenues of the city derived from taxation, and also all those Pueblo lands theretofore conveyed to the Commissioners of the Sinking Fund, who were required to convey, and did convey them to the "Commissioners of the Funded Debt" created for that purpose. See Laws of California for 1851, Chap. 88, page 387, and page 390, § 12 of "An Act to authorize the Funding of the Floating Debt of the City of San Francisco, and to provide for the payment of the same," passed May 1st, 1851. It is a matter of history that under that Act the Commissioners of the Funded Debt sold a vast quantity of real estate, constituting a large portion of the current titles to land, to which there is no title at all in the hands of these grantees, immediate and derivative, except that derived from the CITY OF SAN FRANCISCO. See Wheeler's Land Titles in evidence ut supra. And even as late as the year 1862 the Legislature of California, by "An Act to authorize the Commissioners of the Funded Debt of the City of San Francisco to compromise and settle certain claims to real estate, and to convey such real estate pursuant thereto," passed April 14th, 1862, Laws 1862, chap. CCIII, page 217, and held to be constitutional in Babcock *v.* Middleton, 20 California Reports, 643, referred to and adopted these conveyances of Pueblo lands to the Commissioners of the Funded Debt as a source of title. Can it be possible that all the constituted authorities of Spain, Mexico and California, for a period of more than two hundred and sixty years, have been afflicted with a persistent, pestilent and noxious ignorance on the subject of PUEBLO LANDS?

§ **133.** In the years 1851–52 the creditors of the city, who had obtained judgment on their claims, issued executions upon their judgments, and levied upon these same PUEBLO lands, as if they were the property of the city, and exposed them for sale by the Sheriff. Such sales were restrained by injunction from the District Court, upon the very ground assumed by the authorities of California under the Mexican régime, that the lands were held in trust for the citizens of the Pueblo. §§ 80, 81, of this argument, and which propositions were ten years afterwards sustained by the Supreme Court of California, in the case of Hart *v.* Burnett, 15 California Reports. See City of San Francisco *vs.* Le Roy, case No. 597, 4th District Court; City of San Francisco *vs.* Dunbar, case No. 598, in the same Court.*

RECAPITULATION OF THE ARGUMENT.—PROPOSITIONS OF THE CLAIMANTS.

§ **134.** From the preceding narrative argument we infer :

1. That each Hispano-American Pueblo consisting of ten or more married male heads of families, was entitled to four leagues of land as a part of the patrimony of the Pueblo. See §§ 28, 29, of this argument.

2. That such four leagues of land were to be measured in a square or prolonged form, taking the centre of the Plaza or Public Square of

---

* It is very commonly said that the city has always been unsuccessful in its litigations. The litigation of a municipal corporation is always of a special and troublesome, and generally of a difficult character. With some considerable experience in that respect, I may be permitted to say that the City of San Francisco has been faithfully served by its official servants in the conduct of its law business. Col. Holt, the first City Attorney under the charter, was eminently successful in the management of the vast litigation which the city inherited as a portion of its birthright; and there is probably not one of his successors who can be justly accused of remissness in the discharge of his duties. If I may be permitted to make a grateful suggestion for the benefit of a city to whose kindness I owe so much, it is that the law business of the city can never be perfectly and systematically managed until the office of City Attorney and Counsel is elevated into a DEPARTMENT, with its Bureau in the City Hall, and its records as complete and in as permanent a form as those of any other public office. Then an era of confusion would not attend every change in the *personnel* of the office, and the actual incumbent would always have at his command properly arranged, digested and indexed, all the information belonging to his Department, and a reliable history of every law suit in which the city had ever been engaged. Yet those litigating against the city are evidently interested in having the municipality inadequately defended in its litigation, and the clamor of economy raised by them will probably always prevent the proper means being adopted for the completest vindication of the rights of the city in the courts.

the PUEBLO as a starting point, but that if the sea, mountains, marshes or other wastes intervened, the measurement was to be taken in some other convenient direction; and if waste or other useless lands were still found to be within the boundaries, they were to be included within the lines of the survey, but not to be computed in the calculation of the area. See §§ 28, 30, of this argument.

3. That the conformation of the peninsula of San Francisco is such that there could be only one possible parallel of latitude, which, with the water line surrounding the peninsula, would include the four leagues belonging to the PUEBLO, and therefore it was not necessary that that line should be actually surveyed. *Id certum est quod certum reddi potest.* But that afterwards the Mexican Government made such grants of adjoining lands that there is left for the PUEBLO less than the four leagues to which she is entitled, and the superior authorities have therefore segregated what is left as belonging to the Pueblo, and so reduced that area to certainty. See §§ 30, 39, 123 of this argument.

4. That said four leagues of land were capable of being divided into *solares* or building lots, *suertes* or sowing lots, *propios* or lands to be rented for Municipal Revenue, *ejidos* or commons, and *dehesas* or the large cattle pasture; but that such division was decided by convenience solely, and that the right of PUEBLOS to these four leagues of land did not depend upon the division being actually made. See §§ 10, 11, 14, 15, 16 of this argument, and ADDENDA No. L, page 71, title " Municipal Funds and Revenue."

5. That the PRESIDIOS were recognized as PUEBLOS, and that such PRESIDIAL-PUEBLOS, equally with other PUEBLOS, were entitled to their four leagues of land, to be measured in the same manner. See § 44 of this argument, and ADDENDA No VIII, page 17.

6. That San Francisco was founded in 1776, as a Hispano-American PRESIDIAL-PUEBLO, with eighteen married male soldiers and seven married male colonists, and so as such PUEBLO was entitled to four square leagues of land. See §§ 34 and 44 of this argument. [The words " siete pobladores tambien casados y con familias, seven settlers also married and with families," are not translated in section 44.] That its population in 1825 approached the number of 500 inhabitants, ante § 55, and was never reduced below the " ten male married heads of families " which entitled it to four square leagues of land; even if it were conceded that such a reduction would work a forfeiture of the vested rights of the Pueblo to its lands, which we do not concede. See §§ 28, 34, 73, and ADDENDA No. LXXVI, page 110.

7. That it was an organic feature in the Hispano-American system of administration that populations existing in settlements should be governed by representative and deliberative municipal bodies called AYUNTAMIENTOS or Common Councils; that towns of a certain population were entitled to have Ayuntamientos of their own, as a matter of course; but that if populations were too small to be each entitled to an Ayuntamiento of its own, they were either joined together to form an AGGREGATED AYUNTAMIENTO, or were attached to some PUEBLO which had an Ayuntamiento of its own. See § 47 of this argument.

8. That in the autumn of the year 1834, an Ayuntamiento was organized at San Francisco for the PARTIDO OF SAN FRANCISCO, including small neighboring populations, that is to say, an Ayuntamiento Aggregate, and that this AYUNTAMIENTO AGGREGATE was elected, organized, and entered upon the discharge of its functions. See §§ 47, 70, 71 of this argument.

9. That immediately afterwards it was discovered that the PUEBLO of San Francisco had a population sufficient to entitle it to an Ayuntamiento of its own, and thereupon an Ayuntamiento of the PUEBLO was organized, to which the population of Contra Costa was for awhile attached; namely, a COMPOSITE AYUNTAMIENTO, which superseded the Ayuntamiento of the PARTIDO. See §§ 47, 72, 74, 76, 77 of this argument.

10. That the PUEBLO of San Francisco was a fully organized body politic and CORPORATE, and that it and its Ayuntamiento not only claimed to be such, but were repeatedly recognized as such by the Governor, the Departmental Legislature, and by the citizens of California. See §§ 77, 82, 83, 84, 87, 88, 96, 100, 110, 112, 120, 122 of this argument.

11. That this Ayuntamiento of the Pueblo of San Francisco possessed the power to grant, and did grant lands for building lots, which it could not do unless the PUEBLO OF SAN FRANCISCO was a body politic and corporate, and the owner of such lands. See §§ 83, 84, 87, 98, 100, and ADDENDA No. LXXVIII, pages 113, 114, of this argument. That no measurement of those four leagues of land was actually necessary, but that by the survey of adjoining lands the PUEBLO lands have been effectually segregated from the public domain. See §§ 30, 39, and 123 of this argument.

12. That meanwhile the Governor and Departmental Assembly, assuming to be the superior visitors, inspectors, and directors of said trust, did lawfully grant a large portion of said four leagues of land to citizens of said PUEBLO in fee simple, for purposes of grazing and farming. See §§ 80, 81, 82, 97, 102, 120 of this argument.

13. That in the year 1835 a settlement was begun within the limits of the PUEBLO of San Francisco, on its north-eastern frontage upon the Bay, which was then called YERBA BUENA,* and which is the present site of the most thickly settled portion of the present City of San Francisco. That the population of the PUEBLO OF SAN FRANCISCO gradually shifted itself to YERBA BUENA, and the PUEBLO was known indifferently by the name of PUEBLO of San Francisco, PORT

---

* So named from the fact that that locality abounded in "Yerba Buena—the *good* herb," a species of aromatic mint, reputed to be efficacious as a febrifuge. I believe that the designation of "Yerba Buena," euphonious in itself and replete with historical associations, is now attached to only a disused cemetery, which is about to be appropriated to other uses, and to "Yerba Buena Lodge No. 15," of the Independent Order of Odd Fellows. The island opposite the city, between its water front and Contra Costa, was formerly called "La Isla de Yerba Buena—Yerba Buena Island," but several years ago some experimental Yankee planted there a colony of goats, and since then it has generally been called "GOAT ISLAND." It is to be regretted that the designation Yerba Buena has not been more generally perpetuated.

of San Francisco, YERBA BUENA, and PUEBLO of Yerba Buena. See §§ 120, 111 and 42, 55, 110 of this argument, and ADDENDA No. XXVI.

14. That in the year 1838 the Ayuntamiento of the PUEBLO of San Francisco was suspended, because the requisite basis of population for an Ayuntamiento was raised to 4,000 inhabitants; but that the PUEBLO still retained its character of body politic and corporate, and was administered by Alcaldes and Justices of the Peace with the powers of Ayuntamientos. See §§ 89, 90, 92 of this argument and No. LXIX, page 100, of the ADDENDA.

15. That these Justices of the Peace, thus having the powers of an Ayuntamiento, made and promulgated Municipal Ordinances for the government of the PUEBLO OF SAN FRANCISCO, which were published in that Pueblo. See § 96 of this argument, and ADDENDA No. XLIII, page 62.

16. That the Alcaldes and Justices of the Peace of the PUEBLO OF SAN FRANCISCO continued to grant the lands of the PUEBLO of San Francisco down to the year 1846, and within twenty days of the conquest of California by the Americans, which they could not do unless the PUEBLO of San Francisco continued to exist as a body politic and corporate, and was the owner of said lands. See §§ 100, 83, 84, of this argument, and also ADDENDA No LXXVIII, page 113.

17. That this Pueblo of San Francisco had a complete fiscal organization, with Syndics regularly elected during the existence of the Ayuntamiento, and appointed by the Governor after that time. See ADDENDA, Nos. XXX, page 47; XXXV, page 54; XLV, page 63; LIV, page 75; LXV, page 95.

18. That when California came into the possession of the United States, the constituted authorities of the new Government recognized the PUEBLO of San Francisco, its corporate existence, its right to its lands, and restored its Ayuntamiento; and that the Legislature of California made the same recognition when it raised that PUEBLO to the rank of City. See §§ 126, 127, 129, 130, 131, of this argument.

19. That there was near the Pueblo of San Francisco a Catholic Mission of converted or neophyte Indians, called the Mission of Do-LORES de San Francisco, ["La Mission des Douleurs de Saint François d' Assise—of the *anguish* of Saint Francis of Assise,"] (1 De Mofras, 424;) founded also in the year 1776; see § 34 of this argument. That this Mission was never very prosperous, but from the year 1815 declined rapidly in population. ADDENDA, No. LXXVI, page 110, ante § 115. That the neophyte Indians lived there in a state of COMMUNITY from which they never emerged; §§ 17, 78, 79, 82, 88, 93, 99, 102, 107, 112, 114. That the Mission and Community died of inanition between the years 1840 and 1844, and were lawfully declared extinguished by a formal inquest of office in the year 1845; §§ 115, 116, 117, 120. That it was originally intended that this Mission should become secularized, and be erected into an *Indian Pueblo*, like all other such Missions, § 17, but that as above shown this was never accomplished; and that although it was sometimes called the *Pueblo of*

Dolores, that word *Pueblo* was thus employed only in the sense of " settlement;" §§ 9, 88, 98, 114, 117, and that the Mission of Dolores was never a PUEBLO in the sense of an organized town or body politic or corporate; but on the contrary, as late as the year 1844 its inhabitants, including Prefects, sub-Prefects, Alcaldes, Justices and Regidores, past and present, petitioned the Governor setting forth that the Mission of Dolores had never had the title of PUEBLO, and praying that it might be granted to it in future, which application was not granted; § 114, and ADDENDA, No. LXXI, page 102; and that in the next year, 1845, the said MISSION OF DOLORES, by a formal inquest of law, was forever extinguished, and never reached or could reach the condition of an organized PUEBLO; § 115, and ADDENDA, No. LXII, page 88, Articles 1 and 2; and LXXIII, page 90, Art. 1.

20. That the PUEBLO OF SAN FRANCISCO, and this MISSION OF DOLORES, (otherwise called the ESTABLISHMENT of Dolores) were perfectly distinct, and never confounded with each other, nor has an attempt ever been made to confound them, until long since the conquest of California by the Americans. See §§ 77, 88, 93. 102, 104, 126, 127, 130, 131, 132.

21. That on the 7th day of July, A. D. 1846, [the date of the conquest of California by the Americans] there was a PUEBLO existing at San Francisco.

§ 135. It did not need so long and minute a narrative to sustain the inferences above made, for the law would have presumed all the substantial facts which that narrative has incontestably established. The fact that a town has *de facto* an organization of the usual officers who were elected and served as such, is *prima facie* evidence of the legal organization of such town. Town of Londonderry *vs.* Town of Andover, 28 Vermont Rep. 416. And also that it is a corporation capable of holding and transmitting real estate, and of being by prescription the owner of such real estate. Robie *vs.* Sedgwick, 35 Barbour S. C. R. 319. 2 Kent, 277. Angell & Ames on Corp. 57. Dillingham *vs.* Snow, 7 Mass. 547. Stockbridge *vs.* West Stockbridge, 12 Mass. 400. In order to dedicate property for public use in cities and towns and other places, it is not essential that the property should be vested in a corporate body. It may exist in the public alone; and the sovereign is bound by the dedication, even if there is no actual grant. New Orleans *vs.* The United States, 10 Peters 662. It was therefore wholly unnecessary for the claimants to show that the PUEBLO of San Francisco was an actual legal and fully organized body politic and corporate, the owner of lands which it could grant to its citizens, and which had been completely segregated from the public domain. But those facts were true, and the PUEBLO of San Francisco has shown them by incontestable proofs. What will be the result? The final result cannot be doubted, but meanwhile it is very evident that the United States will advance the following propositions: The Pueblo of San Francisco existed: THEREFORE it did *not* exist. It had the conceded right to grant PUEBLO lands: THEREFORE it had no Pueblo lands. The

7

PUEBLO of San Francisco was a fully organized body politic and corporate: THEREFORE it was the Indian Mission of Dolores which never became a PUEBLO. We must not even smile over these propositions, for they are those of the learned counsel of the United States, who sustain the dignity of the Republic upon their shoulders.

A. D. 1851.

THE UNITED STATES CREATE A COMMISSION TO ASCERTAIN AND SETTLE PRIVATE LAND CLAIMS IN CALIFORNIA.

§ **136.** On March 3d, 1851, the Congress of the United States passed "An Act to ascertain and settle Private Land Claims in the "State of California" (United States Statutes at Large, vol. 9, page 631,) which contains the following enactments:

"SECTION 1. That for the purpose of ascertaining and settling "private land claims in the State of California, a commission shall be, "and is hereby constituted, which shall consist of three Commissioners, "to be appointed by the President of the United States, by and with "the advice and consent of the Senate, which commission shall con- "tinue for three years from the date of this Act, unless sooner discon- "tinued by the President of the United States."

"SEC. 8. That each and every person claiming lands in California "by virtue of any right or title derived from the Spanish or Mexican "government, shall present the same to the said Commissioners when "sitting as a Board, together with such documentary evidence and tes- "timony of witnesses as the said claimant relies upon in support of "such claims; and it shall be the duty of the Commissioners, when "the case is ready for hearing, to proceed promptly to examine the "same upon such evidence, and upon the evidence produced in behalf "of the United States, and to decide upon the validity of the said "claim, and within thirty days after such decision is rendered, to cer- "tify the same, with the reasons on which it is founded, to the District "Attorney of the United States, in and for the district in which such "decision shall be rendered."

"SEC. 14. *And be it further enacted,* [1] That the provisions of this "Act shall not extend to any town lot, farm lot, or pasture lot, held "under a grant from any corporation, or town to which lands may have "been granted for the establishment of a town by the Spanish or Mexi- "can government, or the lawful authorities thereof, nor to any city or "town, or village lot, which city, town or village existed on the seventh "day of July, eighteen hundred and forty-six; but the claim for the "same shall be presented by the corporate authorities of the said town, "or where the land on which the said city, town or village was origin- "ally granted to an individual, the claim shall be presented by or in the "name of such individual [2]; and the fact of the existence of the said "city, town or village on the said seventh July, eighteen hundred and "forty-six, being duly proved, shall be *prima facie* evidence of a grant "to such corporation, or to the individual under whom the said lot- "holders claim [3]; and where any city, town or village shall be in

"existence at the time of passing this Act, the claim for the land
"embraced within the limits of the same may be made by the corpo-
"rate authority of the said city, town, or village.

ANALYSIS OF § 14 OF THAT ACT.

§ 137. The above § 14 contains the provisions under which the
present claim is presented.

1. The FIRST CLAUSE [1] provides that the presentation of a claim
to PUEBLO lands by any PUEBLO existing on July 7th, A. D. 1846,
whether known as city, town or village, and its confirmation, shall in-
nure to the benefit of all persons holding lands by grant from that
PUEBLO ; a most beneficial enactment, preventing a multiplicity of suits,
making one proceeding effectual for a large number of claimants, which
in the case of the Pueblo of San Francisco would probably have
amounted to thousands.

2. THE SECOND CLAUSE [2] provides that when the existence on
the 7th of July, A. D. 1846, of a town established by the Spanish or
Mexican authorities is proved, that fact shall be *prima facie* evidence
of a grant to such town. This enactment seems to have been made for
two purposes : *First*, to satisfy those who it was foreseen would clamor
for a paper or parchment grant, duly engrossed, signed, sealed and delivered ; see ante § 29 of this argument. And such persons are com-
forted with the assurance that such a grant is held *by law* to have been
made, although it cannot now be found. *Secondly*, to relieve all doubts
as to the question of survey, and to answer the objections of those who
might contend that there having been no actual grant, but only a remote
equitable right to a grant which was never carried into execution, this
right has now been lost. To such persons this enactment replies :
"there is presumed to have been a grant ; the PUEBLO is entitled to
the lands ; it is now necessary only to fix their boundaries and issue a
patent for the tract included within them."

3. The Third provision [3] seems to be a general enactment made
for the purpose of providing for such contingencies as might exist
without the knowledge of Congress. Thus a PUEBLO might at the date
of the passage of the Act of Congress exist as a new corporation
created by Act of the Legislature, with a name different from its
PUEBLO name, and in this case the claim might be presented by the
new corporation. There might be a possible case where a PUEBLO
existed before July 7th, 1846, and granted land to its citizens, and yet
fell into decadence and did not exist on July 7th, 1846, but afterwards,
under the Anglo-American dominion, revived, and became incorporated,
and had a corporate existence at the time of the passage of the Act of
Congress ; and in this case also, the claim could be presented by the
new corporation. The phrase "the claim for the land embraced within
the limits of the same," must of course be construed to mean the proprietary limits. No other construction would carry into effect the
purpose of the law, which is, to comply with the duty of the United
States resulting from public law and guaranteed by the Treaty of

Guadalupe-Hidalgo, to confirm to the citizens of California the rights and property possessed by them at the time of the conquest.

THE WHOLE QUESTION DECIDED BY THE SUPREME COURT OF CALIFORNIA.

§ **138.** The Supreme Court of California in the case of Hart *vs.* Burnett, 15 California Reports, 530, has expressly decided the whole question, namely : that San Francisco was a fully organized PUEBLO, and as such entitled to four square leagues of land ; and that decision is followed not only by the Courts of the State, but also by the Circuit Court of the United States for California. We think this decision is binding upon this Conrt. In the complex adjustment of sovereignty under our Federal system, the State Courts of California are the complement of the Federal Courts, that is to say, the State Courts represent that other portion of the judiciary which is necessary to make up a complete judiciary of the sovereign power. The Federal Courts represent in that respect one-half of the judicial power of a complete sovereignty, and the State Courts represent the other half. The comity of nations, which compels Courts representing equal sovereignties to accord a certain deference to each other's decrees, applies in the case at bar not with an equal but with a constraining force, and while this Court is bound to give only an effect of equality to the decrees of its co-ordinate State Jurisdictions of equal rank, it is bound to give a greater effect to the decrees of that State Court of California which is not its co-ordinate, but its superior in rank. District Courts of the State of California are the co-ordinates of the District Courts of the United States. To their decrees, as to those of its co-ordinates, a District Court of the United States for California may, or may not, accord a binding force. But the Supreme Court of the State of California is not the co-ordinate of the District Courts of the United States for the State of California, but is the co-ordinate of the Supreme Court of the United States. When, therefore, the Supreme Court of the State of California has decided a case and the Supreme Court of the United States has not decided to the contrary, we submit that all the District Courts of the United States for California are bound to follow that decision, just as fully as if the Supreme Court of the United States had made it, and that it does not belong to a Court of inferior rank, but only to the judiciary of equal, co-ordinate and complementary rank, to pronounce a dissenting decree. We advance these propositions in all boldness, but with all due respect. Again. When the course of events has called the Supreme Court of Appeals of the State of California to pronounce *first* in affirming a class of titles to lands under a Mexican grant, upon points resting upon municipal law, for a District Court of the United States of one of the Districts of California to pronounce any different decision, would be productive of such disastrous results that the right to do so must be denied upon considerations of convenience alone. In such cases common prudence requires that if an accepted rule of property is to be disturbed, it shall be done only by that Superior Tribunal whose decisions are final.

RÉSUMÉ.

§ **139.** We have shown, then, the ancient immemorial unrepealed laws of Spain and Mexico, never doubted, but always acknowledged, which entitled the PUEBLO of San Francisco to Four Square Leagues of land. We have shown this PUEBLO in existence in the form of a complete and fully organized Municipality, recognized by the Governor, the local Legislature, and by the citizens universally, and afterwards by the United States and the State of California. We have shown this PUEBLO in possession of a portion of these lands, and dealing with them as with its own property; and the possession of a part under color of title, is a constructive possession of the whole. We have shown that the governments of Mexico and of the United States have defined the limits of these lands by surveys of adjacent lands granted by the former government. We have shown the United States coming to the rescue against the most Quixotic assaults, and expressly declaring by law that a grant of lands to the Pueblo shall be presumed. We have shown that the highest Court of the State of California, in the administration of its municipal laws, and compelled to take judicial knowledge not only of the laws but also of the history of the country, has acknowledged all the law and the facts, and conceded and confirmed all the rights for which we contend.

THE QUESTION OF THE FINAL DISPOSITION OF THE PUEBLO LANDS IS NOT TO BE CONSIDERED IN THIS CASE.

§ **140.** The consideration of the legislative direction or control which the Legislature of California in virtue of its right of sovereignty has heretofore asserted, or may hereafter assert over the execution of the trust to which these four leagues of PUEBLO lands are subject for the benefit of the inhabitants of the city, is a mere speculative one, and is not to be regarded in the decision of the case. We have shown that these lands were always held in trust for the benefit of the citizens of the PUEBLO, and that this feature was stamped upon all the colonization laws; see the four league laws, ADDENDA, Nos. I and II; DeNeve's Regulations of 1781, ADDENDA, No. IV; Plan of Pitic, ADDENDA, No. VII; that the Cortez of Spain, as well as the Governors and Departmental Assembly of California exercised the right to modify, direct and control the execution of this trust, §§ 52, 80, 81, of this argument; and that the State of California has succeeded to this sovereign right of inspection and control; New Orleans vs. The United States, 10 Peters 736, 737; Dartmouth College vs. Woodward, 4 Wheaton 518; Hart vs. Burnett, 15 Cal. 530; People vs. Morris, 13 Wend. 325; East Hartford vs. Hartford Bridge Co., 10 Wheaton 511. But what is to be the ultimate disposition of these PUEBLO lands does not concern this Court. When it shall have confirmed to the City of San Francisco the same title and interest which its predecessor had in four leagues of Pueblo lands, it will have done all that the law requires of it, and all that we claim at its hands.

MISCELLANEOUS NOTES.

THE PRESIDIO OF SAN FRANCISCO did not survive the removal of the population from that point to Yerba Buena as stated in §§ 55, 111, 120, and ADDENDA, No. XXVL. Lieutenant Wilkes, who visited San Francisco with his Exploring Expedition in 1841, says: "After passing through the entrance of the bay, we were scarcely able to distinguish the Presidio; and had it not been for its solitary flag-staff, we could not have ascertained its situation. From this flag-staff no flag floated; the building was deserted, the walls had fallen to decay, the guns were dismounted, and every thing around it lay quiet. I afterwards learned that the Presidio was still a garrison in name, and that it had not been wholly abandoned; but the remnant of the troops stationed there consisted of no more than an officer and one soldier." Wilkes' Exploring Expedition, Vol. V, p. 152; Bryant's California, 429. De Mofras, writing in 1842—although his first and probably his only visit to the Presidio was in 1840—writes: "The Presidio of San Francisco is in ruins, and completely disarmed; it is inhabited only by a sub-lieutenant and five farmer soldiers and their families." De Mofras, Vol. I, p. 427. From this condition of ruin and abandonment the Presidio never recovered until after the Anglo-American conquest. It does not seem to be generally known that there was formerly a chapel at the Presidio, which, with the Governor's house enjoyed the distinction of being white-washed; Beechy, Vol. II, p. 9. Farnham's California and Oregon (1844), p. 353.

EJIDOS AS A GENERIC TERM.—I have in the course of the argument several times called attention to the fact that many translators have confounded the terms *ejidos* and *dehesas* when those terms were used as *specific* terms contradistinguished from each other; namely, the *ejidos* as designating the vacant suburbs or commons immediately next to the settled portion of the *Pueblo*, and the *dehesas* indicating the great herd pasture lying beyond. See §§ 14, 15, 103 of this argument. But I have inadvertently omitted to state that *ejidos* was also used as a generic term to designate the whole body of lands to which the *Pueblo* was entitled, which was capable of being divided into—1st. *Propios*, § 10; 2d. *Ejidos*, specific, vacant suburbs or commons, § 14; and 3d. *Dehesas*, the great outside cattle pasture, § 15. *Ejidos*, in a general sense, meaning all the lands of the Pueblo, before they were subdivided, was frequently used by the Governors and Secretaries of State in California before the conquest by the Anglo-Americans. Thus in the case of Doña Martina Castro vs. The United States, No. 343 in this Court, (No. 593 of the Land Commission,) it appears from the *Espediente* (No. 31,) that the Ayuntamiento of the Villa of Branciforte objected to the grant of the lands solicited by Doña Martina, because they might fall within the *ejidos* of that Villa, which had not yet been marked out. Jimeno, the Secretary of State, over date of February 8th, 1844, in a report which the Governor approved, states that the grant had been drawn subject to a tax, in case the lands proved to be within the *ejidos*, and adds: "I understand the town of Branciforte is to have (se le debe señalar) for *ejidos* of its population four square leagues in conformity to the existing law of the Recopilacion of the Indies in Volume II, folios 88 to 149," being the four league law cited in § 28 of this argument. This furnishes an example of the use of *ejidos* in a generic sense; and also shows that the Secretary of State and the Governor of California, in the year 1844, considered that each PUEBLO was entitled to four square leagues of land. So when the Governor in 1840, ADDENDA No. I, p. 70 title COMMONS, reports that none of the towns have their *ejidos* and *propios* marked out, the word *ejidos* is used generically to designate the whole four leagues; and the complaint of the Governor is to the effect that the towns have not yet had their *propios* assigned, and so do not know what municipal revenues can be derived from that source, *because* the great body of the lands of the town—the *ejidos*,—out of which the *propios* are to be assigned, are not yet marked out. I have shown in § 15 that "common lands," present an equivocal translation of the term *ejidos*, for that phrase includes not only the specific *ejidos* which were a portion of the inalienable patrimony of the PUEBLO, but also the *dehesas*, in which the PUEBLO had only a qualified property, subject to the superior legislative control.

ADDENDA.

No. I.

[Recopilacion de Leyes de los Reynos de las Indias. Libro IV, Titulo V, Ley VI Ordenanza del Rey Don Felipe II.]

LEY VI.—*Que la capitulacion para Villa de Alcaldes ordinarios, y Regidores, se haga conforme à esta ley.*

Si la disposicion de la tierra diere lugar para poblar alguna Villa de Españoles, con Concejo de Alcaldes ordinarios, y Regidores, y huviere persona que tome assiento para poblarla, se haga la capitulacion con estas calidades : Que dentro del termino, que le fuere señalado, por lo menos tenga treinta vecinos, y cada uno de ellos una casa, diez bacas de vientre, quatro bueyes, ò dos bueyes, y dos novillos, una yegua de vientre, una puerca de vientre, veinte ovejas de vientre de Castilla, y seis gallinas, y un gallo : assimismo nombrarà un Clerigo, que administre los Santos Sacramentos, que la primera vez serà á su eleccion, y las demás conforme á nuestro Real Patronazgo ; y proveerá la Iglesia de ornamentos, y cosas necessarias al culto Divino, y dará fianzas, que lo cumplirá dentro del dicho tiempo ; y si no lo cumpliere, pierda la que huviere edificado, labrado y grangeado, que aplicamos à nuestro Real Patrimonio, y mas incurra en pena de mil pesos de oro para nuestra Cámara ; y si cumpliere su obligacion, se le dèn quatro leguas de termino y territorio en quadro, ò prolongado, segun la calidad de la tierra, de forma que si se deslindare, sean las quatro leguas en quadro, con calidad de que por lo menos disten los limites del dicho territorio cinco leguas de qualquiera Ciudad, Villa, ò Lugar de Españoles, que antes estuviere poblado, y no haga perjuicio à ningun Pueblo de Indios, ni de persona particular.

[TRANSLATION.]

LAW VI.—*The conditions for a town of Alcaldes with the ordinary jurisdiction and Councilmen (Regidores) shall be agreeably to this law.*

If the nature of the tract of land allow of the settlement of some town (villa) of Spaniards with a Council of Alcaldes of the ordinary jurisdiction and Councilmen (regidores), and there be some person who undertake by contract to settle it, let the agreement be made under these conditions : That within the period of time which may be assigned to him he must have at least thirty settlers, each one provided with a house, ten breeding cows, four oxen, or two oxen and two steers, one brood mare, one breeding sow, twenty breeding ewes of the Castilian breed, and six hens and one cock ; he shall also appoint a priest to administer the Holy Sacraments ; the first time he shall select him, but afterwards the appointment shall be subject to our Royal

1*

Patronage; and he shall provide the Church with ornaments and the things necessary for Divine Worship ; and shall give bonds for the performance of all this within the time agreed upon; and if he should not comply with his obligation he will lose whatever he may have constructed, wrought, or garnered, to be applied to our Royal Patrimony, and will furthermore incur the penalty of one thousand pounds of gold for our treasury; and if he should comply with his obligation, there shall be given to him four leagues of extent and territory in a square or prolonged form according to the character of the land, in such manner that if surveyed, there shall be the four leagues in a square, with the condition that the limits of said territory shall be distant at least five leagues from any city, town, or village of Spaniards previously founded, and that there shall be no prejudice to any Indian town or private person.

No. II.

[Recopilacion de leyes de los Reynos de las Indias, Libro IV, Titulo V, Ley X.]

Ley X.—*Que no haviendo poblador particular, sino vicinos casados, se les conceda el poblar, como no sean menos de diez.*

Quando algunas personas particulares se concordaren en hacer nueva poblacion, y huviere numero de hombres casados para el efecto, se les dè licencia, con que no sean menos de diez casados, y deseles termino y territorio al respeto de lo que està dicho, y les concedemos facultad para elegir entre sí mismos Alcaldes ordinarios, y Oficirles del Concejo annales.

[TRANSLATION.]

Law X.—*If there should be no private contractor for a settlement, but only individual citizens who are married men, let them have leave to found a settlement, provided they are not less than ten.*

When private individuals shall agree to form a new settlement, and for that purpose there shall be a number of married men, let leave be granted to them, provided they be not fewer than ten married men; let there be given them extent of land and territory according to what has been heretofore provided (al respeto á lo que está dicho), and we grant them power to elect among themselves Alcaldes with the usual jurisdiction and annual officers of the Council.

No. III.

[See California Archives, Vol. I, Missions and Colonization, page 812; 1 Rockwell, 444, Halleck; Rep. Ex. Doc. No. 17, 1st Sess. 31st Cong., H. of R., page 133.]

Extracts from " the instructions to be observed by the Commandant appointed to the new establishments of San Diego and Monterey," given by El. Bailie Friar Don Antonio Bucareli y Urusu, dated Mexico, 17th August, 1773.

Article 2. The confusion which has reigned in the accounts, and the want of order which I have observed in everything else, have compelled me to establish this new method, and to appoint Captain Don Fernando Rivèra y Moncada commandant of San Diego and Monterey, because I am well informed of his good conduct or manner of proceeding, and of his knowledge of the new establishments, acquired in the employments and offices which he has therein obtained and in the presidios of California for many years.

ARTICLE 12. With the desire to establish population more speedily in the new establishments, I for the present grant the commandant the power to designate common lands, and also even to distribute lands in private to such Indians as may most dedicate themselves to agriculture and the breeding of cattle, for having property of their own, the love of it will cause them to radicate themselves more firmly; but the commandant must bear in mind that it is very desirable not to allow them to live dispersed—each one on the lands given to them—but that they must necessarily have their house and habitation in the town or mission where they have been established or settled.

ARTICLE 13. I grant the same faculty to the commandant with respect to distributing lands to the other founders (pobladores) according to their merit and means of labor—they also living in the town (pueblo) and not dispersed, declaring that in the practice of what is prescribed in this article and the preceding 12th, he must act in every respect in conformity with the provisions made in the collection of the laws respecting newly-acquired countries and towns, (reducciones y poblaciones,) granting them legal titles for the owner's protection without exacting any remuneration for it or for the act of possession.

ARTICLE 14. The commandant must be carefully attentive that the founders who go to the new establishments have the requisite arms for their defense, and for assisting the garrisons of the presidios or missions in case of necessity, binding them to this obligation as a thing necessary for their own safety and that of all their neighbors.

ARTICLE 15. When it becomes expedient to change any mission into a pueblo, the commandant will proceed to reduce it to the civil and economical government which, according to the laws, is observed in the other pueblos of this kingdom, giving it a name, and declaring for its patron the saint under whose auspices and venerable protection the mission was founded.

No. IV.

[See California Archives, Vol. I, Missions and Colonization,] pages 782, 762, (also 746); 1 Rockwell, 445; Halleck's Report, Ex. Doc. No. 17, 1st Sess. 31st Cong. H. of Rep., pages 134–139.]

Extract from the regulations for the government of the province of California, by Don Felipe De Neve, Governor of the same, dated in the royal presidio of San Carlos de Monterey, 1st June, 1779, and approved by his Majesty in a royal order of the 24th October, 1781.

TITLE THE FOURTEENTH.—POLITICAL GOVERNMENT, AND INSTRUCTIONS RESPECTING COLONIZATION.

¿ 1st. The object of greatest importance towards the fulfillment of the pious intentions of the King, our master, and towards securing to his Majesty the dominion of the extensive country which occupies a space of more than two hundred leagues, comprehending the new establishment of the presidios, and the respective ports of San Diego, Monterey, and San Francisco, being to forward the reduction of, and as far as possible to make this vast country (which, with the exception of seventeen hundred and forty-nine Christians of both sexes in the eight missions on the road which leads from the first to the last named presidio, is inhabited by innumerable heathens) useful to the State, by erecting pueblos of white people, (*pueblos de gente de razon*) who, being united, may encourage agriculture, planting, the breeding of cattle, and successively the other branches of industry ; so that some years hence their produce may be sufficient to provide garrisons of the presidios with provisions and horses, thereby obviating the distance of transportation and the risks and losses which the royal government suffers thereby. With this just idea, the pueblo of San José has been founded and peopled ; and the erection of another is determined upon, in which the colonists (pobladores) and their families, from the provinces of Sonora and Sinaloa, will establish themselves, the progressive augmentation of which, and of the families of the troops, will provide for the establishment of other towns, and furnish recruits for the presidio companies, thus freeing the royal revenue from the indispensable expenses at present required for these purposes ; and it being necessary to establish rules for carrying all this into effect, the following instructions will be observed :

§ 2d. As an equivalent for the $120 and rations, which hitherto have been assigned yearly to each poblador (founder or colonist) for the first two years, and the rations alone for the following one, calculated at a real and a half per diem, free, for the three following ones, they will hereafter receive for each of the first two years $116 and 3½ reals, the rations to be understood as comprehended in this amount : and in lieu of rations for the next three years, they will receive $60 yearly, by which arrangement they will be placed on more favorable terms than formerly, taking into consideration the advance that was charged on what they were paid with, and the discount on the rations furnished, which article they will in future receive at cost from the moment that these regulations be approved and declared to be in force, it being understood that the forementioned term of five years, as regards this emolument, is to be reckoned from the day on which the possession of the house-lots and pieces of [cultivable] land, (*solares y suertes de tierras*,) which are to be distributed to each poblador in the manner hereafter mentioned, to be given ; and the previous time, from the period of their enrolment, must be regulated according to the terms of their respective contracts, and, in order to avoid this expense, measures will be taken to have the new pobladores collocated, and put into possession immediately on their arrival.

§ 3d. To each poblador, and to the community (comun) of the pueblo, there shall be given, under condition of repayment in horses and mules fit to be given and received, and in the payment of the other large and small cattle, at the just prices which are to be fixed by tariff, and of the tools and implements at cost as it is ordained, two mares, two cows and one calf, two sheep and two goats, all breeding animals, and one yoke of oxen or steers, one plow-share or point, one hoe, one *coa*, (a kind of wooden spade with a steel point,) one axe and one sickle, one wood-knife, one musket and one leather-shield, two horses and one cargo mule. To the community (comun) there shall likewise be given the males corresponding to the total number of cattle of different kinds distributed amongst all the inhabitants, one seed jackass, another common one, and three she asses, one boar and three sows, one forge, with its corresponding anvil and other necessary tools, six crowbars, six iron spades or shovels, and the necessary tools for carpenter and cast work.

§ 4th. The house-lots to be granted to the new pobladores are to be designated by government in the situations, and of the extent, corresponding to the locality on which the new pueblos are to be established, so that a square and streets be formed agreeable to the provisions of the laws of the kingdom ; (conforme á lo prevenido por los Leyes del Reyno, y con su arreglo se señalará exido competente para el Pueblo, y Dehesas con les tierras de labor que convenga para propios) ; and conformable to the same, competent common lands (egidos) shall be designated for the pueblo, and pasture grounds, with the sowing lands that may be necessary for municipal purposes (propios).

§ 5th. Each suerte of land, whether capable of irrigation or dependent on the seasons, (de riego de temporale,) shall consist of two hundred varas in length and two hundred in breadth, this being the area generally occupied in the sowing of one fanega of Indian corn. The distribution which is to be made in the name of the King, our master, by the government, with equality, and a proportion to the ground which admits the benefit of being watered, so that after making the necessary demarcation and reserving vacant [baldios] the fourth part of the number which may result, counting with the number of pobladores, should there be sufficient, each one shall have two suertes of irrigable land, and other two of dry ground, delivered to him, and of the royal lands (*realengas*) as many as may be considered necessary [convenientes] shall be separated for the propios of the pueblo, (and of those lots of land reserved for the King, [realengas] as many as shall be considered necessary, etc. See note at end of § 18, page 8). And the remainder of these, as well as of the house-lots, shall be granted in the name of his Majesty, by the governor, to those who may hereafter come to colonize, and particularly to those soldiers who, having fulfilled the term of their engagement, or on account of advanced age may have retired from service, and likewise to the families of those who may die ; but these persons must work at their own expense, out of the funds which each of them ought to possess, and will not be entitled to receive from the royal revenue either salary, rations, or cattle, this privilege being limited to those who leave their own country for the purpose of settling this country.

§ 6th. The houses built on the lots granted and designated to the new pobladores, and the parcels of land comprehended in their respective gifts, shall be perpetually hereditary to their sons and descendants, or to their daughters who marry useful colonists who have received no grants of land for themselves, provided the whole of them comply with the obligations to be expressed in these instructions ; and in order that the sons of the possessors of these gifts observe the obedience and respect which they owe to their parents, these shall be freely authorized, in case of having two or more sons, to choose which of them they please, being a layman, to succeed to the house and suertes of the town ; and they may likewise dispose of them amongst their children, but not so as to divide a single suerte, because each and all of these are to remain indivisible and inalienable forever.

§ 7th. Neither can the pobladores, nor their heirs, impose on the house or parcel of land granted to them, either tax, entail, reversion, mortgage, (*cento, vinculo, fianza, hipoteca,*) or any other burden, although [even if] it be for pious purposes ; and should any one do so in violation of this just prohibition, he shall irremediably be deprived of his property, and his grant shall *ipso facto* be given to another colonist who may be useful and obedient.

§ 8th. The new colonists shall enjoy, for the purpose of maintaining their cattle, the common privilege of the water and pasturage, fire-wood and timber, of the common forest and pasture lands, to be designated according to law to each new pueblo ; (aprovechamiento comun de aguas y pastos, leña y madera del exido y Dehesa que ha de señalarse con arreglo á las Leyes á cada nuevo pueblo) and besides, each one shall privately enjoy the pasture of his own land, but with the condition that as they have to possess and breed all kinds of large and small cattle, and it not being possible that each one can dedicate himself to the taking care of the small stock consigned to them—as by so doing they would be unable to attend to agriculture and the public works—for the present, the small cattle, and the sheep and goats of the community, must feed together, and the shepherd must be paid by such community ; and with respect to collecting together the large cattle, and bringing them to the corral, such as mares and asses, as may be required, this must be done by two of the pobladores, whom they must appoint amongst themselves, or as they may see fit, to look after this business, and thus the cattle of different kinds will be taken care of, and freed from the risk of running wild, at the same time that agricultural and other works of the community will be attended to ; and each individual must take care to mark their respective small cattle and brand the large, for which purpose the records of the necessary branding irons will be made without any charge ; but it is ordained that henceforth no colonist is to possess more than fifty head of the same kind of cattle, so that the utility produced by cattle be distributed amongst the whole of them, and that the true riches of the pueblo be not monopolized by a few inhabitants.

§ 9th. The new colonists shall be free and exempt from paying tithes, or any other tax, on the fruits and produce of the lands and cattle given to them, provided that within a year from the day on which the house-lots and parcels of land be designated to them, they build a house in the best way they can, and live therein, upon the necessary trenches for watering their lands, placing at their boundaries, instead of landmarks, some fruit trees, or wild ones of some utility, at the rate of ten to each suerte ; and likewise open the principal drain or trench, form a dam, and the other necessary public works, for the benefit of cultivation, which the community is bound particularly to attend to ; and said community will see that the government buildings (casas reales) be completed within the fourth year, and during the third a storehouse sufficiently capacious for a public granary, in which must be kept the produce of the public sowing, which at the rate of one almud (the twelfth of a fanega) of Indian corn per inhabitant, must be made from said third year to the fifth, inclusive, in the lands designated for municipal purposes, (propios) all the labor of which, until harvesting the crop and putting it in the granary, must be done by the community, (comun) for whose benefit alone it must serve ; and for the management and augmentation thereof, the necessary laws to be observed will, in due time be made.

§ 10th. After the expiration of the five years they will pay the tithes to his Majesty, for him to dispose of agreeably to his royal pleasure, as belonging solely to him, not only on account of the absolute royal patronage which he possesses in these dominions, but also because they are the produce of uncultivated and abandoned lands which are about to become fruitful at the cost of the large outlays and expenses of the royal treasury. At the expiration of the said term of five years, the new pobladores and their descendants will pay, in acknowledgment of the direct and supreme dominion which belongs to the sovereign, one-half of a fanega of Indian corn for each irrigable suerte of land, and for their own benefit they shall be collectively under the direct obligation of attending to the repair of the principal trench, dam, auxiliary drains, and other public works of their pueblos, including that of the church.

§ 11th. When the hogs and asses shall have multiplied, and the sufficient number of seed asses for covering the mares become adopted, and it be found practicable to distribute these two kinds of animals amongst the pobladores, it must be done with all possible equality, so that of the first kind each one may receive one boar and one sow, and of the second one ass, which the owner will mark and brand.

§ 12th. Within the five years stipulated, the new pobladores shall be obliged to possess two yoke of oxen, two plows, two points or plow-shares for tilling the ground, two hoes, and the other necessary implements for agriculture ; and by the end of the first three years their houses must be entirely finished, and furnished each with six hens and one cock ; and it is expressly forbidden that any one shall, during the forementioned period of five years, alienate by means of exchange, sale, or other pretext, to kill any of the cattle granted to them, or the respective increase thereof, excepting sheep and goats, which, at the end of four years, it is necessary to dispose of, or else they would die ; and therefore they may, at their discretion, dispose of as many of these animals as arrive at that age, but not of any younger ones, under the penalty that whoever shall violate this order, made for his own benefit and for the increase of his prosperity, shall forfeit *ipso facto* the amount of the rations granted to him for one year; and whoever shall receive one more head of such cattle during the same time, in whatever state or condition they may be, shall be obliged to return them.

§ 13th. At the expiration of said five years, the female breeding animals of every kind, excepting swine and asses, of which each poblador is only obliged to possess one sow and one ass, male or female, being preserved; the yokes of oxen or steers designated for their agricultural purposes being provided, and they being furnished with a cargo-mule, and necessary horses, they shall be at liberty to sell their bulls, steers, foals or horses, asses, sheep, castrated goats, and pigs and sows; it being forbidden to kill cows, (except old or barren, and consequently unproductive ones,) sheep or she-goats, which are not above three years old, and to sell mares or useful breeding females, until each poblador be possessed of fifteen mares and one stallion, fifteen cows and one bull, twelve sheep and one ram, and ten she-goats with one buck.

§ 14th. No poblador or resident shall sell a foal horse or mule, or exchange them, except amongst each other, after they are provided with the necessary number, for the remainder must be dedicated solely to the purpose of remounting cavalry of the presidio troops, and will be paid for at the just prices to be established, excepting all particularly fine horses or mules of said pueblos, under the penalty of twenty dollars, to be forfeited by whomsoever may violate this order. For every animal disposed of in any other manner than what is here stipulated, the half to be given to the informer, and the other half to be applied to municipal expenses, (gastos de republica).

§ 15th. The Indian corn, beans, chick-peas, and lentils, produced by the pueblo, (que produzcan las cosechas de los pueblos) after the residents have separated what may be necessary for their own subsistence and for seed, must be bought and paid for in ready money at the prices established, or which may hereafter be established for provisioning the presidio, and from the amount of the same there must be deducted from the amount of each poblador such provident sums as may be considered proper towards refunding the royal revenue the advances made in money, horses, cattle, implements, seeds, and other articles, so that within the first five years the total amount must be paid.

§ 16th. Each poblador and resident head of a family (vecino) to whom house-lots or parcels of land may have been, or in future shall be granted, and their successors, shall be obliged to hold themselves equipped with two horses, a saddle complete, a musket, and the other arms already mentioned, which are to be furnished them at first cost, for the defense of their respective districts, and in order that they may (without abandoning this first obligation) repair to where the governor may, in cases of urgency, order them.

§ 17th. The corresponding titles to house-lots, lands and waters, granted to the new pobladors, or which may hereafter be granted to other residents, (vecinos) shall be made out by the governor, or commissary whom he may appoint for this purpose, records of which, and of the respective branding irons, must be kept in the general book of colonization, to be made and kept in the government archives, as a heading to which a copy of these instructions shall be placed.

§ 18th. And whereas it is expedient for the good government and police of the pueblos, the administration of justice, the direction of public works, the distribution of water privileges, and the carrying into effect the orders given in these instructions, they should be furnished with ordinary alcaldes and other municipal officers, in proportion to the number of inhabitants, the governor shall appoint such for the first two years, and for the following ones, they shall appoint some one from amongst themselves to the municipal offices (los oficios de republica) which may have been established, which elections are to be forwarded to the governor for his approbation, who, if he sees fit, may continue said appointment for the three following years.

NOTE TO § 5.—A defective translation in sec. 5 has produced some confusion. The word "realengas—lands belonging to the King," is translated so obscurely that it seems to include all the lands adjacent to the pueblo and not specifically granted. This is not the case. The provision is that one-fourth of the house-lots and sowing lots (solares y suertes) shall be reserved to the King, and the lots so reserved to the King, (realengas) shall be assigned as *propios* or granted to new settlers. The original Spanish reads as follows: "reservando valdias la quarta parte del numero que resulte, contando con el numero de Pobladores, si alcanzasen, se repartiran á dos suertes á cada uno de regadio, y otros dos de secadal, y de las realengas se separarán las que parecieren convenientes para propios del Pueblo, y de las restantes se hara merced," etc. There is no colon between "secadal" and "y de las realengas," as there is in the translation from Rockwell. Precisely the same language, with the same punctuation, occurs in the Instructions for the foundation of the "Pueblo de nuestra Señora de los Angeles," dated August 26th, 1778, and found in the Archives, vol. I, Missions and Colonization, page 418. *Realengas*, therefore, refers to the solares and suertes so reserved, and to no other lands.

That this is so, clearly appears from the official plan of the pueblo of San José, adopted at its settlement, where three lots are marked Realengo.—*California Archives, Vol. I, Missions and Colonization, page 684.*

No. V.

Exhibit " A " in the Case.

[From California Archives, Vol. I, Provincial Records, pages 10, etc.]

April 15th, 1778.

ESTABLISHMENT OF THE PUEBLOS OF SAN JOSE AND LOS ANGELES.

Governor to Viceroy.

Most Excellent Señor :—Desiring to give due fulfillment to the Superior orders of Your Excellency, notwithstanding the proposition I made in my communication of the———of June of the last year, in relation to the steps that could be taken for the improvements of these establishments, founding two Pueblos on the rivers Guadalupe and Porcincular, they being the best localities on account of the fertility of the soil and the abundance of water for irrigation, in consideration of the delay that must occur in the arrival of the settlers with their families, that I have asked Your Excellency to furnish to perform the duties of laborers, and the importance of losing no time in an enterprise so important, which, if carried out, will in a short time avoid the necessity of transporting grain from San Blas, and in the meantime will cause the arrival or non-arrival of a vessel not to be a matter of life and death : for these reasons I resolved to withdraw nine soldiers (skillful laborers) from the Company of this Presidio and that of San Francisco, to which I added two recruits as settlers, which with the three already on hand, completed the number of fourteen residents (vecinos), which with their families comprise the number of sixty-six individuals, with which I founded the Pueblo of San José de Galvez on the 29th day of November last, near the head of the River Guadalupe, distant 26 leagues from this Presidio, 16 from that of San Francisco, and three-quarters of a league from the Mission of Santa Clara.

To each settler, besides the solares on which they have constructed their houses, lands have been distributed for cultivation, with horses, flocks of all kinds, and utensils, as set forth in the accompanying list.

1 Prov. Rec. 20.

No. VI.

[California Archives, volume I, Missions and Colonizations, page 809; Land Commission Exhibits in Limantour's Cases, Exhibit O, page 59.]

Exhibit " V " in the Case.

Honble. Commandant General. In the instructions which treat of the Political Government and Population of California, and are found inserted in Title 14 of the Regulation of that Peninsula, approved by His Majesty in a royal order of the 24th Oct. 1781, it is directed by Art. 8 that the new settlers shall enjoy, for the maintenance of their stock, the common advantage of waters and pastures, wood and timber of the commons, [exido] forests, and pasture grounds, [dehesas] which in compliance with the laws are to be marked out for every " Pueblo," and that besides each individual shall privately enjoy the pastures of his own lands, with the warning that each settler hereafter, will not exceed fifty head of cattle of each kind in his possession, so that in this manner the usefulness resulting from the stock may be distributed among all, and the true wealth of the Pueblos not confined in a few residents.

By the 5th law and the consecutive ones of tit. 17, lib. 4, of the " Recopilacion " for these territories, it is commanded that the use of the grazing lands [pastos], woods and waters of the Provinces of the Indies be common to all the residents thereof, that they may enjoy them freely with their cattle, revoking when necessary whatsoever ordinances there might exist, this provision to apply not only to the woods, pastures, and water of the " Seignories," (Lugares de Senorios) conceded in these territories, but also to lands and cultivated property, sold and granted, whereon, after the harvest, the pastures remain for common benefit.

The alloting of tracts of land (sitios) for cattle, which some settlers in California claim, and the Governor proposes in his official communication of the 20th November, 1784, cannot, nor ought not to be made to them within the boundaries assigned to each Pueblo, which in conformity with the law 6, tit. 5, lib. 4, of the " Recopilacion," must [deben ser] be four leagues of land in a square or oblong body, according to the nature of the ground, because the petition of the new settlers would tend to make them private owners of the forests, pastures, water, timber, wood and other advantages of the lands which may be assigned, granted, and distributed to them, and to deprive their neighbors of these benefits, it is seen at once that their claim is entirely contrary to the directions of the aforementioned laws, and the express provision in art. 8, of the Instructions for Settlements (Poblaciones) in the Californias, according to which all the waters, pastures, wood, and timber, within the limits which in conformity to law may be allotted to each Pueblo, must be for the common advantage, so that all the new settlers may enjoy and partake of them, maintaining thereon their cattle and participating of the other benefits that might be produced.

By the law 1st, and consecutive ones to the 13th, tit. 12, of the same book 4, the distribution and alloting of Peonias, Cavalerias and Sitios, for tracts " de Ganados Mayores y Menores," is permitted, provided they be given far from the Indian villages and their cultivated fields, obliging the owners to keep as many shepherds and cattle keepers as shall be sufficient to prevent such damages as the cattle might commit, and to satisfy for that which they might cause them, and the concession of the said lands being very useful for the protection of the population in California, where owing to the extent of land and the abundance of its pastures there are means of carrying it into effect without prejudice to the Indians, nor to a third party, and where, through the want of active commerce and of consumption and export of the other produce, the greater wealth of the Pueblos must necessarily consist in the rearing and the increase of cattle ; for these reasons it seems to me your honor can, if you please, decree and command that an order be issued to the Governor of the Californias, Don Pedro Fages, to the effect that alloting at once to each new " Poblacion " the extent of the four leagues belonging thereto, he may measure and mark them out in a square or prolonged body, as the nature of the ground will admit, and that he do not concede within it, nor grant nor distribute any portion whatsoever for farms or for the rearing of cattle to any resident or settler ; the woods, pastures, waters, and other benefits and advantages to be left in common for all the residents and settlers, without any of them exercising dominion, nor own private property thereon. And that in the other lands, outside of the said limits and of the district assigned to each Pueblo, and at such a distance that there cannot result any injury to the Missions, Pueblos, Rancherias (Indian villages) nor to their fields, he do grant and distribute " sitios " for farms, and tracts for rearing cattle, with the express condition that the residents and settlers to whom he may grant them, shall obligate themselves to put as many shepherds and cattle keepers as will be sufficient to prevent damages, and to satisfy the amount which in any event might happen, and (with the condition) that no resident or settler shall have more than three " sitios " tracts, and be obliged to build in each one a stone house, to have thereon two thousand head of cattle at least, and that notwithstanding his grant and concession, the pastures shall remain for the common advantage, and that where there are no (herds of) cattle, " sitios " may be given for sugar plantations and other hereditaments, according as is directed by the laws 12, tit. 12, as in reference to Hispaniola Island. And in law 5, tit. 17, lib. 4, of the " Recopilacion " for these territories, which conditions and laws will be inserted in an express clause in the deeds of grants that may be made ; that as evidence for the residents and settlers who may obtain the same, they may comprehend their obligations, to the fulfilment of which they shall be obliged, and that they may not have any just motive, nor pretext, to allege any right against it hereafter, or else your honor will resolve what may suit your pleasure notwithstanding.

CHIHUAHUA, 27th Oct. 1785.

GALINDO NAVARRO.

A copy according to the original, which I certify.

CHIHUAHUA, 21st June, 1786.
   (Signed)   PEDRO GARRIDO Y DURAN.

I transmit to you the inclosed opinion of the attorney of this Comandancy of the 27th October last year, upon the subject of marking out the lands which some individuals of that province asked, as you reported in your representation No. 204, of the 20th Nov. '84, that you may proceed to grant them agreeably to the requirements of said officer (ministro).

The Lord preserve you many years.

CHIHUAHUA, 21st June, 1786.

   (Signed)   JACOBO UGARTE Y LOYOLA.
Sᵒʳ DON PEDRO FAGES.

No. VII.

[California Archives, Volume I, Missions and Colonization, pages 853, etc. Land Commission Exhibits in Limantour's Cases, Exhibit O, pages 66, etc.]

PLAN OF PITIC.

TRANSLATION.—EXHIBIT Z Z IN THE CASE.

No. 313.

Instructions approved by His Majesty, and made for the establishing of the new town of Pitic, in the Province of Sonora, ordered to be adopted by the other new projected settlements (Poblaciones) and by those that may be established in the district of this General " Comandancia."

1st. Although by the law 6th, title 8th, book 4th, the Viceroys, Supreme Courts (Audiencias) and Governors, are prohibited from granting titles for cities or towns, or from exempting from their principal capitals the settlements (pueblos) of Spaniards or Indians, this decree is limited to those that may have already been established; therefore, as to the new towns and settlements, it is provided that they observe what is decreed in reference to the other laws on the subject, and as the law 2d, title 7th of the same book decrees: that the land, province, and place in which a new settlement (poblacion) shall be made, being chosen, and the convenience and advantages resulting therefrom being inquired into, the Governor, whose district it may be or to which it may be confined, shall determine whether it shall be a city, town, or village, and that in conformity with that which he shall decide, shall be formed the council, the government, and its officers, in using of this power, bearing in mind the extent of the place selected and the advantages offered by its lands, fertilizing through the benefit of irrigation by means of the large canal constructed for that purpose, your honor may declare the new settlement to be a town, designating to it the name it is to have and use for its distinction and recognition.

2d. In conformity with the decree of the law 6th, title 5th, of the same book 4th, relative to the towns of Spaniards that may be founded by agreement or contract, and first in relation to those which for want of contractors shall be erected by private settlers (Pobladores) who may establish themselves and agree to found them, there may be granted to the town in question four leagues of bounds or territory in a square or in length, (que se fundaren y concordaren enformarlas se podrá conceder á la de que se exara quatro leguas determino ó territorio en quadro ó prolongado) as shall be adapted to the better location of the land that shall be selected or marked out so that its true boundaries shall be known, wherein there can be no inconvenience, and inasmuch as it is distant more than five leagues from any other town, city, or village of Spaniards, there shall not result injury to any private individual, nor to any " pueblo " of Indians, on account of that (the village) " de los Seris " remaining within the demarcation as part or suburb of the new settlement, subject to its jurisdiction, and with the advantage of enjoying as neighbors the same benefits public and common that the settlers may have, and of which at present those same natives are wanting, owing to their indolence, their default of application, and of intelligence, reserving to them the faculty of choosing their " Alcaldes and Regidores," with the jurisdiction, economy, and other circumstances prescribed by the laws 15 and 16, title 5, book 6.

3d. The Presidio of San Miguel de Orcavitas having been removed to the locality of Pitic, so that under its protection and guard may be founded the new settlement, conformably to the decree in the articles 1 and 2, title 11, of the new regulation of Presidios of the 10th of September, 1772, and in the 50th article of the old Regulation of the Sōr Viceroy Marquis de Casafuerte of the 20th of April, 1729, which by Royal order of 15th of May, 1779, is ordered to be observed, the Political Government and the Royal jurisdiction, ordinary, civil, and criminal in first instance of the new settlement, belonged to its captain or commandant, who were to exercise the same in the interim of the Presidio being established in that place, with the appeals to the Royal Supreme Court (Audiencia) of the District, but your honor having resolved that the company be considered as detached in the new settlement, and consequently that the use and exercise of the Royal jurisdiction remaineth in charge of the Political Governor of the province of the Alcalde, Mayor, or Lieutenant that you may name, it is necessary that the selection for this office should fall upon one of sufficient instruction and knowledge to promote the advancement of the new settlement, to make the distributions of houses, building lots (solares) and water privileges, and to observe with precision the articles of these instructions and the other orders that may successively be communicated to you.

4th. For your better rule of conduct and government, in conformity with the decree in the laws 10, tit. 15 ; 2 and 19, titles 7th, 1st, 2d and 3d ; tit. 10, book 4, de la Recopilacion, immediately after the number of settlers, shall count thirty residents. there shall be established a council (cabildo) or ayuntamiento, composed of two ordinary alcaldes, six "regidores," one prosecuting (syndico) attorney of the community, and one " mayordomo de propios," to whose charge shall devolve the economical management, the care of provisioning (abastos) and of the cleanliness and police of the new settlement, the mentioned electors being elected the first time by all the residents, and thereafter by the members (vocales) of the Ayuntamiento, in conformity with the decree of the laws on that subject, and the elections shall be returned annually to the Political Governor of the Province, so that in virtue of his approbation the officers elected may take possession and enter upon the discharge of their respective offices.

5th. The two ordinary alcaldes shall also, by way of precaution, and jointly with the first alcalde or commissioner, exercise the royal jurisdiction, ordinary, civil, and criminal in the first instance, subject to the appeals to the Royal Supreme Court, to the Governor, or to the Ayuntamiento, in the cases wherein they correspond to each and every one, by the laws of the kingdom, as prescribed in the first and following title 3d, book 5th.

6th. The tract of four leagues granted to the new settlement being measured and marked out (demarcado y amojonado que sea el terreno de cuatro leguas concedido á la nueva poblacion) its pastures, woods, water privileges, hunting, fishery, stone quarries, fruit trees, and other privileges, shall be for the common benefit of the Spaniards and Indians residing therein, and in its suburb or village, " de los Seris," (y en su razzia ó Aldea de los Seris) as shall also be the pastures of the lands and estates (heredades), the grain sowed therein being harvested, as directed by the laws 5th and following title 17th, book 4th, de la Recopilacion.

7th. The residents and natives shall enjoy equally the woods, pastures, water privileges, and other advantages of the royal and vacant lands that may be outside of the land assigned to the new settlement, in common with the residents and natives of the adjoining and neighboring pueblos, which bounty and privilege shall continue as long as they are not changed or altered by His Majesty, in which case they shall conform to that which has been provided in the Royal orders that may be issued in favor of the new possessors or owners (proprietarios).

8th. The place which has been considered more appropriate to locate the new settlement, having been selected and marked out, the commissioner shall superintend its establishment; all the houses and other buildings thereof, which shall successively be constructed, shall conform to the sketch or plan made by the extraordinary engineer, Don Manuel Mascaro, which, in order that it be taken in consideration, shall be annexed and made a guide to these instructions and municipal ordinance, according to which plan the streets shall run in a straight line most suitable to facilitate the traffic and communication of the citizens and settlers, and their regularity and symmetry contributing to embellish the settlement, its cleanliness and health to the benefit of those that they may fix themselves therein.

9th. The space of ground that every block shall comprise being marked out in the plan or sketch, and as it is not easy to determine the building lot (solar) that will be sufficient for every resident settler, on account of the inequality that may exist between the families, and the means of those who may conclude to become so, to the prudent arbitration of the commissioner is left the power of granting to them the building varas, which according to their families, wealth, and other just considerations, he shall deem each one might need, cultivate, and build upon ; for which purpose, and so that all may possess that which may be corresponding to their means, there can be distributed to them a block, half of a fourth, or eighth portion, which are the divisions most suitable to carry out the object of making uniform, as far as possible, the buildings of the settlement.

10th. So as to avoid difficulties which the voluntary marking out of lots might occasion, owing to the preference or ameliorations of the one over the other, the distribution shall be made between the first settlers casting lots as prescribed in the law 11, title 7th, book 4th, de la Recopilacion.

11th. The extraordinary engineer, Don Manuel de Mascaro, having marked out the place in which the new settlement shall be located, there shall be left for the four fronts of its circumference commons (ejidos) suitable for the settlers to amuse themselves, drive out their cattle without doing injury, and so that as they increase hereafter there may be land to grant them, so that they might build their houses and habitations as provided by the laws 7th, 13th and 14th of the forementioned title 7th, book 4th, of the Recopilacion.

12th. The same shall also proceed to mark out and lay out the pasture grounds, which shall be made sufficient so that the work-oxen and the cattle for the provisioning of the new settlement may pasture abundantly and with ease, endeavoring to choose for that purpose the lands abounding in pastures, and that may not be of the best quality to produce wheat or other grains and vegetables useful to the consumption and subsistence of the settlers and their families, as provided in the forementioned laws 7th and 14th, title 7th, book 4th, of the Recopilacion.

13th. The laying out of the commons (ejidos) and of the common pasture grounds being completed (evacuado el señalmiento de los ejidos y a la dehesa comun ó Prado Boyal) the commissioner shall make a careful calculation of all the useful and productive land, which by means of the ditch can be irrigated, and of the balance, which, without possessing this advantage, he may consider adaptable to cultivatible lands and crops depending on the seasons (de temporal) and dividing the other into equal (suertes) of four hundred varas in length and two hundred in breadth, which is that which is generally contained in land sown with a fanega of corn : he shall ascertain the number of suertes of both kinds there may be to distribute to the new settlers and to those that may join them and increase their numbers hereafter.

14th. The "suertes" having thus been divided from those most useful and adjoining the Pueblo, and that have the advantage of irrigation, there shall be marked out and laid out eight "suertes" that shall remain applied to the funds, (de propios) the proceeds of which shall be administered by the "mayordomo" whom the ayuntamiento may appoint, whose duty it shall be to render accounts annually that will be examined and approved, referring them previously to the prosecuting Syndic, or agent of the community, so that in his defense he may make the notes or investigations he may deem justifiable and corresponding ; and admitting that their proceeds should be used for the public benefit of all the inhabitants under the rules which are established for the security of his faithful management and legitimate disbursing, and that actually there is no public fund with which to defray the expenses of their first plowing, sowing, and crops, the settlers and residents will be under the obligation to aid in performing them personally, or by means of their (peons) laboring men, yokes of oxen and cattle, in the equitable manner that the commissioner may direct, and who shall distribute the work in such manner that all may participate in it equally, without excepting any settler or resident, with the understanding that this arrangement shall be limited to the first plowing, sowing and crops, with the proceeds of which shall be defrayed the costs of the next, bearing the net balance to the benefit of the common fund (fondo propios) to convert it to the object of the public good, notwithstanding that by the laws of the kingdom these species of property are appropriated.

15th. The making out and adjudging of the eight " suertes " of irrigable land for the benefit of the common fund (propios) of the new settlement being ascertained, the remaining " suertes " that may be useful in its district, be they irrigable or arrable, shall remain to the benefit of the settlers to whom they shall be distributed and granted as they establish themselves therein, and as it is not possible to establish a fixed rule on the number of "suertes " that can be distributed and granted to every settler, to the wise judgment of the commissioner is left the power of regulating and granting to them those which he may consider sufficient for the maintenance of the family of every one, taking in consideration the number of persons composing it, those existing among them fit for labor and cultivation, the whole of the agricultural implements and other utensils which each one might own to undertake it, and finally their respective industry, as it is just that he who possesses the same should obtain in recompense thereof a larger number of " suertes " than those who by indifference and inapplication shall leave without cultivation those " suertes " which shall have been marked out to them. Under these considerations the first distribution among the actual settlers shall be completed, not exceeding three " suertes " which can be granted to every one, leaving the remaining others so as to distribute them to those who hereafter shall have joined the settlement—to the sons of families who having actually settled belong to the class of residents, or to the same settlers who by the industry and application with which they have devoted themselves to the cultivation of the first distributed " suertes " deserve an augmentation of other " suertes," which never can exceed the same number which in the first distribution shall have been marked out to them.

16th. As it is very inconvenient for the settlers that the number of " suertes " that may be distributed to them should be united and contiguous to each other, so that in this way they may better attend to their cultivation without the diversity of attention occasioned by the distance of lands one from another, the commissioner shall make it his duty to bear in mind this consideration, so as to adapt to the settlers, as much as possible, the advantage of the assemblage of " suertes," or at least the less distance that can be made to exist between those which may be distributed to them, and so as to avoid the differences that may from the improvements of some lands with regard to others, after they shall have been divided in the manner hereafter provided, he (the commissioner) shall proceed to make the first distribution, casting lots for the same among the settlers, as is provided with regard to the (solares) town lots in the article 10 of these instructions.

17th. The commissioner in whose charge shall be the new settlement and the distribution of lands and town lots (solares), shall make a book or register (quaderno) in which shall appear the original steps of distribution that were taken, which book shall be kept in the archives of the Ayuntamiento of the new settlement; and with regard to those steps, he shall give to each settler an attestation or certificate, explaining with brevity, distinctness, and clearness the extent and boundaries of the (solar) town and "suertes" which he may have respectively assigned to them, which instrument shall serve them as a title in fee for themselves, their children and descendants, warning them that for this purpose they shall keep it, and that if they were to lose it by some unintentional accident, they may have recourse to the commissioner or to the Ayuntamiento to give them a true copy of the proceedings, which for this purpose shall remain in the archives.

18th. Thus in the original proceedings of distribution, as in the certificates or titles in fee which shall have been given to the settlers, the commissioner shall also make kown that the (solares) town lots and lands shall be distributed and granted in the name of His Majesty perpetually—forever and ever—and by right of inheritance. for themselves, their children and descendants, with the positive conditions that they shall keep arms and horses and be ready to defend the country from the insults of the enemies that might commence hostilities against it, and to march against them whenever they shall be ordered ; that they shall build and occupy their houses and reside with their families in the new settlement at least for the space of four years ; that during this time they cannot alienate, hypothecate, nor subject to any incumbrance whatsoever the lands and town lots (solares) which shall have been granted to them, even should it be for a pious purpose ; that within the precise space of two years they shall work and cultivate the lands which shall have been donated to them, and they shall at least commence building the houses upon the town lots which shall have been marked out to them, under the penalty that whosoever shall abandon them over this length of time shall lose both, and they can be given to another more diligent : that having fulfilled these conditions, and resided for four years with house and family in the new settlement, they shall acquire the real ownership of the lands and town lots which shall have been distributed to them, and of the houses and edifices in which they shall have worked, and they shall be empowered hereafter with the authority to sell them, and to dispose of them at their own free will, as they would of a thing of their own, as provided by the law 1, title 12, book 4 of the Recopilacion, but under the condition that they never can sell or alienate them to a church. monastery, ecclesiastic community, nor to any of those called mortmain, as provided in the law 1st of the same title and book, under the penalty that he who shall contravene the same shall lose the lands and edifices, which in this case can be distributed to others ; and finally, that within the three months that the grant and distribution shall have been made to them, they shall be under the obligation to take possession of the building lots and lands which shall have been marked out to them, and to plant all the bounds and limits thereof with fruit trees or other which may be useful to the supplying of the settlement with provisions, by which means its district shall enjoy a good and peaceable management, and they shall avail themselves of the fruit, wood and timber which shall be produced for their domestic uses and for the farming utensils which they need indispensably, as provided in the law 11th of said title and book.

19th. The advantage of irrigation being the principal means of fertilizing the lands, and the most conducive to the increase of the settlement, the Commissioner shall take particular care to distribute the waters so that all the land that may be irrigable might partake of them, especially at the season of spring and summer, when they are most necessary to the cultivated land in order to insure the crops, for which purpose, availing himself of skillful or intelligent persons, he shall divide the territory into districts (partidos) or hereditaments, marking out to each one a trench or ditch starting from the main source, with the quantity of water which might be regulated as sufficient for its irrigation, at the said periods and at the other seasons of the year that they may need them, by which means each settler shall know the trench or ditch by which his hereditament shall be irrigated, and that he cannot and shall not have the power to take the water of another, nor in a greater quantity than that which may fall to his share, for which purpose and that it may not increase in injury to the owners situated on the land beyond or still lower, it shall be proper for the trenches or partitions to be constructed in the main ditch made of lime and stone at the cost of the settlers themselves.

20th. In order that these (the settlers) might enjoy with equity and justice the benefit of the waters in proportion to the need of their respective crops, there shall be named annually by the Ayuntamiento one Alcalde (or Mandador) for each trench, to whose charge shall fall the care of distributing them in the estates (heredades) comprised in the "partido" or hereditament, which shall be irrigated by them in proportion to their need for this benefit, designating by a list which he shall make out the hours of day and night at which each owner (heredado) shall irrigate his lands sown with grain ; and in order that by the carelessness or indolence of the owners (dueños) those (the lands) that may need them shall not remain without irrigation, nor the crops be lost, whereby independent of the private injury may also result that of the public and community, produced by the want of provisions and supplies, it shall also come within the duty of the Alcalde, or Mandador, for each trench to have a servant (peon) or day-laborer knowing the hour of the day or night designated for the irrigation of each tract of land or corn-field, who, in default of its owner, shall take care to irrigate it ; the just price of his labor, which shall be caused to be paid to him by the owner of the land or estate (heredad) irrigated, to be thereafter regulated by the Commissioner or by the Justice.

21st. The repairs and cleansing out which the main ditch may need for its conservation, shall be done at the expense of the whole neighborhood at the periods which the Commissioner and Ayuntamiento shall designate, every resident aiding therein by his assistance and personal labor, or in default thereof by the quantity which by partition and an equitable distribution shall be designated to him to pay and satisfy the servants (peons) ; and with regard to the repairs and cleansing out of the distributing dams and ditches destined to the irrigation of the "partidos" or hereditaments in which the land is to be divided, it shall be the duty of the "hacenderas," or owners, whose lands (suertes) and possessions shall be irrigated by them (the dams and ditches), amongst whom shall be divided the expenses which they may occasion *pro rata* to the number of "suertes" which each one shall possess in said "partido," or hereditament, belonging to the (cavildo) Council or Ayuntamiento, in common with the Commissioner, to determine upon those in which, without injury to the cultivated lands, the above mentioned cleansing out and repairs shall be made.

22d. So as to avoid the damages and injuries which through the negligence of their owners the large cattle and the sheep do on the cultivated lands, there shall be appointed annually by the Ayuntamiento two Alcaldes (Guardias de Campo), that the one shall exercise his functions by day, and the other by night ; and like public officers, who shall swear before the Ayuntamiento to well and faithfully perform their duty, their depositions shall be credited unless a proof is proffered against the same sufficient to justify the contrary, and both shall be under the obligation to watch by day and by night that the cattle do not occasion damages in the cultivated lands of the neighborhood, and to apprehend those that they may encounter so doing, which they will drive to a "corral" which shall be made for the purpose, and to be called "Corral del Consejo," reporting and denouncing them immediately to justice, so that under their sworn authority they proceed summarily and effectively, and make known and value the damage they may have occasioned, and to oblige the owner of the apprehended cattle to pay the same and to satisfy him (the Alcalde) for the cultivated land which may have suffered the same.

23d. As it is not sufficient to prevent and avoid the damages which the cattle frequently occasion on the cultivated lands, to compel its owners to the payment of the value at which they (the damages) shall be estimated, it becomes necessary to recover it to impose upon them some other moderate pecuniary fine, which, exacted irremissibly in all cases of contravention, obliges them to heed them and not to reiterate them; and to regulate the above mentioned pecuniary fine a thorough knowledge of the country, of the condition of its inhabitants, and of the value of the cattle being indispensable, this subject shall be reserved to the Ayuntamiento, so that in common with the Commissioner they fix and determine upon the fine to be imposed and exacted in cases of contravention, taking care that the fine be greater for those who shall occasion damage by night, on account of the greater difficulty of their being apprehended and punished.

24th. And lastly, as it is peculiarly the province of the (Cavildos) Councils, or Ayuntamientos, as being the best informed of that which becomes the community and public which they represent, to determine and resolve upon the subjects and measures which they may consider most useful and conducive to their better management and economical and political government, and which being approved by the highest authority appertain to the class of municipal ordinances which are to be observed as the particular laws of every settlement, so far as they are not in opposition to the general laws established by the sovereign, this Ayuntamiento of the new settlement shall be vested with this same power, and in using of this power and acting in common with the Commissioner of its establishment, they shall fix and promulgate the articles, or municipal ordinances, which they may consider most useful and necessary, and which they shall report to this Superior Government, so that in virtue of its approval they be valid and observed.

CHIHUAHUA, 14th of November, 1789.   JUAN GASIOT,
                                             Y. MIRALLES.

No. VIII.

[California Archives, Vol. 1, Missions and Colonization, page 850; 1 Rockwell, 451; Halleck's Report, Ex. Doc. No. 17, 1st Sess. 31st Cong., H. of Rep., page 451.]

In conformity with the opinion of the assessor of the *comandáncia general*, I have determined in a decree of this date that, notwithstanding the provisions made in the 81st article of the ordinance of *intendentes*, the captains of presidios are authorized to grant and distribute house-lots and lands to the soldiers and citizens (soldados y vecinos) who may solicit them to fix their residences on.

And considering the extent of four common leagues measured from the centre of the presidio square, viz : two leagues in every direction, to be sufficient for the new pueblos to be formed under the protection of said presidios, (que van formandose á su abrigo) I have likewise determined, in order to avoid doubts and disputes in future, that said captains restrict themselves henceforward to the quantity of house-lots and lands within the four leagues already mentioned, without exceeding in any manner said limits, leaving free and open the exclusive jurisdiction belonging to the *intendentes* of the royal hacienda, respecting the sale, composition, and distribution of the remainder of the land in the respective districts.

And that this order may be punctually observed and carried into effect, you will circulate it to the captains and commandants of the presidios of your province, informing me of having done so.

God preserve you many years.

CHIHUAHUA, October 22, 1791.

                                        PEDRO DE NAVA.

Senor DON JOSEPH ANTONIO ROMEN.

2*

No. IX.

EXHIBIT B IN THE CASE.

[California Archives, Vol. I, Missions and Colonization, page 874.]

JULY 1ST, 1796.

Report of Don Pedro de Alberni, who had been ordered by Governor to make a careful examination of the country, and report the most suitable location for the Villa of Branciforte, ordered to be established by the Viceroy.

Having examined the points set forth in the foregoing Superior Official Communication, as well as those requiring me to set forth all that I might think necessary, I reply as follows: The principal object and view of the whole matter may be reduced to the project formed by Don José Mᵃ Beltram, and forwarded by the Royal Tribunal de Cuentas to the Most Excellent Viceroy, in relation to the establishment of a Villa or Poblacion; and its being necessary to remember that, in order to attain the desired end, an eye must be had to such favorable circumstances as are required to give to the inhabitants of the same the necessary advantages, such as a plentiful supply of water, wood, irrigable and arable lands, forests, pastures, stone, lime, or earth for adobés; and having been commissioned to this end for the examination, which I made with the Señor Governor Don Diego de Borica, of the country from the Mission of Santa Cruz, Arroyo del Pajaro, and the Mission of Santa Clara, to the place of the Alameda, and the country around the Presidio and Fort of San Francisco, and the Mission of the same name. After a careful and scrupulous examination of these places with the Engineer Extraordinary, Don Alberto de Cordoba, I found that the place of the Alameda, although it contains a creek, still that it affords but little water, and that the channel is so deep [low?] that it is difficult to obtain water therefrom for irrigating the extensive plains of what appears to be good lands; but as the place is without fuel, timber, and pasturage, which cannot be obtained save at the distance of many leagues, it is clear that it is unsuitable for the project under consideration.

In the District of the Presidio of San Francisco, as also in that of the Fort or Battery, and in those of the Mission, at the distance of a league, there is not only wanting irrigable lands, but there is a very small extent of such as are *de temporal* (suitable for grain). The water is so scarce that it is scarcely sufficient for the few families that reside at the Presidio, and from a few holes (positos) from which at intervals they obtain water with much labor, they have to supply themselves. Groves or timber is found at a distance of twelve or fourteen leagues, and pasturage for the little stock of the garrison is only found at a distance of five or six leagues. The wood used in cooking is some *matorrales*, or chiamisos, as it is there called, which grows upon the sand hills. And therefore I am convinced that the worst place or situation in California is that of San Francisco for the establishment of such a villa as is proposed by the Señor Contador, Don José Mᵃ Beltram.

No. X.

[Leyes Vigentes, page 28; 1 White's Recopilacion, 416; 1 Rivera Nueva Coleccion de Leyes y Decretos Mexicanos, 890.]

Decree of the Spanish Cortes of May 23d, 1812.

FORMATION OF THE CONSTITUTIONAL AYUNTAMIENTOS.

The general and extraordinary Cortes, convinced that it is equally important to the welfare and tranquility of families, and the prosperity of the nation, that Common Councils (Ayuntamientos) be established as soon as practicable in such towns (pueblos) where it is proper that they should be instituted and which have not hitherto enjoyed the benefit thereof, as well as to avoid the doubts which might arise in the execution of what has been prescribed on this subject in the Constitution, and to establish a uniform rule for the appointment, form of election, and the number of its members, decree as follows :

1. Every town (pueblo) which has no Common Council, (Ayuntamiento) and the population of which does not amount to one thousand souls, and which, on account of the peculiar condition of its agriculture, industry, or population, requires a Common Council, (Ayuntamiento) will make the same known to the Deputation of the Province, in order that by virtue of this information they may apply to the Government for the requisite permission.

2. Towns (pueblos) which do not find themselves in this situation shall be united to the Councils (Ayuntamientos) to which they have hitherto belonged, as long as the improvement of their political condition shall not require other measures, uniting those newly formed to those nearest them in their Province, or to those which have lost their jurisdiction for want of population.

3. By virtue of the provision of the 312th article of the Constitution, the functions of the regidores and other perpetual officers of the Common Councils (Ayuntamientos) cease as soon as the Constitution and this decree shall have been received in each town, and they shall be elected according to an absolute plurality of votes as prescribed in the 313th and 314th articles of the Constitution, as well in those towns (pueblos) where all have the quality of being perpetual, as in those where some only enjoy this privilege ; for the information of those towns wherein the election may be carried into effect four months before the expiration of the year, it is ordered that said election be renewed at the end of the month of December of the same year, as to one-half, those to go out who were last elected ; but in those towns wherein the elections take place when less than four months are required to terminate the year, those elected will continue in their employment until the end of the next year, when one-half of them will cease to hold their offices.

4. As it cannot fail to be proper that there should exist between the government of the towns and its inhabitants, (el gobierno del pueblo y su vecindario) such proportion as is compatible with good order and its better administration, there shall be one Alcalde, two Regidors, and one Procurator Syndic, in all towns which do not have more than two hundred inhabitants ; one Alcalde, four Regidors, and one Procurator, in those the population of which exceeds two hundred but does not exceed five hundred inhabitants ; one Alcalde, six Regidors, and one Procurator, in those which possess five hundred but the population of which does not amount to one thousand inhabitants : two Alcaldes, eight Regidors, and two Procurator Syndics, in towns having from one thousand to four thousand inhabitants, and the number of Regidors will be augmented to twelve in those towns which have more than four thousand inhabitants.

5. In the capitals of the Provinces there must be at least twelve Regidors, and should they possess more than ten thousand inhabitants their number will be sixteen.

6. In following out these principles in making the elections to fill these offices, it is ordered that the election take place on some day of festival *in the month of December*, by the inhabitants who are in the exercise of the rights of citizenship, of nine electors in the towns which have less than one thousand inhabitants, of sixteen in those having more than one thousand and less than five thousand inhabitants, and of twenty-five electors in those towns having a greater number of inhabitants.

7. This election being completed, there shall be formed on another day of

festival *in the month of December* the Board of Electors, presided by the political chief, if there be any, and if not by the oldest of the Alcaldes, and in the absence of the Alcalde by the oldest Regidor, in order to deliberate on the persons most suitable for the government of the town, (pueblo) and they cannot adjourn without having completed the election, which must be transcribed in a book kept for this purpose, and signed by the President and the Secretary, who shall be likewise Secretary of the Council, (Ayuntamiento) and said election shall be immediately published.

8. In order to facilitate the appointment of the electors, especially where the population is numerous, or where the divisions or distances of the towns or parishes, (los pueblos ó parroquías) which must unite in order to form their Council, might create difficulties or delays, Boards are to be formed in each parish composed of all the inhabitants domiciliated therein, which must be previously convoked, and must be presided by the political chief, Alcalde or Regidor, and each one of them must elect the number of electors to which it is entitled, in the proportion which its population bears to the total population, and the act of the election must be transcribed in a book kept for this purpose, and be signed by the President and the Secretary, which the Board may appoint.

9. A parish Board (Junta de parroquía) cannot be held in towns not having fifty inhabitants, and those being in this predicament must unite among themselves, or with such as are nearest ; but all such towns as have hitherto enjoyed the privilege of nominating electors for the appointment of Justices, Councils, or deputies in common, shall retain this privilege.

10. If, notwithstanding what has been provided in the preceding article, there should still be a greater number of parishes than there are electors, still an elector is to be nominated by each parish.

11. If the number of parishes should be less than the number of electors, each parish will elect one, two, or more, until it has completed the requisite number ; but if an elector were yet wanting, he must be appointed by the parish having the largest population ; and if another be still wanting, he must be elected by the parish having the next largest population, and so successively.

12. Inasmuch as it may happen that there exist in the ultramarine provinces some towns (en las provincias de ultramar algunos pueblos) which, owing to peculiar circumstances, ought to have Common Councils for their better government, but whose inhabitants are not in the enjoyment of the rights of citizens, they have nevertheless the right to elect among themselves the officers of their Councils, in conformity to the rules herein prescribed for other towns.

13. The Common Councils will not in future have any permanent Assessors with fixed salaries.

No. XI.

[Leyes Vigentes, pages 56. etc.]

Decree of the Cortes of Spain of the fourth of January, 1813.

On reducing the vacant land (baldios) and other common lands to private property, cultivable lots to be granted to the defenders of the country, and to citizens who are not proprietors. (Sobre reducir los baldios y otros terrenos comunes a dominio particular: suertes concedidas a los defensores de la patria y a los ciudadanos no proprietarios.)

The Cortes general and extraordinary, considering that the reduction of common lands (terrenos communes) to private property is one of the measures most imperiously demanded for the welfare of the PUEBLOS, and the improvement of agriculture and industry, and wishing, at the same time, to derive from this class of lands aid to relieve the public necessities, a reward to the worthy defenders of the country, and relief to the citizens not proprietors, decree :

1. All vacant land (baldios) or lands belonging to the Royal patrimony (realengos) and lands the revenue whereof goes to the use of the pueblo governments, (propios y arbitrios) wooded or otherwise, as well in the Peninsula and adjacent islands *as in the provinces beyond the sea*, except the necessary suburbs (egidos) of the PUEBLOS, shall be reduced to private property, providing however that in disposing of lands the revenue whereof goes to the use of the pueblo governments, (propios y arbitrios) the yearly revenue derived therefrom shall be supplied by the most appropriate means, to be proposed by the respective provincial deputations, and approved by the Cortes.

2. In whatever manner these lands may be distributed it shall be in fee simple absolute and by metes and bounds, (acotados) so that their owners may inclose the same, without prejudice to the ravines, cross roads, watering places for cattle, (abrevaderos) and easements, (servidumbres) and enjoy them freely and exclusively, and dedicate them to any use and cultivation they may think best ; but they shall never entail them, nor transfer them at any time, nor under any title to be held in mortmain (manos muertas).

3. In the transfer of said lands, the residents of the pueblos within the limits whereof said lands may be shall be preferred, and the commoners of said pueblos in the enjoyment of said vacant land (baldios).

4. The Territorial Deputations shall propose to the Cortes, through the Regency, the best time and means to carry out these dispositions in their respective provinces, in accordance with the circumstances of the district, and also the lands which may be indispensable to reserve for the pueblos, that the Cortes may decide what would be suitable for each district.

5. This business is recommended to the zealous attention of the Regency of the kingdom, and of the two Secretaries of State, that they may present it and explain it before the Cortes whenever proposals may be made by the Territorial Deputations.

6. Without prejudice to the foregoing provisions, one-half of the vacant land (baldios) and lands belonging to the Royal patrimony (realengos) of the monarchy, except the suburbs of the pueblos, (egidos) is hereby reserved, to be in whole or in part, as may be deemed necessary, hypothecated for the payment of the national debt, preferring the payment of the claims against the nation which may be held by the citizens (vecinos) of the pueblos to which the lands may belong ; and in the latter class, preferring such claims as proceed from any supplies furnished to the national armies, or war loans made by said residents since the first day of May, 1808.

7. In selling on account of the public debt said one-half of the vacant land (baldios) and lands belonging to the Royal patrimony, (realengos) or the part which may be deemed necessary to hypothecate, the citizens (vecinos) of the respective pueblos shall be preferred in the purchase thereof, and the commoners in the enjoyment of the aforesaid lands ; and both shall be allowed to pay the full price of said lands with claims duly liquidated held by them on account of said supplies and loans, and in default thereof with any other legitimate national claim they may hold.

8. There shall be comprised within said half of vacant land (baldios) and lands belonging to the Royal patrimony (realengos) the portion already justly and legally sold in some of the provinces for the expenses of the present war.

9. Out of the remainder of the vacant land (baldios) or lands belonging to the Royal patrimony, (realengos) or lands the revenue whereof goes to the use of the pueblo governments, (propios y arbitrios) there shall be given gratis one lot of the best land for cultivation to each Captain, First or Second Lieutenant,

who on account of old age, or having become an invalid in the military service, shall have been honorably discharged from the service, be they either citizens or foreigners, provided that in the districts of their residence there should be any of this class of lands.

10. The lots to be granted in each PUEBLO to the officers or soldiers shall be equal in value, proportionate to the extent and quality of the same, and larger in some districts and smaller in others, according to the circumstances of the same, and the greater or less extension of the lands ; providing, however, if possible, that each lot may be such that if reasonably cultivated it shall suffice to the support of an individual.

11. These lots shall be designated by the constitutional Common Councils (Ayuntamientos) of the respective pueblos to which the lands may belong, as soon as the interested parties present before them the documents proving their good performance in and honorable discharge from the service, and above all the statements of District Attorneys (Procuradores Sindicos) shall be heard summarily and officially without exacting fees or reward of any kind. The proceedings (expediente) shall immediately be sent to the Territorial Deputation that it may approve it and correct any error.

12. The granting of these lots, (suertes) which shall be denominated patriotic rewards, shall not at present be extended to any other individuals, except those now serving or who may have served in the present war, or in the pacification of the actual revolts in some of the provinces beyond the sea. But it comprises the Captains, First and Second Lieutenants, and rank and file, who having served in either may have been honorably discharged, having a genuine discharge, for having been disabled on the battle-field, and not otherwise.

13. It also comprises individuals not military, who having served as guerrillas, or contributed in any other manner to the national defense in this war, or in the American revolts, have been or may become mutilated or disabled in consequence of any conflict in war.

14. These favors (gracias) shall be granted to the aforementioned parties, though they may on account of their services and brilliant exploits enjoy other privileges.

15. Out of the remainder of the vacant land (baldios) and lands belonging to the Royal patrimony (realengos) there shall be segregated those most fit for cultivation, and one lot (suerte) only, proportionate to the extent thereof, shall be given gratis and by lottery to every resident of the respective PUEBLOS, owning no other land, and who may apply for the same, provided the whole amount of lands so segregated and distributed shall not exceed one-fourth of said vacant land (baldios) and lands belonging to the Royal patrimony (realengos) ; and if these should not be sufficient, the lot shall be given in the lands the revenue whereof goes to the use of the pueblo governments, (propios y arbitrios) imposing upon the same a redeemable tax (cañon) equivalent to the revenue derived from the same for the five years next preceding the end of the year 1817, so that the municipal funds may not decrease.

16. If any of those favored by the preceding articles should fail to pay said tax (cañon) for two consecutive years, if the lands belong to the class the revenue whereof goes to the use of the PUEBLO governments, (propios) or if he had it for his own benefit, it shall be given to a more industrious resident having no land of his own.

17. All the proceedings for these grants shall be made by the Common Councils (Ayuntamientos) without any costs, and shall in like manner be approved by the Provincial Deputations.

18. All lots granted in accordance with articles 9, 10, 11, 12, 15, shall be in fee simple absolute (plena propiedad) to the grantees and their successors upon the terms and conditions expressed in article the second ; but the owners of these lots cannot dispose of them before four years have elapsed from the date

of the grant, nor entail them, nor transfer them at any time under any title to be held in mortmain (manos muertas).

19. Any of the aforementioned grantees or their successors establishing upon the land granted his permanent habitation, shall be for the period of eight years exempted from the payment of any tax or impost upon said land and the product thereof.

20. This decree shall be circulated, not only throughout all the pueblos of the monarchy, but also throughout the national armies, it being everywhere published, so that it may come to the notice of all individuals composing the same.

No. XII.

[Colleccion de Ordenes y Decretos de la Soberana Junta Provisional Gubernativa y Soberanos Congresos Generales de la Nacion Mexicana, Vol. III, page 64, etc.; 1 Rockwell, 451; Halleck's Report, ut supra, Appendix 4.]

Decree of the 18th August, 1824, respecting Colonization.

The sovereign general constituent Congress of the United Mexican States has been pleased to decree—

1st. The Mexican nation promises to those foreigners who may come to establish themselves in its territory, security in their persons and property, provided they subject themselves to the laws of the country.

2d. The objects of this law are those national lands which are neither private property nor belonging to any corporation or pueblo, and can therefore be colonized. (Son objeto de esta ley aquellos terrenos de la nacion, que no siendo de propiedad particular, ni pretenecientes á corporacion alguna ó PUEBLO, pueden ser colonizados.)

3d. To this end the Congress of the States will form, as soon as possible, the laws and regulations of colonization of their respective demarcation, with entire conformity to the constitutive act, the general constitution, and the rules established in this law.

4th. Those territories comprised within twenty leagues of the boundaries of any foreign nation, or within ten leagues of the seacoast, cannot be colonized without the previous approval of the supreme general executive power.

5th. If, for the defense or security of the nation the federal government should find it expedient to make use of any portion of these lands for the purpose of constructing warehouses, arsenals, or other public edifices, it may do so, with the approbation of the general Congress, or during its recess with that of the government council.

6th. Before the expiration of four years after the publication of this law, no tax or duty (direcho) shall be imposed on the entry of the persons of foreigners, who come to establish themselves for the first time in the nation.

7th. Previous to the year 1840, the general Congress cannot prohibit the entry of foreigners to colonize, except compelled to do so, with respect to the individuals of some nation, by powerful reasons.

8th. The government, without prejudicing the object of this law, will take the precautionary measures which it may consider necessary for the security of the federation, with respect to the foreigners who may come to colonize. In the distribution of lands, Mexican citizens are to be attended to in preference ; and no distinction shall be made amongst these, except such only as is due to private merit and services rendered to the country, or inequality of circumstances, residence in the place to which the lands distributed belong.

10th. Military persons who are entitled to lands by the promise made on the

27th of March, 1821, shall be attended to in the States, on producing the diplomas granted to them to that effect by the supreme executive power.

11th. If by the decrees of capitulation, according to the probabilities of life, the supreme executive should see fit to alienate any portion of land in favor of any military or civil officers of the federation, it may so dispose of the vacant lands of the territories.

12th. No person shall be allowed to obtain the ownership of more than one league square, of five thousand varas (5,000) of irrigable land (de regadio), four superficial ones of land dependent on the seasons (de temporal), and six superficial ones for the purpose of rearing cattle (de abreradiso).

13th. The new colonist cannot transfer their possessions in mortmain (manos muertas.)

14th. This law guaranties the contracts which the grantees (empresarios) may make with the families which they may bring out at their expense; provided they be not contrary to the laws.

15th. No one who, by virtue of this law, shall acquire the ownership of lands, shall retain them if he shall reside out of the territory of the republic.

16th. The government, in conformity with the principles established in this law, will proceed to the colonization of the territories of the republic.

No. XIII.

EXHIBIT ○ IN THE CASE.

[California Archives, Vol. IV, San José Dep. S., page 278.]

NOVEMBER 6TH, 1828.

Governor Echandia says Comandantes of Presidios cannot grant lands.

" Under this date, I say to Lieutenant Don Ygnacio Martinez, Com^{te} of the Presidio of San Francisco, that which follows :

"The Englishman, William Willis, resident for many years in the pueblo of San José Guadalupe, presented himself before this Government, asking the concession of a place named Laguna de los Bolbones, and in consequence of the Bando, lately published, and other considerations influencing this Superior Government in favor of its ancient and new inhabitants, the following decree was made on his petition : 'Port of San Diego, June 7th, 1828.—Inasmuch ' as there are in the pueblo of San José Guadalupe lands sufficient on which the ' petitioner can maintain his flocks and herds, in accordance with the late Bando ' published in relation to the matter, the place petitioned for cannot be granted.' On this refusal, this individual, maliciously disregarding the authority of the Government, presented himself to the Comandante of San Francisco, setting forth that the said place pertained to his jurisdiction, and asking him to concede to him *ad interim* that which he was unable to obtain from the proper source, who was weak enough to accede to his petition, and grant to him the land (a thing that no Comandante of this Territory has any authority to do) by decree on his petition, dated the twenty-fifth of August last past, not even in the character of a loan for one year. Wherefore, as soon as you receive this you will cause to appear before you the said William Willis, and will exact from him a fine of fifty dollars," etc.

No. XIV.

[California Archives, Vol. II, Missions and Colonization, page 1, etc.; 1 Rockwell, 453; Halleck's Report, ut supra, Appendix 5.]

General rules and regulations for the colonization of territories of the republic. Mexico, November 21, 1828.

It being stipulated in the 11th article of the general law of colonization of the 18th of August, 1824, that the government, in conformity with the principles established in said law, shall proceed to the colonization of the territories of the republic ; and it being very desirable, in order to give to said article the most punctual and exact fulfilment, to dictate some general rules for facilitating its execution in such cases as may occur, his excellency has seen fit to determine on the following articles :

1st. The governors (gefes politicos) of the territories are authorized (in compliance with the law of the general Congress of the 18th of August, 1824, and under the conditions hereafter specified) to grant *vacant lands* (terrenos valdios) in their respective territories to such contractors (empresarios,) families, or private persons, whether Mexicans or foreigners, who may ask for them, for the purpose of cultivating and inhabiting them.

2d. Every person soliciting lands, whether he be an *empresario,* head of a family, or private person, shall address to the governor of the respective territory a petition, expressing his name, country, profession, the number, description, religion, and other circumstances of the families or persons with whom he wishes to colonize, describing as distinctly as possible, by means of a map, the land asked for.

3d. The governor shall proceed immediately to obtain the necessary information whether the petition embraces the requisite conditions required by said law of the 18th of August, both as regards the land and the candidate, in order that the petitioner may at once be attended to ; or if it be preferred, the respective municipal authority may be consulted, whether there be any objection to making the grant or not.

4th. This being done, the governor will accede or not to such petition, in exact conformity to the laws on the subject, and especially to the beforementioned one of the 18th of August, 1824.

5th. The grants made to families or private persons shall not be held to be definitely valid without the previous consent of the territorial deputation, to which end the respective documents (espedientes) shall be forwarded to it.

6th. When the governor shall not obtain the approbation of the territorial deputation, he shall report to the supreme government, forwarding the necessary documents for its decision.

7th. The grants made to *empresarios* for them to colonize with many families shall not be held to be definitely valid until the approval of the supreme government be obtained ; to which the necessary documents must be forwarded, along with the report of the territorial deputation.

8th. The definitive grant asked for being made, a document signed by the governor shall be given, to serve as a title to the party interested, wherein it must be stated that said grant is made in exact conformity with the provisions of the laws in virtue whereof possession shall be given.

9th. The necessary record shall be kept in a book destined for the purpose, of all the petitions presented, and grants made, with the maps of the lands granted, and the circumstantial report shall be forwarded quarterly to the supreme government.

10th. No *capitulization* shall be admitted for a new town, except the *capitulizator* bind himself to present, as colonists, twelve families at least.

11th. The governor shall designate to the *new colonist* (nuevo poblador) a proportionate time within which he shall be bound to cultivate or occupy the land on the terms and with the number of persons or families which he may have *capitulized* for, it being understood that if he does not comply, the grant of the land shall remain void; nevertheless, the governor may revalidate it in proportion to the part which the party may have fulfilled.

12th. Every new colonist, after having cultivated or occupied the land agreeable to his *capitulization*, will take care to prove the same before the municipal authority, in order that, the necessary record being made, he may consolidate and secure his right of ownership, so that he may dispose freely thereof.

13. The reunion of many families into one *town* (poblacion) shall follow, in its formation, interior government and policy, the rules established by the existing laws for the other towns of the republic, special care being taken that the new ones are built with all possible regularity.

14th. The *minimum* of irrigable land to be given to one person for colonization shall be 200 varas square, the *minimum* of land called *de temporal* shall be 800 varas square, and the *minimum* for breeding cattle (*de abrevadero*) shall be 1,200 varas square.

15th. The land given for a house-lot shall be 100 varas.

16th. The spaces which may remain between the colonized lands may be distributed among the adjoining proprietors who shall have cultivated theirs with the most application, and have not received the whole extent of land allowed by the law, or to the children of said proprietors, who may ask for them to combine the possessions of their families ; but on this subject particular attention must be paid to the morality and industry of the parties.

17th. In those territories where there are missions, the lands occupied by them cannot be colonized at present, nor until it be determined whether they are to be considered as the property of the establishments of the neophytes, catechumens, and Mexican colonists.

No. XV.

[See the same: Halleck's Report, Appendix, No. 13; 1 Rockwell, 455; Jones' Report, page 59.]

Decree of the Mexican Congress relating to the Secularization of the Missions of California.

ARTICLE 1. The Government will proceed to secularize the Missions of Upper and Lower California.

ART. 2. In each of said Missions shall be established a parish, served by a secular clergyman, with a stipend of from two thousand to two thousand five hundred dollars a year, as the Government shall decide.

ART. 3. These Parochial Curates shall not recover or receive any fees for marriages, baptisms, or under any other name. As regards fees for processions, they shall be entitled to receive such as may be specifically named in the list made out for that object, as concisely as possible, by the Reverend Bishop of the Diocese, and approved by the Supreme Government.

ART. 4. The churches which have served in each Mission shall serve as parish churches, with the sacred vases, ornaments, and other articles, which each possesses at present, and such additional furniture belonging to said church as the Government may deem necessary for the more decent use of said parish.

ART. 5. The Government shall cause to be laid out a *campo santo* [cemetery] for each parish out of the way of the population.

ART. 6. Five hundred dollars a year are appropriated for the service and worship in each parish church.

ART. 7. Of the houses belonging to each Mission, the most suitable shall be selected as the residence of the Curate, the land appropriated to him not to exceed two hundred yards square, and the rest shall be specially devoted to a town house, primary school, and public establishments and offices.

ART. 8. In order to provide promptly and effectively for the spiritual wants of both the Californias, there is established in the capital of the Upper a vicarship, which shall have jurisdiction over the two Territories, and the Reverend Diocesan shall endow it with the most ample powers.

ART. 9. Three thousand dollars are appropriated as an endowment to this vicarship, the Vicar being required to discharge his duties free of charge under any pretext or name, not even for paper.

ART. 10. If for any other cause whatever the Parochial Curate of the capital, or any other parish in the district, shall act as Vicar, there shall be paid to him one thousand five hundred dollars, besides the stipend of his curacy.

ART. 11. There shall not be introduced any custom which shall require the inhabitants of California to make offerings, however pious they may be, although they may be termed *necessary ;* and neither time nor the will of the said inhabitants shall give them any force or weight whatever.

ART. 12. The Government shall take effectual care that the Reverend Diocesan shall contribute, so far as he is concerned, to fulfill the objects of this law.

ART. 13. The Supreme Government shall provide for the gratuitous transportation, by sea, of the new Curates that may be appointed and their families, and besides may give to each one, for his traveling by land, from four to eight hundred dollars, according to the distance and the number of his family which he brings.

ART. 14. Government shall pay the traveling expenses of the religious [regulars] (religiosos) Missionaries who move; and that they may be accommodated on land as far as their colleges or convents, may give to each from two to three hundred dollars, and, at discretion, so much as may be necessary to such as have not sworn to support the independence, that they may leave the Republic.

ART. 15. The Supreme Government shall pay the expenses arising under this law out of the products of the securities, capitals, and rents, which are regarded as the pious fund in the Missions of California.

August 17th, 1833.

No. XVI.

EXHIBIT No. 5 TO DEPOSITION OF R. C. HOPKINS IN THE CASE.

[California Archives, Vol. III, Departmental State Papers, page 558.]

MAY 18TH, 1834.

Governor Figueroa to Com^te Vallejo.

The Military Comandante of that place (San Francisco) has been considered as one encharged with the administration of justice, which functions were, in the time of the Spanish Government, attributed to that officer on account of there being no constitutional Alcalde, on whom the law of the ninth of October, 1812, conferred the jurisdiction *contensiosa*.

Thus it is that the Military Comandantes have continued exercising these functions until Ayuntamientos should be established at the points where none existed. Under this view of the matter, it is for you, in the character of Judge of First Instance, to carry out the provisions of the law of the twenty-second of July, 1833, in that Presidio and its *comprehension* (jurisdiction).

It belongs also to the Military Comandante of that Presidio to exercise the political government of the same, for the want of local authorities. It is his duty to make out a list of the inhabitants, in the manner prescribed by law, which I will expect you to forward to me without delay, informing me at the same time if, in your opinion, an Ayuntamiento may be established, that I may take such steps as may be necessary in order to carry out the matter.

Signed with Rubrica of Figueroa.

No. XVII.

EXHIBIT No. 6 TO DEPOSITION OF R. C. HOPKINS IN THE CASE.

[California Archives, Vol. XIV, Angeles Official Correspondence.]

Governor Figueroa's Decree of August 6th, 1834, respecting Constitutional Ayuntamientos.

FIGUEROA'S REGULATIONS.

The Most Excellent Territorial Deputation, under date of the second instant, was pleased to resolve as follows:

1st. There shall be a Constitutional Ayuntamiento in the "vecindario" of San Diego, composed of one Alcalde, two Regidores, and one Sindico Procurador.

2d. There shall be a Constitutional Ayuntamiento in the "vecindario" of Santa Barbara, composed of one Alcalde, four Regidores, and one Sindico Procurador.

3d. The Constitutional Ayuntamiento of the pueblo of Los Angeles shall be increased by one Alcalde of the second nomination and two Regidores.

4th. The Constitutional Ayuntamiento of this capital by one Alcalde of the second nomination and two Regidores.

5th. The officers referred to in the foregoing articles shall be elected on the days designated in the law of the twelfth of June, 1830, and shall enter upon the duties of office on the first of January, 1835, excepting those for Santa Barbara, who from the present date (such as are elected) shall exercise all the functions awarded to them by decree of the twenty-third of June, 1813.

All of which I forward to you for your information and further ends, requiring you to see that the same be fulfilled.

God and Liberty!

MONTEREY, August 6th, 1834.

JOSE FIGUEROA.

To the Constitutional Alcalde of Los Angeles.

No. XVIII.

DOCUMENT "A P L" IN THE CASE.

[California Archives, Vol. II, Missions and Colonization, page 538. This is very badly
translated as will be seen where the mistranslations are italicised and the Spanish terms
inserted in parentheses.]

AUGUST 6TH, 1834.

DECREE OF GOVERNOR FIGUEROA, RESPECTING TOWN PROPERTY, MUNICIPAL TAXES, ETC.

José Figueroa, Brigadier General of the Mexican Republic, Commander-in-Chief, Inspector and Superior Political Chief of the Territory of the Upper California.

The Right Honorable Territorial Deputation being desirous to provide the *Towns and Cities* (los Pueblos) with necessary funds for their expenses and works of public benefit, has been pleased to resolve the following :

A plan of ways and means to raise municipal funds (propios y arbitrios) for the AYUNTAMIENTOS OF THE TERRITORY OF THE UPPER CALIFORNIA.

Art. 1st. The Ayuntamientos will proceed by ordinary channels to solicit, that, to each *Town and City*, lands for common and for Town and City property be *assigned*. (Se señalen á cada pueblo terrenos para ejidos y para propios—that lands for *ejidos* and *propios* be designated to each *pueblo*.)

2d. Town and City landed property (los terrenos de propios) so to be assigned to each Town and City, will be subdivided into middling and small sized lots ; and the same may be rented or leased to the highest bidder or bidders. Actual possessor or possessors of town or city property (propios) will pay such annual ground rent as at the discretion of the Ayuntamientos after an investigation of three intelligent and honest men having been had, may be imposed upon them.

3d. Upon the concession of a building-lot for the erection of houses or places of abode, the party and parties interested will pay six dollars and a quarter for each building-lot of one hundred varas square ; and so on ; progressively or diminutively he or they will pay at the rate of one quarter of a dollar for each front vara.

4th. The Constitutional Ayuntamientos within their respective demarcation may for the time being allow to be used such branding irons as at the instance of the parties, may be filed for registration ; and collect at the time of allowing the same for each of such branding irons the sum of one dollar and a half to be applied to municipal funds.

5th. The Political Chief (Governor) will please to order so as to be publicly known that a party now using a branding-iron which is not so registered, shall produce the same in the town or city house of the proper jurisdiction, for the purpose of obtaining a proper license upon being so registered; for which an equal sum as assigned in the 4th Article is likewise to be paid.

6th. For slaughtering each head of cattle, being for the public supply or market, the owner or owners will pay half a real, and the like sum for slaughtering each sheep ; and two reals each hog or pig.

7th. For each clothing store the owner or owners will pay one dollar monthly ; and for each of the groceries of liquor stores, or stores for any other trade, half a dollar.

8th. For each of the weighing or measuring prices, when sealed by the inspector, he or they will pay one real.

9th. From the manager or managers of rope-dances, comedy, and puppet plays, two dollars will be collected for each performance.

10th. For billiard places, they will pay one dollar monthly.

11th. In the ports of Monterey, San Francisco, Santa Barbara, San Pedro and San Diego, every national vessel, not being a vessel of war, will pay as municipal duty, half a real for each package landed for commercial purposes ; and foreign vessels of the like class will pay one real for a package landed in said ports.

12th. It will be solicited from the Supreme Government that the two reals tunnage-duty on foreign vessels, which, according to the 4th Article of the Custom House regulations of 16th of November, 1827, were allowed to the States, be granted to this Territory for municipal funds, which are to supply the treasury of the Deputation.

13th. Enterprisers of fishing and shooting of otters, will pay for each skin of the size of a vara, and so on, four reals, and the like sum for each of the beaver's skins.

14th. All fines or pecuniary penalties which may hereafter be imposed for light offenses by the Constitutional Alcaldes, and even by the Political Chief, will be applied to municipal funds.

15th. The municipal duty heretofore paid on national liquors, will be from the time of the passing hereof, reduced to three dollars on a barrel of brandy, two dollars on each of the "*angelica,*" and one dollar and a half on each of wine, which duty will be paid at the port where the same may be introduced by the importer or importers.

16th. On foreign brandy hereafter introduced for commercial purposes into this Territory, one dollar will be paid for a gallon as municipal duty ; at the like rate it will be paid on gin ; and on wine and beer it will be at the rate of four reals a gallon.

17th. A voluntary contribution is established to every vessel, national and foreign, anchoring in the bay of Monterey, for the exclusive purpose of building a wharf ; each captain, supercargo, or owner of vessel will give what he may spontaneously please ; the produce of this contribution will be collected and kept by the harbor-master under his charge ; and the same will be employed on the construction of such a wharf, and on this work being finished, said contribution to cease.

18th. For each public sale wherein commercial goods are sold to the highest bidders, the auctioneer or auctioneers will pay three dollars as municipal duty.

19th. Taking into consideration the want of funds for ordinary expenses and principal works of the town, according to the power 4th, article 335 of the constitution in force, and after the assent of the Political Chief is given thereto, the taxes, customs and excise determined in Articles 3, 4, 5, 6, 7, 8, 9, 10, 13, 14, 15, 16, 17, and 18, will be enforced, which the said Political Chief will have published on the usual places for observance.

20th. Account will be given to the Supreme Government of this designation, to solicit from the General Congress the approval thereto.

21st. The Political Chief will notify the controller of the Marine Custom House to report to the " Ayuntamiento " of the Capital, the quantity and kind of liquors that he may hereafter guage from each vessel, in order the same may in view of said report take such measures as may be deemed most proper to avoid fraud.

And for the purpose that it may be publicly known, this will be published, and due observance given thereto, by posting the same on the public places, and in a circular to those who are to watch the observance thereof.

Given at Monterey, on the 6th day of August, 1834.

JOSE FIGUEROA.

Agustin V. Zamorano, Secretary.

No. XIX.

[Halleck's Rep., Appendix No. 14; 1 Rockwell, 456; and from the end of Art. 23d, Jones' Rep., page 65.]

Governor Figueroa's Provisional Rules for the Secularization of the Missions.

ARTICLE 1. The Governor, agreeable to the spirit of the law of the seventeenth August, 1833, and to the instructions which he has received from the Supreme Government, will, with the coöperation of the Prelates of the Missionary Priests, partially convert into pueblos the Missions of this Territory, beginning in the next month of August, and commencing at first with ten Missions, and afterwards with the remainder.

ART. 2. The Missionary Priests will be exonerated from the administration of temporalities, and will only exercise the functions of their ministry in matters appertaining to the spiritual administration until the formal division of parishes be made, and the Supreme Government and Diocesan provide Curates.

ART. 3. The Territorial Government will reassume the administration of temporalities in the directive part, according to the following bases.

ART. 4. The Supreme Government will, by the quickest route, be requested to approve of these Provisional Regulations.

DISTRIBUTION OF PROPERTY AND LANDS.

ART. 5. To every individual head of a family, and to all those above twenty-one years of age, although they have no family, a lot of land, whether irrigable or otherwise, of not exceeding four hundred varas square, nor less than one hundred, shall be given out of the common lands of the Missions; and in community a sufficient quantity of land shall be allotted them for watering their cattle. Common lands shall be assigned to each pueblo, and, when convenient, municipal lands also.

ART. 6. One-half of the self-moving property (cattle) shall be distributed among the said individuals, in a proportionable and equitable manner, at the discretion of the Governor, taking as a basis the last accounts of all kinds of cattle presented by the Missionaries.

ART. 7. One-half or less of the chattels, instruments, and seeds, on hand and indispensable for the cultivation of the ground, shall be divided proportionably among them.

ART. 8. The remainder of all the lands, landed property, cattle, and all other property on hand, will remain under the care and responsibility of the Mayordomos, or other officers whom the Governor may name, at the disposal of the Supreme Federal Government.

ART. 9. From the common mass of this property the subsistence of the Missionary Padres, the pay of the Mayordomos, and other servants, and the expenses of religious worship, schools, and other objects of policy and ornament, shall be provided.

ART. 10. The Governor, having under his charge the direction of temporal affairs, will determine and regulate, according to circumstances, all the expenses necessary to be laid out, as well for the execution of this plan as for the conservation and augmentation of this property.

ART. 11. The Missionary Minister will select the locality in the Mission which may best suit him for his own habitation and that of his servants and attendants; and he shall be furnished with the necessary furniture and implements.

ART. 12. The library, sacred dresses, ornaments, and furniture, of the church, shall be put in charge of the Missionary Padre, under the responsibility of the person who acts as subscriber, and whom the Priest himself shall elect, and a reasonable salary be given for his troubles.

ART. 13. General inventories shall be made of all property on hand in each Mission, with due separation and explanation of the different branches ; of the books, debit and credit, and all kinds of papers ; of the amount owing by and to the Missions ; which document and account shall be forwarded to the Supreme Government.

POLITICAL GOVERNMENT OF THE PUEBLOS.

ART. 14. The political government of the pueblos shall be organized in perfect conformity with the existing laws ; the Governor will give the necessary instructions to have Ayuntamientos established and elections made.

ART. 15. The economical government of the pueblos shall be under the charge of the Ayuntamientos ; but as far as regards the administration of justice in contentious affairs, they will be subject to the primary Judges of the nearest towns constitutionally established.

ART. 16. The emancipated Indians will be obliged to assist at the indispensable common labor which, in the opinion of the Governor, may be judged necessary for the cultivation of the vineyards, orchards, and corn-fields, which for the present remain undisposed of, until the resolution of the Supreme Government.

ART. 17. Said emancipated Indians will render to the Missionary Priest the necessary personal service for the attention of his person.

RESTRICTIONS.

ART. 18. They cannot sell, burden, or alienate, under any pretext, the lands which may be given them ; neither can they sell their cattle. Whatever contracts may be made against these orders shall be of no value ; the Government will reclaim the property as belonging to the nation, and the purchasers shall lose their money.

ART. 19. The lands whose owners shall die without heirs shall revert to the possession of the nation.

GENERAL ORDERS.

ART. 20. The Governor will name such Commissioners as he may see fit to carry this plan and its incidents into effect.

ART. 21. The Governor is authorized to resolve any doubt or matter which may arise relative to the execution of these regulations.

ART. 22. Until these regulations be put in force the Reverend Missionary Padres are prohibited from slaughtering cattle in large quantities, except the common and ordinary number accustomed to be killed for the subsistence of the neophytes, without allowing any waste.

ART. 23. The debts of the Mission shall be paid in preference, out of the common mass of the property, at the time and in the manner that the Governor shall determine.

That the fulfillment of this law may be perfect the following rules will be observed :

1st. The Commissioners, so soon as they shall receive their appointments and orders, shall present themselves at the respective Missions, and commence the execution of the plan, being governed in all things by its tenor and these regulations. They shall present their credentials respectively to the Priests under whose care the Mission is, with whom they shall agree, preserving harmony and proper respect.

2d. The Priests shall immediately hand over and the Commissioners receive the books of accounts and other documents relating to property claims, liquidated and unliquidated ; afterwards, general inventories shall be made out, in accordance with the 13th Article of this regulation, of all property—such as houses, churches, workshops, and other local things—stating what belongs to each shop—that is to say, utensils, furniture, and implements; then, what belongs to the homestead; after which shall follow those of the field, that is to say, property that grows, such as vines and vegetables, with an enumeration of the shrubs, if possible, mills, etc.; after that, the cattle, and whatever appertains to them; but as it will be difficult to count them, as well on account of their number as for the want of horses, they shall be estimated by two persons of intelligence and probity, who shall calculate, as nearly as may be, the number of each species, to be inserted in the inventory. Everything shall be in regular form in making the inventory, which shall be kept from the knowledge of the Priests, and under the charge of the Commissioner or Steward; but there shall be no change of the order of the work and services, until experience shall show that it is necessary, except in such matters as are commonly changed whenever it suits.

3d. The Commissioner, with the Steward, shall dispense with all superfluous expense. establishing rigid economy in all things that require reform.

4th. Before he takes an inventory of articles belonging to the field, the Commissioner will inform the natives—explaining to them with mildness and patience that the Missions are to be changed into villages, which will only be under the government of the Priests so far as relates to spiritual matters; that the lands and property for which each one labors are to belong to himself, and to be maintained and controlled by himself without depending on any one else; that the houses in which they live are to be their own, for which end they are to submit to what is ordered in these regulations, which are to be explained to them in the best possible manner. The lots will be given to them immediately, to be worked by them as the 5th Article of the regulations provides. The Commissioner, the Priest, and the Steward, shall choose the location, selecting the best and most convenient to the population; and shall give to each the quantity of ground which he can cultivate, according to his fitness and the size of his family, without exceeding the *maximum* established. Each one shall mark his land in such manner as may be most agreeable to him.

5th. The claims that are liquidated shall be paid from the mass of property; but neither the Commissioner nor the Steward shall settle them without the express order of the Government, which will inform itself on the matter, and, according to its judgment, determine the number of cattle to assign to the neophytes, that it may be done, as heretofore, in conformity with what is provided in the 6th Article.

6th. The necessary effects and implements for labor shall be assigned in the quantities expressed by the 7th Article, either individually or in common, as the Commissioner and Priest may agree upon. The seeds will remain undivided, and shall be given to the neophytes in the usual quantities.

7th. What is called the priesthood shall immediately cease; the female children whom they have in charge being handed over to their fathers, explaining to them the care they should take of them, and pointing out their obligations as parents. The same shall be done with the male children.

8th. The Commissioner, according to the knowledge and information which he shall acquire, shall name to the Government, as soon as possible, one or several individuals, who may appear to him suitable and honorable, as Stewards, according to the provisions of the 8th Article, either from among those who now serve in the Missions or others; he shall also fix the pay which should be assigned them, according to the labor of each Mission.

9th. The settlements which are at a distance from the Mission, and consist of more than twenty-five families, and which would desire to form a separate community, shall be gratified; and the appropriation of lands and other property shall be made to them as to the rest. The settlements which do not contain twenty-five families, provided they be permanently settled where they now live, shall form a suburb, and shall be attached to the nearest village.

10th. The Commissioner shall state the number of souls which each village contains, in order to designate the number of municipal officers, and cause the elections to be held, in which they will proceed conformably, as far as possible, to the law of June 12, 1830.

11th. The Commissioners shall adopt all executive measures which the condition of things demands, giving an account to the Government, and shall consult upon grave and doubtful matters.

12th. In everything that remains, the Commissioners, the Priests, Stewards, and natives, will proceed according to the provisions of the regulation.

JOSE FIGUEROA.

Augustin V. Zamorano, Secretary.

Monterey, August 9, 1834.

No. XX.

REGULATIONS OF THE MISSIONS WHICH HAD BEEN SECU-LARIZED, NOV. 3D, 1834.

[Halleck's Rep. App. 15 ; Jones's Report, page 60, No 10 ; 1 Rockwell, 461.]

In the extraordinary session of the most excellent California deputation held in Monterey on the 3D *OF NOVEMBER,* 1834, *the following regulations were made respecting the missions which had been secularized, agreeably to the supreme order of the* 17th *August,* 1833, *and the provisional regulations of Governor Figueroa of the 9th August,* 1834 :

ARTICLE 1. In accordance with the 2d article of the law of the 17th August, 1833, the amount of $1,500 per annum is assigned to the priests who exercise the functions of parish priests in the curacies of the first class, and $1,000 to those of the second class.

ART. 2. As curacies of the first class shall be reputed San Diego, San Dieguito, San Luis Rey, Las Flores, and ranches annexed ; San Gabriel and Los Angeles ; Santa Barbara, the mission and presidio annexed ; San Carlos, united to Monterey ; Santa Clara, joined to San José de Guadalupe, and San José, San Francisco Solano, San Rafael, and the colony. And the following shall be reputed of the second class : San Juan Capistrano, San Fernando, San Buenaventura, San Ynes and la Purisima, San Luis Obispo, San Miguel, San Antonio and La Solidad, San Juan Bautista, Santa Cruz, *San Francisco de Assis,* and the presidio.

ART. 3. Agreeably to the 8th and 9th articles of said law, the reverend father commissary prefect, Father Francisco Garcia Diego, shall establish his residence in the capital, and the governor (gefe politico) shall request the reverend diocesan to confer upon said prelate the faculties appertaining to a foraneous vicar. He shall enjoy the salary of $3,000 assigned to him by said law.

ART. 4. The foraneous vicar and the curates shall be judged, in all other respects, by said law of the 17th August, 1833.

ART. 5. Until the Government can furnish permanent parish priests, the respective prelates of the missionaries (religions) shall do so provisionally, with the approbation of the governor.

ART. 6. With respect to article 6th of said law, the $500 per annum shall be paid for public worship and for servants in each parish.

ART. 7. From the common stock of the property of the *extinguished* [suppressed] mission, the salaries of the foraneous vicar, the curates, and for religious worship, shall be paid either in cash (should there be any) or in produce or other articles at current prices. The governor will give the necessary orders to have this carried into effect.

ART. 8. The 17th article of the provisional regulations of secularization, which imposed upon Indians the duty of giving personal service to the priests, is annulled.

ART. 9. With respect to the 7th article of said law, the governor will order localities to be appointed for the habitation of curates, for the court-house, schools, public establishments, and workshops.

ART. 10. The other matters to which the observations of the reverend padre, Fr. Narcisco Daran, extend, as they are of easy resolution, will be settled by the governor, who is authorized to do so by the provisional regulations.

ART. 11. This law, together with the opinion of the committee appointed to examine the above rations of Padre Daran on the provisional regulations, shall be communicated to the prelates for them to make it known to their subordinates.

ART. 2, (addition to). The curacies which embrace two or more inhabited places will recognise the first one mentioned as the principal, and there the parish priest will reside, and in San Diego and Santa Barbara the missions will be the places of residence.

No. XXI.

EXHIBITS NOS. 1 AND 2 TO THE DEPOSITION OF M. G. VALLEJO.

DECEMBER, 1834.

Order for election of an Ayuntamiento for the Partido of San Francisco, and election of the same.

No. 1.   { Seal of the Political Government }
         { of Upper California. }

The most excellent Territorial Deputation, using the powers conferred on it by the law of the 23d of June, 1813, on yesterday passed the following instructions:

" 1st. The Political Chief will direct that the partido of San Francisco proceed to the election of an Ayuntamiento constitutional, which shall reside in the Presidio of that name, composed of an Alcalde, two Councilmen, and a Sindic Procurer, regulating itself in all respects, so as to be able to verify it, by the existing Constitution and the law of June 12, 1830.*

" 2d. That account be given by the proper way to the Supreme Government for the due approbation."

And I transcribe it to you for your information and compliance, recommending that the election be carried into effect on the day appointed by the said law of the 12th of June.

I also notify you that the Ayuntamiento, when installed, will exercise the political functions with which you have been charged, and the Alcalde the judicial functions which the laws, for want of a *Judge of Letters*, confer on

---

* This should be July 12, 1830. See the Original Coleccion de Decretos por 1829–1830, pages 113, etc.

him ; you remaining restricted to the military command alone, and receiving in anticipation the thanks due for the prudence and exactness with which you have carried on the political government of that demarcation.

God and Liberty!

Monterey, November 4, 1834.

JOSE FIGUEROA.

To the Military Comandante of San Francisco.

No. 2.

In the Presidio of San Francisco, the 7th day of December, 1834, the Municipality of the Demarcation assembled in the house of the *Comandancia*. The corresponding order of convocation being previously given for the purpose of holding the primary *Junta* for voting for the electors who are to meet in secondary (junta) on the first following Sunday, for the purpose of electing the individuals who are to compose the new Ayuntamiento for this *Comprehension*, and who are to hold office for the coming year of 1835, in compliance with what is ordered by the Political Chief, on the 4th of November of this year, in virtue of the resolution on the matter by the most excellent Territorial Deputation, after the election of four secretaries, proceeded to the election of twelve electors, which number according to the assembled Municipality was found to correspond to it, and having counted the votes from which there resulted by majority. Citizens: Ygnacio Peralta with 27 votes; Francisco Sanchez with 23 ; Francisco Soto with 20 ; Joaquin Castro with 19 ; José de la Cruz Sanchez with 17 ; Francisco de Haro with 16 ; Manuel Sanchez with 15 ; Juan Miranda with 15 ; Antonio Castro with 12 ; Manos Briones with 9, and Apolonario Miranda with 9 ; from which it resulted that the said gentlemen were elected ; and they were notified of it, and the act being concluded, the President and Secretaries signed the present act.

FRANCISCO DE HARO,
FRANCISCO SANCHEZ,
JOAQUIN CASTRO,
JUAN MIRANDA.

No. XXII.

EXHIBIT No. 5 TO DEPOSITION OF M. G. VALLEJO.

Approval of choice of Alcalde for Contra Costa, by Governor Figueroa.

{ Seal of the Political Government }
{ of Upper California. }

The appointment you have made in favor of the citizen Gregorio Briones, as auxiliary Alcalde in the Contra Costa, seems to me very well, and consequently has my approval. I say this to you in answer to your official note on the matter of the 22d ultimo.

God and Liberty!

Monterey, January 31st, 1835.

JOSE FIGUEROA.

Señor Constitutional Alcalde of San Francisco de Asis.

No. XXIII.

EXHIBIT No. 14 TO DEPOSITION OF R. C. HOPKINS.

Order of Governor Figueroa for the election of an Ayuntamiento for the PUEBLO of San Francisco, January 31st, 1835.

[SEAL.]
Con el ofo de V. de 23 del que acaba es en mi poder el Padron general de los habitantes que tiene esa poblacion de San Francisco de Asis.

Como esta prevenido por la ley de 23 de Mayo de 1812, que se reputa vigente que cada pueblo tenga su Ayuntamiento y correpondiendole á ese por su senso un Alcalde, dos Regidores, y un Sindico Procurador, dispondra V. que desde luego se verifiquen las elecciones para la formacion del Ayuntamiento con total arreglo á la ley de 12 de Junio de 1830.

Dios y Libertad!

MONTEREY, Erno 31 de 1835.

JOSE FIGUEROA.

SR DN JOAQUIN ESTUDILLO, Comandante de Sⁿ Francisco de Asis.

[TRANSLATION.]

[SEAL.]
With your official note of the 23d of the ending month, is in my possession the general list of the inhabitants of the population of San Francisco de Asis.

By the law of 23d of May, 1812, which is considered in force, it is provided that each pueblo shall have its Ayuntamiento, and according to the census of that town there shall be elected one Alcalde, two (Regidores) Directors, (y un Sindico Procurador) and one Attorney-General, therefore you will dispose hereafter the election to verify the formation of the Ayuntamiento with all the rule of the law of 12th June, 1830.

God and Liberty!

MONTEREY, January 31st, 1835.

JOSE FIGUEROA.

SR DON JOAQUIN ESTUDILLO, Cᵗᵉ de San Francisco de Asis.

No. XXIV.

EXHIBIT F TO DEPOSITION OF R. C. HOPKINS IN THE CASE

[California Archives, Vol. VI, Prefecturas and Juzgados, Benicia, 122.]

Governor Figueroa decides, August 6, 1835, that the distribution of house-lots and sowing-lots at Yerba Buena does not belong to the Ayuntamiento.

JULY 15TH, 1835—F.

Justice Haro to Governor Figueroa.

COURT OF FIRST INSTANCE }
OF SAN FRANCISCO DE ASIS. }

Don José Joaquin de Estudillo has presented himself to me, asking permission to build his house on the beach (playa) of Yerba Buena, the anchorage of vessels, and that there be also conceded to him sowing lands. Your Señoria will inform me if this Ayuntamiento has authority to permit him to do so, and also to concede him lands for cultivation in that vicinity.

God and Liberty!

SAN FRANCISCO DE ASIS, July 15th, 1835.

FRANCISCO DE HARO.

Reply of Governor Figueroa.

MONTEREY, August 6th, 1835.

Let him be answered that the distribution of lands for house-lots and for purposes of cultivation, in the place of Yerba Buena, does not belong to the Ayuntamiento.

No. XXV.

EXHIBIT No. 12 TO THE TESTIMONY OF R. C. HOPKINS.

Espediente relative to the place called Laguna de la Merced, solicited by José Antonio Galindo.

August to Sept., 1835.

STAMP THIRD. TWO REALS.

Provisionally authorized by the Administration of the Maritime Custom House of Monterey, of Upper California, for the years eighteen hundred and thirty-four and eighteen hundred and thirty-five.

A. RAMIREZ,
FIGUEROA.

Señor Political Chief:

The citizen, José Anto. Galindo, before your Lordship in due form of law appears, and exposes that, finding himself with a numerous family, which consists of his mother, three brothers, and two sisters, he is in need, for their subsistence, of a tract of land, which is vacant, lying near San Francisco AND Dolores (que se aya valdia en las immidaciones de S. Francisco *y de* Dolores), which tract of land is one league in width, and a half league, more or less, in length. The corresponding sketch he herewith presents, according to the law of the eighteenth of August, 1824; wherefore, he prays your Lordship that due action be taken on this petition, by which he shall receive a favor. I swear it is not in malice, etc.

SAN FRANCISCO, August 15, 1835.

(Signed)   JOSE ANTO. GALINDO.

MONTEREY, September 5, 1835.

In conformity with the laws and regulations on the matter, let the Ayuntamiento of San Francisco report whether the interested party in this petition has the requisite qualifications to be attended to in his petition (informe el Ayuntamiento de San Francisco si el interasado obtiene los requisitos); whether the land he solicits is within the twenty border leagues, or ten littoral ones, mentioned in the law of the eighteenth of August, 1824; whether it is the property of any individual, Mission, corporation, or pueblo, and whatever else may be conducive to elucidate the matter; which being done, let the espediente (record) of proceedings pass to the Superintendent of the same, in order that he may state what he may see proper in the matter.

D. José Castro, first member of the most excellent Territorial Deputation and Political Chief *ad interim* of the Territory of Upper California: thus ordered, decreed, and signed, of which I certify.

(Signed)   JOSE CASTRO. [Rubric.]

In accordance with the superior decree of the fifth of September of the present year, which appears on the margin of the petition made by the citizen José Antonio Galindo, in solicitation of the tract of land La Laguna de la Merced, the municipal authorities (Ayuntamiento) of this demarcation reply as follows: That the petitioner possesses the qualifications of being a Mexican citizen by birth, and of having served the nation in the capacity of a soldier, and of being an honest man, and that he supports his mother, an aged widow, with other children, contributing by his aid to the support of all, and in the preservation of the property which they possess. The land which he solicits is not comprehended within the twenty bordering leagues, but it is within the ten littoral ones; but it has belonged to the Mission of San Francisco, from which it is distant, to the west, a little more than one league in a straight line. It is not farming land, not irrigable, nor is it irrigable farming land, but it is pasture land, for it can only be used to raise a small number of cattle at the said Laguna, for all the land is sandy, and produces pasture only fit for horses and cattle. For the purpose of cultivation it is altogether useless and barren.

This is all that this corporation can say in relation to the matter to which the said superior order refers.

SAN FRANCISCO, September 10, 1835.

(Signed)   FRANCISCO DE HARO.
F. SANCHEZ, Secretary.

Señor Political Chief, ad interim:

In obedience to the superior decree of your Lordship, which provides that this record of proceedings (espediente) be transmitted to the Superintendent of this Mission, in order that he may state what he may see proper, I will say that the petitioner possesses the necessary qualifications to be attended to; that he is a Mexican citizen by birth, and has served in the military career. The land which he solicits belongs to this community; it is grazing land; it is not within the twenty bordering leagues, but it is within the ten littoral leagues.

It is at the distance of a little more than a league from said Mission, and is not in the occupation of the same; but as the commons (ejidos) which shall belong to this place when it shall be constituted into a town (pueblo) are not yet designated (pero con motivo no estan aun señalados los ejidos ó propios que me parecen quedaran á esta cuando se erije en pueblo), I do not know whether the said commons will embrace the said tract of land, and for this reason I cannot say with certainty whether the said place may be granted without prejudice to this community.

DOLORES, September 13, 1835.

(Signed)   GUMDO. FLORES.

STAMP THIRD. TWO REALS.

Provisionally authorized by the Administration of the Maritime Custom House of Monterey, of Upper California, for the year eighteen hundred and thirty-four and eighteen hundred and thirty-five.

           ANGELO RAMIREZ,
           CASTRO.

MONTEREY, September 22, 1835.

Let this be transmitted to the Alcalde of this capital, before whom the interested party, Don José Antonio Galindo, will produce an information of three competent witnesses, who shall be examined upon the following points :

1st. Whether the petitioner is a Mexican citizen by birth; if he is a married man; has any children; and if he is of good conduct.

2d. Whether the land he solicits is the property of any individual, Mission, corporation, or *pueblo ;* if it is farming, irrigable land, or not irrigable grazing land, and what may be its extent.

3d. Whether he has personal property to occupy it, or can acquire it.

These proceedings being concluded, the espediente shall be returned for final action to Don José Castro, first member of the most excellent Territorial Deputation and Superior Political Chief, *ad interim*, of Upper California: thus ordered, decreed, and signed, which I attest.

(Signed)   JOSE CASTRO.
F. DEL CASTILLO NEGRETE, Secretary.

MONTEREY, September 22, 1835.

Fees $4.00. Let the interested party be notified to produce the witnesses to be examined on the points comprised in the preceding superior decree; let the required information be taken, and let the record of proceedings be returned to the Señor Superior Political Chief, that it may have the due effect.

In assistance : JOSE M. MALDONADO,   E. D. SPENCE.
      J. J. ESTADILLO.

On the same date, the citizen José Antonio Galindo being present, the foregoing order was communicated to him; and apprised of it, he said that he hears it, and that he presents as witnesses Messrs. Francisco Sanchez, José Fernandez, and Guadalupe Barcenos; and he did not sign this, because, as he said, he did not know how; and I did it with those of my assistance according to law.

                                                E. D. SPENCE.
In assistance : JOSE M. MALDONADO,
      J. J. ESTADILLO.

Immediately after, the citizen Francisco Sanchez being present, I administered to him the legal oath, which he made according to law, under which he offered to say the truth to the extent of his knowledge to the questions that should be put to him; and being asked for his name, state, age, country, and religion, he said that his name is as above said, that he is a married man, twenty-nine years of age, a native of San Francisco in Upper California, and Roman Apostolic Catholic.

Being interrogated upon the points prescribed by the superior decree of the twenty-second instant, he answered to the first, that he is a Mexican by birth, that he has no children, and is not married, and that he is of good conduct; and he answers to the second, that he knows that the lands which the party solicits belongs to the Mission of San Francisco de Asis, that it is pasture land, and that its extent may be in length one league, and the greatest width half a league; and he replies to the third, that he has farming stock, and possesses property; that all he has said is the truth, under the oath which he has taken, which he confirmed and ratified after this deposition was read to him, and he signed it with me, and those of my assistance.

(Signed)   DAVID SPENCE,
In assistance :   FRANCISCO SANCHEZ.
   (Signed)   J. M. MALDONADO,
             J. J. ESTADILLO.

On the same date, Don José Fernandez being present, I administered to him the legal oath, under which he promised to answer the truth, to the extent of his knowledge, to the question that might be put to him; and being asked as to his name, state, age, country, and religion, he answered, that his name is the same before mentioned, that he is a married man, of the age of thirty-six, a native of Cadiz, and an Apostolic Roman Catholic.

Being interrogated to the same points as the preceding witness, he said to the first, that the party is a Mexican citizen by birth, that he is not married, nor has he any children, and that he is of good conduct; and he answers to the second, that he knows that the tract of land which he solicits belonged formerly to the Mission of San Francisco, that he does not know whether at present it belongs to the Mission or not, that it is pasture land, and that its extent may be three-quarters of a league in length and one-quarter of a league in width; and he replies to the third, that he has personal property to occupy it; and that what he has said is the truth, under the oath he has taken, which he confirmed and ratified after this deposition was read to him, and he signed it with me, and those of my assistance.

(Signed)   . D. E. SPENCE.
In assistance :
    (Signed)   J. M. MALDONADO,
                    JOSE J. CARRILLO.

Immediately after, I administered the legal oath to the citizen Guadalupe Barcenos, under which he promised to speak the truth, to the extent of his knowledge, in answer to the questions that might be put to him; and being interrogated as to his name, age, country, and religion, he said, that his name is the same before mentioned, that he is a married man, and twenty-three years of age, native of San Francisco, and Apostolic Roman Catholic.

Being interrogated to the same points as the two former witnesses, he said to the first, that the petitioner was a Mexican citizen by birth, that he is not married, and is of good conduct; and he answers to the second, that he knows that the land which he solicits belongs to the Mission of San Francisco, but is not occupied by the same, that it is only pasturing land, and that its extent may be one league in length, and in breadth in some places half a league; and replies to the third, that he has sufficient personal property to occupy it; and that what he has said is the truth, under the oath which he has taken, which he confirmed and ratified after this deposition was read to him; and he did not sign because he said he knew not how, and I did it, with those of my assistance.

(Signed)   E. SPENCE.
In assistance :
    (Signed)   J. W. MALUVUNDE,
                    J. J. ESTUDELLO.

On the same date, the information required being ended, this record of proceedings is returned to the same Supreme Political Chief, in compliance with what has been prescribed by the preceding decree; in witness whereof, I note it down and affix my rubric.

R.   [L. S.]

MONTEREY, September 23, 1835.

In view of the petition with which this (espediente) record of proceedings begins the report of the municipal authority of this capital, the testimony of witnesses, together with whatever else was thought to the purpose, in conformity with the provisions of the laws and regulations on the matter, José Antonio

Galindo is declared owner in full property of the land known by the name of La Laguna de la Merced.

Subject to the conditions that may be stipulated, let the corresponding dispatch be issued, and note of it be taken in the respective book, and the espediente to be submitted to the most excellent Territorial Deputation for approval.

Señor Don José Castro, first member of the excellent Territorial Deputation and Political Chief, *ad interim*, of Upper California : thus ordered, decreed, and signed, which I attest.

  (Signed)   JOSE CASTRO.

                MONTEREY, September 25, 1835.

In session of this day, this espediente was referred to the Committee on Vacant Lands.

  (Signed)   CASTRO.

Due note has been taken upon page 74.

No. XXVI.

EXHIBIT No. 6 TO DEPOSITION OF M. G. VALLEJO IN THE CASE.

OCTOBER, 1835.

The Ayuntamiento of San Francisco authorized to grant building lots.

  { Seal of the Political Government }
  {   of Upper California.   }

The most excellent Territorial Deputation, in session of the twenty-second of September, approved that the AYUNTAMIENTO OF THAT PUEBLO may grant lots which do not exceed one hundred varas, for the building of houses in the place named Yerba Buena, at the distance of two hundred varas from the shore of the sea, paying to the Ayuntamiento the fees which may be designated to him [it ? que se la señale] as pertaining to the propios and arbitrios, and being subject to observe the order for forming the town in lines, [en linea de major policia] in accordance with the ordinance regulating the Police, which I communicate to you that you may make it known to the inhabitants of that PUEBLO, in order that they may not apply with their memorials to this Political Government, as it is one of the favors which the Ayuntamiento can grant.

           God and Liberty!

MONTEREY, October 27, 1835.

               JOSE CASTRO.

Señor Alcalde de San Francisco de Asis.

No. XXVII.

EXHIBIT DOC. 9, FILED JANUARY 2d, 1857.

Summons to the Mayordomo of the Mission of Dolores to settle the boundaries of the Buri Buri Rancho, November 2d, 1835.

Nov. 2d, 1835—Sanchez Rancho.

TRIBUNAL OF FIRST INSTANCE
OF THE PORT OF SAN FRANCISCO DE ASIS. }

Having to give possession to Don José Sanchez of the Rancho Buri Buri and the lands which pertain to it, according to the title of concession, which he has presented, and the plat (diseño) accompanying it, and he (esta parte) having already appointed his surveyor, according to previous arrangement, it remains for you, as the party in charge of that pueblo (ese pueblo) and community, and the only co-terminous neighbor (unico colindante) of Don José Sanchez, to proceed to appoint also your surveyor, who must appear before this Tribunal (Juzgado) to-morrow morning at eight o'clock, in order that he and the other surveyor appointed by said Señor Sanchez may accept the appointment, and take an oath to execute this commission faithfully, according to custom ; consequently it will remain for me to appoint the day and hour when, with the assistance of all, I shall cause the said admeasurement and possession of the said Don José Sanchez to be perfected.

God and Liberty !

San Francisco, November 2d, 1835.

FRANCISCO HARO.

To the Mayordomo of the Pueblo of Dolores,
DON GUERMECINDO FLORES.

No. XXVIII.

SUSPENSION OF SECULARIZATION OF THE MISSIONS.

Mexican decree of the 7th November, 1835.

[Halleck's Rep. App. 16; Jones's Report, page 63, No. 14; 1 Rockwell, 462.]

The President *ad interim* of the Mexican republic to the inhabitants thereof. Know ye that the General Congress has decreed the following :

" Until the curates mentioned in the 2d article of the law of August, 1833, shall take possession, the government will suspend the execution of the other articles of said law, and maintain things in the state they were in before said law was enacted."

No. XXIX.

TRANSLATION OF DOCUMENT "C P L," IN THE CASE.

May to December, 1835.

RECORD OF PROCEEDINGS HAD BY THE RESIDENTS IN THE VICINITY OF SAN FRANCISCO, PRAYING THAT THEY MIGHT BE ALLOWED TO BELONG TO THE JURISDICTION OF SAN JOSE GUADALUPE.

[*An eminent specimen of the "circumlocution," or official style of translation as practiced by strangers to both languages.*]

To H. E. the Governor :

The residents in the adjoining Ranchos of the North, now belonging to the jurisdiction of the port of San Francisco, (el vecindario de los Ranchos del Norte, pertenciente á la jurisdiccion del puerto de San Francisco,) with due respect to Y. E. : That being so great detriment and on seeing the evils resulting from belonging to this jurisdiction, whereby they are obliged to represent to Y. E. that it causes an entire abandoning of their families for a year to those who attend the Judiciary functions and others who are called and are obliged to cross the Bay, properly speaking, for to go to such a port by land, we are sure there are more than 40 leagues on going and coming back, and to go by sea we are exposed to be wrecked ; and as to abandoning our families, as above stated, it is evident that they will remain [without] protection from the malevolent persons, the detention and loss of labors and properties, being exposed to injury by animals ; although there is no lodging to be had in that port, where for a year an Ayuntamiento should be, with their families, after making a heavy transportation of necessary provisions for the term of their employment : wherefore, in view of the above statement, they pray Y. E. to be pleased to allow them to belong to the authority of this Town (pueblo) of S. Jose, recognizing a Commission of Justice, that this may correspond to that of the said San Jose as Capital, regarding the inhabiting, in these Ranchos the majority of the Vicinity and families.

Wherefore we humbly pray Y. E. to accede in favor of the parties interested a favor that we hope to receive.

RANCHOS OF THE NORTH, SAN ANTONIO, SAN PABLO, AND THE ADJACENT, May 30, 1835.

ANTONIO MN. PERALTA,	ANTONIO YGERCE,†
JOAQN. YSIDRO CASTRO,	YGNACIO PERALTA,
BLAS NARBOES,†	DOMINGO PERALTA,†
Z. BLAS ANGELENO,	BUNO VALENCEA,†
SANUAGO MESA,†	JOAQN. MORAGO,†
JUAN JOSE CASTRO,	RAMON FORERO,†
GABRIEL CASTRO,	JOSE DUARTE,†
ANTONIO CASTRO,	FRANCO. PACHECO,†
CANDELARCO BALENCEN,	BARTOLO PACHECO,†
JOSE PERALTA,	MEREANO CASTRO,†
FERNANDO FELES,	FELEPE BRIONES,†
ANTONIO AMEJAR,†	JULIAN VELES,†
JUAN BERNAL,†	RAFAEL FELES,†
BISENTE PERALTA,	FRANCO SOTO,†
MARCANO CASTRO,†	FRANCO AMIGO.†

SUBSTANCE (EXTRACTO : SYLLABUS).

The residents of the adjoining Ranchos of the North, petition that they be exempted from belonging to the jurisdiction of San Francisco on account of the long distance, where they live, and great detriment resulting from causes as stated. They pray that they may be allowed to belong to the jurisdiction of the Town (pueblo) of San Jose Guadelupe, it being near [nearer] their places, (mas inmediato).

MONTEREY, Augt. 12th, 1835.

Let it be kept to be reported to the Deputation.

SEPT. 1st, 1835.

On this day the same was reported and referred to the Committee on Government. CASTRO.

Most Excellent Sir:

The Committee on Government being required to report upon the memorial which the parties subscribed thereto made to the Political Chief on the 30th day of May last, finds that the said memorial is grounded upon good reasons and public convenience, but as the subject should be considered upon proper reports for a due determination, the Committee is of opinion that the reports of the Ayuntamientos of the Towns of San Jose and San Francisco (los Ayuntamientos de los PUEBLOS de San José y San Francisco) are required for that purpose. Therefore the Committee offers for the deliberation of the most Excl. Deputation the following propositions:

1st. That this Espediente be referred to the Ayuntamientos of the Towns of San Jose and San Francisco, (los Ayuntamientos de los PUEBLOS de San José y San Francisco) in order that they report upon said memorial.

2d. That after which the same be returned for determination.

MONTEREY, Sept. 5, 1835.

MAN^L. JIMENO.

SALVEO PACHECO.

MONTEREY, Sept. 10th, 1825.

At the Session of this day the Most Excellent Deputation has approved the two propositions made in the report of the Committee on Government.

MANUEL JIMENO.

MONTEREY, Sept. 28th, 1835.

Let this Espediente be forwarded to the Ayuntamiento of the Town (pueblo) of San José Guadelupe for a report upon the prayer of the foregoing memorial and to that of San Francisco, (AL de San Francisco) for the like purpose.

The Ayuntamiento of the latter Town will moreover give a list of the residents of the vicinity of the same, (un padron de los vecinos de ese Pueblo).

Don Jose Castro, senior member of the M^t. Excellent Territorial Deputation and Superior Political Chief of the Upper California, thus commended, decreed and signed this which I attest.

JOSE CASTRO.

FRAN^{co}. DEL CASTELLO NEGRETE, Sec'y.

In pursuance of the foregoing Sup^r. Order of Y. E., this Ayuntamiento begs to state the following: That with regard to the residents on the Northern Vicinity, now under the jurisdiction of San Francisco, and who in their memorial prayed to be exempted from belonging to that jurisdiction owing to most notable detriment occasioned to them now and then from having indispensably to cross the Bay or to travel upwards of 40 leagues, while on half their way they can come to this Town, (pueblo) under the jurisdiction of which they formerly were, which was most suitable and less inconvenient to them—this Ayuntamiento thinks that their prayer should be granted—if it is so found right.

TOWN (PUEBLO) OF SAN JOSE GUADALUPE, Nov. 4th, 1835.

ANTONIO Mᴬ. PICO,
IGNACIO MARTINEZ, Sec'y.
JOSE BERREYESA.

In pursuance of the direction in the Superior decree of the Political Chief *ad interim*, dated the 28th day of September of the present year, and issued on that day upon the memorial made by the residents and the adjoining Ranchos of San Pablo and San Antonio, the Ayuntamiento of San Francisco (el Ayuntamiento de San Francisco) begs to state the following :

That in the opinion of the said Ayuntamiento the reasons assigned by the memorialists from being exempted from belonging to this jurisdiction are frivolous ; for what evils and detriments can result to them ? Which are the evils and detriments they have actually suffered ? And again, when then they will voluntarily make at least a little sacrifice for the good of their country ? What excitement can move them for the aggrandizement of the same ? How are they sure that only those of those Ranchos will be called to function in the Ayuntamiento for a year, and even taking it for granted that it is so, are they the first who, to fulfil the duty of good citizens, leave their home, and family, and interest ? And yet, can they compare a service to be done by traveling 40 leagues, as they state, and leaving their private business for some days, months, or even the whole year, with that of others, who, for the like purpose of serving their country, have traveled of leagues in the interior of the Republic to go where they are called by law ? there have been several others of this very Territory, who, as electors, have left their homes, family, and interest, have traveled from San Francisco to San Diego, and other deputies to the General Congress have done the same from the Upper California to Mexico ; and how many are expected to make equal sacrifices for such a permanent interest of the public good and aggrandizement of the nation, of those who are to be terrified with most evident dangers of the sea, and traveling by land to the place where they are required by law to be.

The memorialists believe that only their private interest and family deserve their particular attention and appreciation, and that the constitutional laws have dispensed with or exonerated them from suffering as other wives and sons by the same laws willingly, as when their husbands, fathers, and brothers, or rather their benefactors, engage themselves in service of the country—but surely another kind of patriotism and public spirit move and excite this kind of servants or citizens.

The memorialists further say that they are exposed to be wrecked, for the place of their residence is beyond the sea, from where they have to come over in case they are appointed to aid in the Ayuntamiento : which are those Peraltas and Castros that have been wrecked on attending to their business affairs every time that any vessel comes to anchor in the Bay of Yerba Buena [?] Or how are they sure that wreck will only wait them when they are called to attend the service of their country ? (Llamados por la ley hacer alguno servicio á su *pueblo*.) The fact is, that up to this time no such event has ever been heard or known of having occurred said gentlemen or others, on going on board of vessel in the Bay, or coming over to the Presidio.

They further say that there is no lodging to be had in the Presidio, where they could live for a year ; if they are required to attend the Ayuntamiento, which is untrue, (although allowing them to say so) for they depart from truth and purity, which they ought to have before an authority (as likewise to put in their memorial the names of other persons who did not know it, which can be referred to them,) for it is evident that the commandant of the Presidio found residences to the officers of the present Ayuntamiento, as soon as the same was installed. In conclusion, Sir, the land or coast where the memorialists live, had belonged to the jurisdiction of the Presidio since the former time, as besides the Bay of San Francisco is the one forming that of the same port; the Ranchos of Castros, which lies in the front of the same Presidio, (a little to the north) is only distance by sea scarcely two leagues, and that of Peraltas on the west, a little more than two leagues, which was undoubtedly the fact and principles upon which the Honorable Deputation grounded its resolution of the latter part of 1834, (depending upon that vicinity to proceed to the formation of the Ayuntamiento (reporting to the Supreme Government and the Commanding General and Political Chief, being then the late Don Jose Figueroa, supported by the same reasons to as the corporation (la corporacion) proceeded to the complying of the resolution)—thus ordering the commandant only of San Francisco by as besides the said late Jose Figueroa had to cause the limits of the jurisdiction of San Francisco to be marked out (although for the time being) as proved by his official note now in this archive, that portion of land and vicinity was also incorporated. All this is brought to the superior knowledge of your Excellency in order that, notwithstanding the above statement, Y. E. may direct what may be deemed proper on the subject.

PORT OF SAN FRANCISCO, Dec. 20, 1835.

FRANCISCO DE HARO.

FRAN^{co}. SANCHEZ, Sec'y.

No. XXX.

EXHIBIT No. 3 TO DEPOSITION OF M. G. VALLEJO IN THE CASE.

Election of Electors of the Ayuntamiento in the Pueblo of San Francisco, IN DECEMBER, 1835 FOR 1836.

In the PUEBLO of San Francisco de Asis, on the 13th day of the month of December, 1835, the Municipality of this Demarcation in the *Plaza* of said PUEBLO. The corresponding call being previously made by billets by its constitutional Alcalde, for the purpose of holding the primary *junta* to elect nine electors, which correspond according to the number of inhabitants of this section, and the said constitutional Alcalde having begun the matter as President, the said election took place by means of billets, which were successively presented, all the citizens concurring; which being made public by the Secretary, who was also the Secretary of the Ayuntamiento, they in continuation took notes, from which there resulted by majority for electors. Citizens Bartolo Bajorques with 16 votes; José de la Cruz Sanchez, 14; Felipe Briones, 14; Gabriel Castro, 13; Manuel Sanchez, 11; Francisco Sanchez, 11; Ygnacio Peralta, 11; Joaquin Estudillo, 11; Candalario Valencia, 10; who were officially notified, and understood their appointments, and were to meet on Sunday, the 27th of the present month, in order to hold the electoral Junta, for the election of Alcalde, second Regidor, and Sindic Procurador, for the following year of 1836; and the act being concluded, the Junta dissolved, and the President and Secretary signed.

FRANCISCO DE HARO, President.

FRANCISCO SANCHEZ, Secretary.

No. XXXI.

EXHIBIT S TO DEPOSITION OF R. C. HOPKINS.

Espediente of De Haro for the Rancho San Pedro.

MARCH 7TH, 1836.

Seal of the Third Class. Two Reales.

Provisionally authorised by the Maritime Custom House of Monterey of Upper California, for the years 1834 and 1835.

To the Superior Political Chief:

Francisco de Haro, appears in due form before your worship, and represents, that in consideration of having, more than a year since, presented himself to the Superior Power of the Territory, soliciting the grant of the tract of land of San Mateo, or San Pedro, or El Corral de tierra on the coast, (either one or the other) ; having in view the fact that the first is occupied by the Indians of the Pueblo of Dolores for the purpose of cultivation, and the third also occupied by the cattle of the same Pueblo, and being well satisfied, as has been well known for many years, that the tract of San Pedro is vacant and unoccupied, he therefore presents himself to the kindly consideration of your worship, soliciting that by virtue of your power you will grant to him the aforesaid tract of San Pedro, its extent being two leagues from North to South (according to the map which accompanies this), so that he may place thereupon the stock that he possesses, this being sufficient for the place.

Wherefore he solicits of your Excellency the said favor, which is just, not sought through malice, is necessary, etc.

Port of San Francisco, 22d of November, 1835.

FRANCISCO DE HARO.

———

In conformity with the superior decree of your worship, commanding the Administrator of this Mission to report with regard to this expediente, I have to say, that the petitioner possesses the requisite qualifications, being a Mexican citizen by birth. The land that he solicits belongs to this community, is pasture land, suitable for crops, and irrigable ; it is not included in the twenty leagues (limitrofes) but in the ten litorally ; it is a little more than four leagues distant from this place and is now occupied by horses, being the most convenient spot for this place, and the coast, it serves as a middle point for the use of both ; moreover the common lands (ejidos y propios) which I think will belong to this place, after it shall have become a Pueblo, have not yet been designated.

It is certain that the said community has alwáys occupied the land, and everything is as I have stated it.

San Francisco de Asis, March 7, 1836.

GUEN^{DO.} FLORES.

———

MONTEREY, March 14, 1836.

In view of the preceding report, the petitioner's request cannot be granted. Let him be notified to that effect, and the espediente recorded in the archives. Señor Don Nicolas Gutierrez, Political Chief (ad interim) of the Territory, thus orders, decrees, signs and duly attests.

NICOLAS GUTIERREZ,

FRANCISCO DEL CASTILLO,

NEGRETE.   Secretary.

At the same date the party interested was duly notified by means of a dispatch.

CASTILLO.

No. XXXII.

Order for the Resurvey of the Buri-Buri Rancho.

MARCH 15TH, 1836.

EXHIBIT NO. 1 TO DEPOSITION OF R. C. HOPKINS, IN THE CASE.

[SEAL.] *Under this date I have written as follows to the constitutional Alcalde of the Port of San Francisco, [al Alcalde Constitutional del Puerto de San Francisco.]*

" By the proceedings heretofore had in regard to the possession held by the " Indians who occupy the tract of land lying between the first willow-grove " (el primer sausal) and San Mateo, contiguous to the Rancho of Buri-Buri " which belongs to Don José Sanchez, it appears that these Indians are in " lawful possession of this tract of land, according to the distribution which was " made conformably to the Regulation of Secularization. But having pro- " ceeded to the survey of four leagues of land granted by the Government to " Don José Sanchez in the place called Buri-Buri without prejudice to the co- " terminous neighbors (los colindantes), the result is that in order to complete " the said four leagues of land they have measured as far as ' Laguna de las " Salinas,' including within these boundaries the lands occupied by these " Indians. For this reason the survey is wrongly made, because it has intruded " into the lands of strangers and, consequently, another survey should be had, " completing the four leagues of land in some other direction (por otro rumbo) " as may be most suitable, leaving free the lands which the Indians now occupy, " and without causing damage to any other co-terminous neighbor."

This I transcribe for your information, at the same time notifying the person who occupies the land in question that there shall be marked out to him the portion of land which belongs to him, in order to prevent controversies, and that every one may know what his boundaries are.

Dios y Libertad!

Monterey, March 15, 1836. NICOLAS GUTIERREZ.

Señor Administrator de San Francisco de Assis.

NO. XXXIII.

EXPEDIENTE OF THE **PRESIDIAL PUEBLO** OF MONTEREY RESPECTING ITS **EJIDOS**, OR SUBURBS.

March 1836.

[EXHIBIT " H " TO DEPOSITION OF R. C. HOPKINS.]

Constitutional Ayuntamiento of Monterey.

On the 5th of December last, the Ayuntamiento of this port stated to your Antecessor (predecessor) as follows :

4*

" In session of the 5th of this month, the Ayuntamiento approved of the proposition made by the Committee on Vacant Lands, in the report made by them in the espediente containing the petition of Gabriel Espinosa for a (solar) town lot, for building and laboring purposes, in a spot that belongs to the (ejidos) common lands, which proposition says " let inquiry be made (by means of an oficio) of the Superior Political Chief, whether it is his duty to grant the lands referred to, or whether it solely belongs to the Ayuntamiento to dispose of their common lands." In accordance with this decree, I call upon your worship's attention to the matter, renewing the assurances of my respect :"
And as up to date, no answer has been received, and as the expediente, containing the petition of the said Espinosa, which gave rise to this consultation, has been impeded, together with other proceedings of the same nature, the Ayuntamiento decided to transmit this to your worship, that you might advise them as to the matter ; wherefore I now do so, renewing the assurances of their consideration.

JOSE R. ESTRADA.

Jose Maria Maldonado, Secretary.

To the Superior Political }
Chief of the Territory : }

Monterey, Jan. 19, 1836.

[Marginal Decree.]
Let this be transmitted to the Assessor Attorney General of the Territory, for his report.

GUTIERREZ.

To the Ayuntamiento :

It appears that Ramon Estrada, in soliciting the place called del toro, made his application to the Government, and the same course was taken by Juan Antonio Muños with respect to the land called " La puerta del rey i Nacional," both of which are included in the limits of this Port.
If Senor Espinosa solicits a town lot, for building a house, and land for cultivation, under a lease for a limited time, the Corporation may grant it to him ; but if he desires the absolute ownership of the same, he must take the same course as the others above mentioned. Notwithstanding, the vote of the Ayuntamiento has passed to the Assessor's office, and I am waiting to inform you of the reply. God and Liberty.
Monterey, Jan. 19, 1836.

NICOLAS GUTIERREZ.

The Ayuntamiento of this Port :

Monterey, Jan. 23, 1836.

In session of to-day the Ayuntamiento decided to suspend the discussion relative to common lands (ejidos) until the arrival of the " Consulta " and the report thereupon.

ESTRADA.

Jose Maria Maldonado, Secretary.

Senor Political Chief :

The power inherent in the Territorial Political Chiefs, with respect to granting lands, should only apply to such lands as can be granted for the purpose of colonization, and which do not belong to any private individual or corporation ; and, as the (ejidos) common lands, as well as all lands belonging to the " fundo legal," are the absolute property of the Ayuntamiento, it is clear that, when such lands are in question, there should be no intervention whatever on the part of the Political Chiefs. The law, 4 title 16, lib 7, of the Novisima Recopilacion, confers upon the Ayuntamientos of Municipalities the management of the lands of their fundos, and consequently authorizes them to lease them, putting them up at public auction, and advertising them by the public crier for nine days, afterwards appointing the day for their auction, and adjudging them to the best and highest bidders, provided that they shall not be persons prohibited by law 7, tit. 9, of the books aforesaid (who are "all the members of the Ayuntamiento, including its Secretary") which lease shall endure for five years, in accordance with the Royal Resolution, published in Council on the 27th of May, 1763, which revoked in this respect the instructions given by Charles the Third, for the Administrative Government of the property belonging to the "propios and arbitrios" of the Ayuntamientos, in which it was only permitted to lease for one year.

By virtue of which the Assessor General of the Courts of 1st Instance of the Territory, gives, as his opinion, that your Excellency may return the present consultation to the noble Ayuntamiento, whence it proceeded, in order that, if it meets with your approbation, that body may submit itself to the aforesaid Supreme Resolutions.

MONTEREY, Jan. 20, 1836.   COSURE PEÑA.

In my former official note I promised to return you an "oficio," with the opinion of the Senor "Asesor," into whose hands it passed. This being ready, I transmit it to you, in company with the following declaracion relative to the subject.

The Pueblos that have their Jurisdictional, but not their Municipal Boundary defined, should (by means of the Political Government) send their petition to the Deputation (which petition will be granted by that body ; for this purpose an exact map of the tract petitioned for must be enclosed, as was done in the last year, by this illustrious corporation, when it solicited that its municipal boundaries might be defined. The municipal termino having been defined, and the expenses of the Ayuntamiento being high, it may solicit, through the same channel, that within the boundary assigned, certain lands may be assigned to it as "propios," and the Ayuntamiento may propose, in their petition, those which appear to be the most appropriate. To this effect it will annex to its petition a general account, including both its petty and extraordinary expense, graduated for the term of five years, so that the Deputation and Political Chief, being satisfied with them, may grant the petition. The "termino municipal" and the "terrenos propios" having been defined, the Ayuntamiento may define or assign that which it requires for "ejidos." It results that there is a great difference in the significations of "Termino Jurisdiccional," "Jurisdicion," "Termino Municipal," "Terrenos de propios," and "Ejidos."

For your better comprehension I will make a brief explanation :

By "termino Jurisdiccional," "Jurisdiccion," "Partido," or "Distrito," is understood all that is comprised within the limits, to which the jurisdiction of the Alcalde or Judge of the Pueblo extends.

By "termino Municipal," that land, which has been assigned to the Pueblos for the relief of their herds, within which neither the cattle nor inhabitants of neighboring pueblos can enter, for the purpose of grazing or cutting wood, without being denounced, unless they have some letter of commonalty.

The "terrenos de propios" are lands assigned to the Ayuntamiento, so that, by leasing them to the best bidders, for a term not exceeding five years, they may defray their expenses by the proceeds ; and the Ayuntamiento may propose the amount of rent, mentioning it in the petition which is presented. The lands that remain, after the assignment of the "propios," and that are not granted to any person, remain as vacant lands, at the disposal of the government; and as to those granted and confined within the " termino Municipal," a " censo " may be imposed upon them by assigning them as " de Propios," care being taken that all be conformable to the " reglamento of propios."

And by "Ejidos," are understood lands that are immediate to, and in the circumference of the Pueblo, which serve both for the relief and the convenience of the inhabitants, (poblacion) who may keep therein a few milch cows and horses for their use, and to form walks or alleys which may adorn the entrance of the place, so that the ejidos may have a quarter or a half league around the town, which is sufficient for its ventilation, and the Ayuntamiento may dispose of these lands for building lots.

If any further doubt should occur you may consult me upon the matter, so that everything may be duly explained. God and Liberty !

Monterey, Jan. 25, 1836.

                                   NICOLAS GUTIERREZ.

To the Illustrious Ayuntamiento of this Port.

                                   Monterey, Jan. 30, 1836.

In session of to-day, this was referred to the Committee on Lands.

          JOSE MARIA MALDONADO, Secretary.

Illustrious Ayuntamiento :

The committee on vacant lands (valdios) have duly considered the " consultar " that the illustrious Ayuntamiento submitted to the Political Chief, and the report as to how this corporation should act with regard to its propios and ejidos, and the committee cannot, beyond a doubt, approve of any other course than that minutely set forth in the report of the Political Governor, of January 25 last.

The Committee, therefore, submits to this illustrious body the following proposition :

That the expediente pass to the proper committee, that it may proceed to the formation of a general account of the expenses of the Municipality, in the forms prescribed by the Political Governor in his report of the 25th of January last.

Monterey, March 11, 1836.

                                   SANTIAGO WATSON.

Bonifaciode }
Madariaya }   Monterey, March 21, 1836.

In session of to-day, the Illustrious Ayuntamiento approved of the following proposition :

1st. It approves of the proposition which concludes the foregoing report of the committee.

2d. Therefore, let the expediente pass to the Committee of Finance " (de contaduria)" in connection with those of " Arbitrios " and " Valdios," (vacant lands) in order that the first and second may set forth the expenses of this municipality, and that the third may prepare the maps of the lands to be solicited as " propios " of this pueblo and frame the petition to be presented to the Excellent Territorial Deputation. And by virtue of and in compliance with this decree, let the expediente pass to the aforesaid committees, who are requested to give the matter their prompt attention and report thereon as speedily as possible.

                                   ESTRADA.

Jose Maria Maldonado, Secretary.

No. XXXIV.

GRANT OF LAND BY THE AYUNTAMIENTO OF SAN FRANCISCO TO WILLIAM RICHARDSON IN 1836.

[Exhibit Y Z in the case.]

Most Illustrious Ayuntamiento :

William Richardson, a citizen and resident of this Port, in due form represents that he is resolved to establish himself in Yerba Buena, and for that effect requires to build a house, for which he applies to your Superiority, by using your faculties to deign to grant him a lot of one hundred varas square, in Yerba Buena, in front of the Plaza and anchorage of the ships.

For which effect I request that you will deign to grant this my petition, which is on common paper, there being no stamp as corresponds.

San Francisco, June 1, 1836.

(Signed,)   WM. RICHARDSON.

This Corporation being satisfied of the good services that the party requesting has rendered to this jurisdiction since his arrival in this country, with his different trades as bricklayer, surgeon and carpenter, and having married one of the first in the country, and that the said party has resolved to follow his good conduct, this Corporation has concluded to grant to Mr. William Richardson the lot of one hundred varas square, which he requests in Yerba Buena, so that he may establish himself there with his family.

Date as above.

JOSE JOAQUIN CARRILLO,
Alcalde Constitutional.

No. XXXV.

Exhibits No. 8 and 9 to Deposition of M. G. Vallejo.

ELECTION FOR THE AYUNTAMIENTO OF 1838.

December 3d, 1837.

In the Pueblo of San Francisco de Asis, on the third day of the month of December, one thousand eight hundred and thirty-seven, the municipality of this comprehension being assembled in the *plaza* of said Pueblo, for the purpose of celebrating the " Junta primaria," according to custom and the laws on the matter ; the act of voting having first taken place for president, secretaries, and the corresponding inspectors, and consequently the first in continuation (proceeded) to take the votes, according to the order of the tickets previously distributed by the committee appointed for this purpose, and in conclusion of every act. The regulation of suffrages being made, it resulted in favor of each one of the citizens present; from it then resulted electors by the majority of votes given, citizen Francisco Guerrero with 29 votes, Francisco de Haro with 26, Vicente Miramontes with 21, Antonio Maria Peralta with 20, Jose Antonio Alviso with 17, Juan Bernal with 16, Leander Galindo with 15, Juan Cornelio Bernal with 14, Domingo Sais with 13, which was made known to them for their information, by means of an official letter which will serve them for credentials, and this act being concluded, the Junta was dissolved, and there was recorded officially all that had been done, which was signed by the president, secretaries and inspectors, this day of its date.

President,
FRANCISCO DE HARO
Secretaries,
FRANCISCO G. PALOMARES,
FRANCISCO SANCHEZ.
Inspectors,
ANTONIO MARIA PERALTA,
J. DE LA C. SANCHEZ.

JANUARY 8TH, 1838.

In the Pueblo of San Francisco de Asis, on the eighth day of the month of January, one thousand eight hundred and thirty-eight, the electors of this municipality, citizens Francisco de Haro, Francisco Guerrero, Antonio Maria Peralta, José Cornelio Bernal, José Antonio Alviso, Juan Bernal, Leandro Galendo, Domingro Sais and Vincente Miramontes, being assembled in the Constitutional Hall of said Pueblo to celebrate the secondary Electoral Junta, the reading of the Act of the previous Sunday the 3d (inst.), was proceeded to, and having been approved in continuation (they proceeded) to the appointment of the committee to examine the credentials of said Señores, which were also approved; in continuation the voting for Alcalde was commenced by means of tickets, and the computation of votes being made, citizen Francisco de Haro resulted (elected) by a majority of four votes; for which reason, and because no objection was presented against the person elected, he remained in effect elected Alcalde for the present year of 1838. In continuation they proceeded to vote for 2d Regidor, and being performed in the same terms as the preceding, and the computation of votes made, citizen Domingo Sais received the majority of four votes, wherefore he was elected 2nd Regidor; in continuation the voting was continued for "Sindico Procurador," in the same form as those before appointed, and from it resulted citizen José Rodriguez, uniting the majority of five votes, and in effect he was elected "Sindico." Lastly, having asked if there was any objection against any of those elected, and none having been presented, they were approved, and the whole act was considered as concluded, and it was recorded officially, which the President and Secretary signed this day of its date.

IGNACIO MARTINEZ,
FRANCISCO SANCHEZ.

No. XXXVI.

GRANT OF LAND BY FRANCISCO SANCHEZ, MILITARY COMMANDANT, TO APOLONARIO MIRANDA, NOVEMBER 16, 1838.

PREFECT'S GRANT OF 100-VARAS, OJO DE AGUA DE FIGUEROA.

[Exhibit W in the Case.]

To the Military Commandant:

Apolinario Miranda, a Corporal of Squadron of the Company of San Francisco, comes before your Excellency and presents himself by means of this writing, and states that he is about leaving the service and he is desirous of establishing himself and family in the Presidio, and finding that you have the power to grant lots, he requests that you will grant to him the lot known as the " Ojo de Figueroa," where he has provisionally built a house.

To which effect he humbly begs that you will attend to his request, by which he will receive a favor and justice.

Presidio of San Francisco.

APOLONARIO MIRANDA.

——

San Francisco, November 16, 1838.

I hereby grant unto the party interested the lot he requests, as regulated by laws, and it comprises one hundred varas square.

SANCHEZ.

——

No. XXXVII.

GOVERNOR ALVARADO'S REGULATIONS RESPECTING MISSIONS, JANUARY 1839.

[Halleck's Rep. App. 17; 1 Rockwell 462; Jones' Report, page 66; App. 17.]

The fact of there not having been published in due season a set of regulations, to which the management of the administrators of the missions ought to have been subject from the moment the so-called secularization was attempted, having caused evils of great transcendency to this Upper California, as these officers, authorized to dispose without limit of the property under their charge do not know how to act in regard to their dependence upon the political government and that of the most excellent department junta, not being at present in session to consult with respecting the necessary steps to be taken under such circumstances, since the regulations of said secularization neither could nor can take effect on account of the positive evils attending the fulfilment thereof, as experience itself has demonstrated, has induced this government, in consideration of the pitiful state in which said establishments at present are, to dictate these provisional regulations, which shall be observed by said administrators, who will subject themselves to the following articles :

Article 1. All persons who have acted as administrators of missions will, as soon as possible, present to the government the accounts corresponding to their administration for due inspection, excepting those persons who may have already done so.

Art. 2. The present administrators who, at the delivery of their predecessors, may have received said documents as belonging to the archives, will return them to the parties interested, who, in virtue of the foregoing article, will themselves forward them to government, they being solely responsible.

Art. 3. Said officers will likewise remit those belonging to their administration up to the end of December of last year, however long they may have been in office.

Art. 4. Said officers will remit, as soon as possible, an exact account of the debts owing by and to the missions which at different times have been contracted.

Art. 5. Under no title or pretext whatsoever shall they contract debts, whatever may be the object of their inversion, nor make sales of any kind either to foreign merchants or to private persons of the country, without the previous knowledge of government, for whatever may be done to the contrary shall be null and without effect.

ART. 6. The amounts owed by the establishments to merchants and private persons cannot be paid without an express order from government, to which must likewise be sent an account of all such property of each mission as it has been customary to make such payments with.

ART. 7. Without previous permission from said government, no kind of slaughtering of cattle shall take place, except what is necessary for the maintenance of the Indians, and the ordinary consumption of the house; and even with respect to this, the persons in charge will take care that, as far as possible, no female animals be killed.

ART. 8. The traffic of mules and horses for woolen manufactures, which has hitherto been carried on in the establishments, is hereby absolutely prohibited; and in lieu thereof, the persons in charge will see that the looms are got into operation, so that the wants of Indians may thus be supplied.

ART. 9. At the end of each month, they will send to government a statement of the ingress and egress of all kinds of produce that may have been warehoused or distributed, it being understood that the Indians at all times are to be provided for in the customary manner with such productions; to which end the administrators are empowered to furnish them with those which are manufactured in the establishment.

ART. 10. The administrators will in this year proceed to construct a building, on account of the establishment, to serve them for habitation, and they may choose the locality which they may deem most convenient, in order that they may vacate the premises which they now occupy.

ART. 11. They shall not permit any individual of those called *de razon* (white people) to settle themselves in the establishments while the Indians remain in community.

ART. 12. They will at an early period present a census of all the inhabitants, distinguishing their classes and ages, in order to form general statistics; and they will likewise mention those who are emancipated and established on the lands of said establishments.

ART. 13. The establishments of San Carlos, San Juan Bautista, and Sonoma are not comprehended in the orders of this regulation. The government will regulate them in a different manner; but the administrators, who at different times may have had the management of their property, will be subject to the orders contained in articles 1 and 2.

ART. 14. They will likewise remit an account of all persons employed under them, designating their monthly pay, according to the orders which may have been given, including that of the reverend padres, with the object of regulating them according to the means of each establishment; and these salaries shall not be paid now nor hereafter with self-moving property; (cattle).

ART. 15. The administrators will, under the strictest responsibility, fulfil these orders, with the understanding that, in the term of one month, they shall send the information required of them.

ART. 16. Government will continue making regulations respecting everything tending to establish the police to be observed in the establishments, and the manner to be observed in making out the accounts.

ART. 17. For the examination of these accounts, and everything thereto relating, the government will appoint a person with the character of inspector, with a competent salary, to be paid out of the funds of said establishments; and this person will establish his office where the government shall appoint, and have regulations given therefor in due time.

No. XXXVIII.

EXHIBIT NO. 10 TO DEPOSITION OF M. G. VALLEJO.

ORDER FOR CONSTITUTIONAL ELECTIONS JANUARY 17TH, 1839.

Juan Baptiste Alvarado, Governor ad interim, of the Department of the Californias:

Whereas, it has become necessary to give due fulfilment to the law of November 30th, 1836, sent in the last mail by the Supreme Government for its observance in the Department, directing its proper fulfilment, and that the elections be commenced for the organization of the Constitutional system, and desirous that in conformity to it there be established the authorities who are to act, I have ordered that for that object there be observed, in this Alta California, the following articles :

1st. The Constitutional Elections will be proceeded with conformably to the law of November 30th, 1836.

2d. These elections will commence the first Sunday of next March, and will terminate the third of the same month.

3d. According to the order which the Towns hold, there will be named an elector for each one of the following : San Francisco, San José, Villa of Branceforte, Monterey and Santa Barbara, Los Angeles, and San Diego.

4th. In accordance with the foregoing article, the Port of San Diego will recognize the city of Los Angeles as the head (cabecera) of Partido ; the Villa of Branceforte, Monterey ; and the frontier of the north of San Francisco, the Port of that name.

5th. This government will place itself in agreement with the Political Chief *ad interim*, of Baja California, in order that directing the corresponding elections in these towns (pueblos) full compliance may be made with what is directed by the laws.

And that it may come to the notice of all, I order that it be published by proclamation, and be posted in the usual public places.

SANTA BARBARA, January 17, 1839.

JUAN B. ALVARADO.

[The following endorsement is on the outside of the within document :]

I transmit to you this proclamation to which official communication of the 17th of January, 1839, refers, and to which I annex it ; in order that being advised of its contents you may return it to me to record it.

HARO.

To the person in charge (Sor Encargado) of Contra Costa, Citizen Yg° Peralta.

No. XXXIX.

GOVERNOR ALVARADO'S REGULATIONS RESPECTING MISSIONS, MARCH, 1839.

Regulations of Governor Alvarado respecting the missions of California, obligations of the mayordomos, inspectors, &c., dated March 1, 1840.

[Halleck's Rep. App. 18 ; 1 Rockwell, 466 ; Jones' Report, page 68 ; Appendix, 18.]

Experience having proved in an undoubted manner that the missions of Upper California, for want of regulations organizing the management of the persons in charge of them, have in a short time suffered reverses and losses of great moment, the many abuses which were found to exist in the administration of the property of said missions obliged this government to issue the regulation of 17th January last year; but as it has been found that those have not been sufficient to root out the evils which are experienced, particularly on account of the high salaries with which the establishments are burdened, and which they cannot support, and being desirous to establish economy and a regular administration until the supreme government determine what it may deem proper, I publish the present regulations which are to be strictly observed :

ARTICLE 1. The situations of administrators in the missions of Upper California are abolished, and in their stead mayordomos are established.

ART. 2. These mayordomos will receive the following salaries : Those of San Diego and San Juan Capistrana, $180; those of Santa Barbara, San Luis Obispo, San Francisco de Asis, and San Rafael, $240; those of San Buenaventura, La Purissima, San Miguel, and San Antonio, $300; those of San Fernando and Santa Frues, $400; those of San Luis Rey and San Gabriel, 420; the one of Santa Clara, 480 ; and the one of San Jose $600.

ART. 3. The former administrators may occupy said situations, provided, that they be proposed in the manner pointed out by these regulations.

ART. 4. The situation of inspectors and the office established agreeable to the 17th article of the regulations of the 17th of January last year, shall continue, with a salary of $3,000 per annum, and his powers will be hereafter designated.

OBLIGATIONS OF THE MAYORDOMOS.

ART. 5. To take care of everything relative to the advancement of the property under their charge, acting in concert with the reverend padres in the difficult cases which may occur.

ART. 6. To compel the Indians to assist in the labors of the community, chastising them moderately for the faults they may commit.

ART. 7. To see that said Indians observe the best morality in their manners, and oblige them to frequent the church at the days and hours that have been customary, in which matter the reverend padres will intervene in the manner and form determined in the instructions given by the inspector to the administrators.

ART. 8. To remit to the inspector's office a monthly account of the produce they may collect into the storehouses, and an annual one of the crops of grain, liquors, &c., and of the branding of all kinds of cattle.

ART. 9. Said account must be authorized by the reverend padres.

ART. 10. To take care that the reverend padres do not want for their necessary aliment, and furnish them with everything necessary for their personal subsistence, as likewise to vaqueros and servants, which they may request for their domestic service.

ART. 11. To provide the ecclesiastical prelates all the assistance which they may stand in need of when they make their accustomed visits to the missions through which they pass ; and they are obliged under the strictest responsibility to receive them in the manner due to their dignity.

ART. 12. In the missions where the said prelates have fixed residence, they will have the right to call upon the mayordomos at any hour when they may require them, and said mayordomos are required to present themselves to them every day at a cartain hour, to know what they may require in their ministerial functions.

ART. 13. To furnish the priest of their respective missions all necessary assistance for religious worship; but in order to invest any considerable amount in this object, they will solicit the permission to do so from government through the medium of the inspector.

ART. 14. To take care that in the distribution of goods received from the respective office to the Indians, the due proportion be observed amongst the different classes and description of persons, to which end the reverend padres shall be called to be present, and they will approve of the corresponding list of distribution.

ART. 15. To observe all the orders which they receive from the inspector's office emanating from the government, and to pay religiously all drafts addressed to them by said conduct and authorized by said government.

ART. 16. They will every three months send to the respective office a list of the goods and necessaries they may stand in greatest need of, as well for covering the nakedness of the Indians and carrying on the labor of the establishment, so as to provide for the necessities of the priests and religious worship, so that comparing these requisitions with the stock on hand, the best possible remedy may be applied. They will take care to furnish the necessary means of transport and provisions to the military or private persons who may be traveling on the public service, and they will provide said necessaries as well for the before mentioned persons, as for the commanders of stations who may ask for assistance for the troops ; and send in a monthly account to the inspector, that he may recover the amount from the commissariat.

ART. 18. They will likewise render assistance to all other private individuals who may pass through the establishments, charging them for food and horses an amount proportioned to their means.

ART. 19. They will take care that the servants under them observe the best conduct and morality, as well as others who pass through or remain in the establishments ; and in urgent cases they are authorized to take such steps, as they may consider best adapted to preserve good order.

ART. 20. They may without any charge make use of the provisions produced by the establishments for their own subsistence and that of their families.

ART. 21. They may employ as many servants as they consider necessary for carrying on the work of the community, but their situations must be filled entirely by natives of the establishments themselves.

ART. 22. Said mayordomos are merely allowed to request the appointment of a clerk to carry on their correspondence with the inspector's office.

ART. 23. After the mayordomos have for one year given proofs of their activity, honesty, and good conduct in the fulfilment of their obligations, they shall be entitled (in times of little occupation) to have the government allow the Indians to render them some personal services in their private labors ; but the consent of the Indiians themselves must be previously obtained.

ART. 24. The mayordomos cannot make any purchase of goods from merchants, nor make any sale of the produce or manufactures of the establishments, without previous authority from government. (Second.) Dispose of the Indians in any case for the service of private persons without a positive superior order. (Third.) Make any slaughtering of cattle, except what shall be ordered by the inspectors, to take place weekly, extraordinarily, or annually.

OBLIGATIONS OF THE INSPECTORS.

ART. 25. To make all kinds of mercantile contracts with foreign vessels and private persons of the country for the benefit of the missions.

ART. 26. To provide said establishments with the requisite goods and necessaries mentioned in the lists of the mayordomos, taking into consideration the stock of each establishment.

ART. 27. To draw the bills for the payment of the debts contracted by his office and those already due by the establishments.

ART. 28. He shall be the ordinary conductor of communication between the government and the subaltern officers of said missions, as well as between all other persons who may have to apply to government respecting any business relative to said establishments.

ART. 29. He will pay the salaries of the mayordomos and other servants, take care that they fulfil their obligations, and propose to government, in conjunction with the reverend padres, the individuals whom they may consider best qualified to take charge of the missions.

ART. 30. He will determine the number of cattle to be killed weekly, annually, or on extraordinary occasions.

ART. 31. He will form the interior regulations of his office, and propose to government the subalterns which he may judge necessary for the proper management thereof.

GENERAL ORDERS.

ART. 32. All merchants and private persons who have any claims on said missions, will in due time present to the inspector an account of the amounts due to them, with the respective vouchers, in order that the government may determine the best manner of settling them, as the circumstances of said mission may permit.

ART. 33. With respect to the missions of San Carlos, San Bautista, Santa Cruz, La Solidad, and San Francisco Solano, the general government will continue regulating them as circumstances may permit.

ART. 34. Officers and magistrates of all kinds are at liberty to manifest to government the abuses they may observe in those charged with fulfiling these regulations, so that a quick remedy may be applied.

ART. 35. The government, after previously hearing the opinions of the reverend padres, will arrange matters respecting the expenses of religious worship and the subsistence of said padres, either by fixing a stated amount for both objects, or in some other manner which may be more convenient towards attending to their wants.

ART. 36. All prior regulations and orders conflicting with the present are annulled ; and if any doubt occur respecting their observance, the government will be consulted through the established channel.

ART. 37. During the defect or temporary absence of the mayordomos, the reverend padres will in the mean time take charge of the establishments.

No. XL.

JUSTICE DE HARO TO THE GOVERNOR.

PETITION FOR LOTS IN YERBA BUENA, REFERRED TO GOVERNOR, FEBRUARY 27TH, 1839.

[California Archives, Vol. I, Juzgados, p. 282. Exhibit J to deposition of R. C. Hopkins in the Case.]

Juzgado of San Francisco.

I submit for the consideration of your Excellency the petitions of the citizens Valencio and Jose Rodriquez for solars at the point of Yerba Buena, where, as they represent to me, they desire to settle. Your Excellency will resolve in relation to said petition, what may be judged proper. God and Liberty.

SAN FRANCISCO, February 27th, 1839.

FRANCISCO DE HARO.

No. XLI.

NO JAIL AT SAN FRANCISCO IN FEBRUARY, 1839.

[Exhibit K to Deposition of R. C. Hopkins in the Case. California Archives, Vol. I, of Juzgados, page 283.]

JUSTICE DE HARO TO GOV. ALVARADO. NO MEANS OF SECURING A CRIMINAL IN SAN FRANCISCO.

Juzgado of San Francisco.

From the scattered condition of the inhabitants of the place, from the fact that each one has his agricultural and stock interests at a great distance, (from this place) it results, that there are very few remaining to guard the criminal José Anto. Galindo, and these cannot spare the time from their personal business. These facts induce me to consult your Excellency in relation to the removal of the said Galindo to the Pueblo of San José, since at that place there is a " pueblo unido," (united people) possessing the means of obtaining assistance and other circumstances wanting at this place, such as a jail and means of subsistence ; for these reasons I think it advisable to remove said Galindo to San José. Your Excellency will be pleased, however, to resolve in relation to the matter, and determine what is necessary to be done in the premises.

God and Liberty.

SAN FRANCISCO, February 27th, 1839.

FRANCISCO DE HARO.

No. XLII.

ALCALDE DE HARO TO GOV. ALVARADO. REPORT OF PETITION OF FELIPE GOMEZ FOR LOT IN DOLORES, APRIL 20TH, 1839.

[Exhibit L to Deposition of R. C. Hopkins. California Archives, Unbound Documents.]

In compliance with the Superior Decree of the 20th of March, ulto. of this year, which is found upon the margin of the petition of Felipe Gomez for a house lot in the ex-mission of San Francisco de Asiz, I have to say : That in view of its being named as the *cabecera* of the Partido, with the title of Establishment of Dolores, and that this circumstance gives it a character of Pueblo, and believing for this reason that the inhabitants who petition (for lots) may establish themselves in the same, there may be conceded to the petitioner the lot for which he asks, notwithstanding he does not designate a fixed place, or the number of varas. In case your Excellency shall see proper to concede the same, you will be pleased to dictate the necessary measures for the survey of the same, and the order to be observed with this and successive petitioners.

ESTABLISHMENT OF DOLORES, April 20, 1839.

FRANCISCO DE HARO.

No. XLIII.

GUERRERO, JUSTICE OF THE PEACE OF SAN FRANCISCO, PROCLAIMS CERTAIN MUNICIPAL LAWS FOR THE GOVERNMENT OF THE **PUEBLO OF SAN FRANCISCO,** MAY 26, 1839.

[Exhibit No. 15 to Deposition of R. C. Hopkins, California Archives, Vol. V, Monterey, page 413.]

Francisco Guerrero, Justice of the Peace of this Section of San Francisco, of the Department of Alta California, desiring to promote the order and good management of the PUEBLO under his charge, in conformity with Article 29th of the Sixth Law of the 30th of November, 1836, makes known :

ART. 1st. That any one intending to open a public store shall apply to this Juzgado for a license, in order that he may know the Municipal taxes, according to the bando heretofore published by the Most Excellent Deputation, and the restrictions to be observed in his mercantile business, since without the said license nothing can be sold. Neither can any one who does not own property sell cattle, without acquainting this Juzgado of the fact.

2d. That no hides shall be delivered unless they have the mark established by the Illustrious Ayuntamiento ; and persons making payments of hides shall give a memorandum that they have a right to do so, and if they do not they cannot remain in the Juzgardo until they have justified themselves.

3d. No transactions shall be had with the children of a family, nor servants or domestics, without the knowledge of their parents, since otherwise they will be responsible under the law ; and the same rules are applicable to anything stolen or taken without the knowledge of the owner.

4th. That all persons who may own stock in this community must have their brands and marks, which shall be registered, so that their property shall be known, which must not be without a mark ; inasmuch as it is necessary, when stock belonging to any one beyond this section is placed in the same, to make known when they are entered and when withdrawn, otherwise they cannot be claimed, nor can the charges be made unless notice is given as to their admission.

5th. No person who may have stock in this community shall mark their stock in the fields (campo,) nor brand beyond the time for branding, without informing this Juzgado, or the Admr. of the Establishment of Dolores, the stock of the inhabitants (vecindario) being in his charge, nor sell any unmarked stock without proof that the same is his property.

6th. That all the inhabitants owning stock shall meet at the Rodees which are given, at the appointed times, or shall send some one in their place, in case they shall not be able to attend, otherwise they shall pay one dollar to one who shall be appointed ; whereupon, on the meeting of the vecindario [inhabitants,] persons shall be appointed to take charge, who will be accompanied by the persons designated for the punctual discharge of their duties.

7th. The wood-cutters shall pay fifty cents for each wagon going beyond the demarcation of the PUEBLO.

And in order that this may reach the notice of all, for its due fulfillment, it shall be posted in the public places. Given in the PUEBLO of San Francisco on the 26th of May, 1839.

FRANCISCO GUERRERO.

V. Monterey, 413.

No. XLIV.

GUERRERO, JUSTICE TO THE PEACE OF SAN FRANCISCO TO PREFECT CASTRO, ABOUT SOLARES AT THE MISSION, JULY 15, 1839.

[Exhibit **N** to Deposition of R. C. Hopkins. California Archives, Vol. V, Monterey, p. 408.]

Juzgado de Paz of San Francisco:

The residents [vecinos] of this municipality have made various verbal representations to me, to the end, that through me they might receive the necessary license to establish themselves in this Establishment, where they are desirous of uniting themselves to form a settlement. This project is of public utility, which will result beneficially to the inhabitants, and the Government can be better administered in all its branches. All are now dispersed, [todos se hayan dispersos,] and this condition of society is not the best for the present age, in which civilization is an object that particularly attracts the attention of the Departmental Government. I submit this proposition to your *Señoria* [worship,] in order that on placing the matter before his Excellency, the Governor, he may be pleased to provide in favor of the inhabitants that make this representation through me, conceding to them the solares which they need in the said Establishment on which to build their houses, if the same should be within your authority ; or operate, if it should be necessary, and his Excellency should think it proper, in concert with the Most Excellent Departmental Junta.

On saying this to your Señoria [worship,] I have the honor to protest the assurances of my esteem and regard.

God and Liberty.

San Francisco, July 15, 1839.

FRANCISCO GUERRERO.

No. XLV.

GUERRERO, JUSTICE OF THE PEACE, NOMINATES TO THE PREFECT, JUAN FULLER, AS SYNDIC OF SAN FRANCISCO, JULY 20, 1839.

[Exhibit No. 17 to Deposition of R. C. Hopkins, California Archives, Vol. V, Monterey, page 422.]

JUZGADO OF SAN FRANCISCO. [JUZGADO DE PAZ DE S. F.]

It is necessary to appoint a Sindico Procurador for this place [punto,] for the better management of the Municipal rents ; wherefore, I hope your Excellency, in the exercise of your authority, will be pleased to make the appointment.

I would propose to your Excellency, the appointment of Don Juan Fuller, as a suitable person to fill said office.

God and Liberty.

San Francisco, July 20, 1839.

FRANCISCO GUERRERO.

To the Sor Prefect of the 1st District.

No. XLVI.

ESPEDIENTE HAD BY CITIZEN CORNELIO BERNAL, ON AP-
PLICATION FOR THE PLACE CALLED LAS SALINAS. (177.)

[Exhibit No. 13 to Deposition of R. C. Hopkins.]

1835–1840.

STAMP THIRD, TWO REALS.

*Provided provisionally by the Marine Custom House of Monterey, for the
years 1839 and 1840. Anto. Ma. Asio.*

Alvarado, Marine Custom House of }
Monterey. [Place of Eagle.] }

José Cornelio Bernal, a resident of San Francisco, before your worship
appears and says : That having made an application for the rancho called
Las Salinas to the late Governor Don José Figueroa, and the said Don
José Figueroa having given me a document therefore, by way of a loan,
I have resided in the said ranch up to the present time; and I have consulted
with the visitor and the superintendent of the said mission, they say that it does
not need the said tract : and annexing hereto the document and sketch, as
necessary, I pray your worship will be pleased to grant this my prayer, a favor
which I hope to receive through the well known kindness of your worship. I
swear as required, &c.

MONTEREY, October 3, 1839.
At the request of the petitioner, I signed.

JORGE ALLEN.

[The following order was written on the margin of the above petition.]

SAN JUAN DE CASTRO, October 4, 1839.

Let the Justice of the Peace of San Francisco report on the subject-matter
of this petition, and next let it be transmitted to the Superintendent of the Establishment of Dolores, in order to state what may occur to him. In the absence of the Prefect. JUAN ANZAR.

———

JUSTICE COURT OF SAN FRANCISCO, }
October 8, 1839. }

In accordance with the foregoing order regarding the application, I have to
say, that it is sometime ago that citizen José Cornelio Bernal has possessed,
with his cattle, the tract of land called the Rincon de las Salinas, and there are
on the same private stock. It is dependent on the seasons ; it is not comprehended within the twenty border leagues, but in the littoral ones ; and the said
Bernal is recommendable for the services that he has rendered and is rendering
in this municipality.

F. GUERRERO.

———

SUPERINTENDENCY OF THE ESTABLISHMENT OF DOLORES, }
October 8, 1839. }

In conformity with the preceding order of 4th of October of the present
year, the undersigned states, with regard to the application made by citizen
José Cornelio Bernal, that this establishment is not in need of the tract of land
petitioned by the said party, for the greater number of cattle belonging to the
establishment is on the place called Los Pilarcitos, on the coast.

Stamp third, two reals.

Provisionally provided by the Marine Custom House of Monterey, for the years 1839 and 1840.

ALVARADO, ANTONIO MARIA ASIO.

JOSE DE LA C. SANCHEZ.

MONTEREY, October 10, 1839.

Upon viewing the petition wherewith this espediente begins, the report of the Justice of the Peace of San Francisco, and that of the Superintendent of the Mission of San Francisco, and other proceedings which were had, and ought to have been viewed in conformity with the law and regulation, I do declare Don José Cornelio Bernal owner in full property of the place called Las Salinas, with the Potrero Viejo, bounded by the Mission of San Francisco, the sea, and the lands of the Visitacion. And its extent is one league, a little more or less, as explained in the sketch which is annexed to this espediente, to be subject to the conditions which shall be set out in the title.

Don Manuel Jimeno Casarin, Chief Member of the Honorable Junta of the Department of California, in exercise of the government of the same, thus did command it, decree and sign.

MANUEL JIMENO.

FRANCISO C. ARCE, Chief Officer.

OFFICE OF THE SEC'Y OF THE DEPART. JUNTA OF CAL. }
MONTEREY, May 19, 1840. }

Account having been given of the (Espediente) to the Honorable Departmental Junta, the same resolved, at the session of this day, that it should be referred to the Committee on Agriculture.

JOSE Z. FERNANDEZ, Sec'y.

On the 22d instant the Committee returned it with the accompanying opinion.

FERNANDEZ.

MONTEREY, January 2, 1835.

[Place of a Stamp.]

As from the foregoing reports it appears that the tract of land petitioned by José Cornelio Bernal is the property of the Pueblo of San Francisco De Asis, to which it serves as ejidos for the cattle of the community, (es de la propiedad del pueblo de San Francisco de Asis á quien sirve de ejidos para los ganados del comun,) his application is not admissible, as it cannot be granted in full property : but the party may retain his cattle there in the same way as the other citizens do, (que los demas ciudadanos,) or apply for another place not appropriated, in which case it will be granted. Let this determination be made known to the party, and the espediente be filed. Don José Figueroa, Brigadier-General, Commanding-General, and Governor of the Territory of Upper California, thus commanded it, decreed, and signed, which I attest.

JOSE FIGUEROA.

AGUSTIN V. ZAMARANO, Secretary.

It agrees literally with the original, from which I caused the present copy to be made, at the request of the party, at Monterey, the 3d day of January, 1835. Citizens Brinfario Madacarga and José Ma. Castro, of this place, being witnesses thereto, which I attest.

JOSE FIGUEROA.

5*

Excellent Sir :—The Committee on Agriculture, instructed with reporting upon the application of Don Cornelio Bernal, upon viewing the proceedings had thereon, presents for the determination of your Excellency the following articles :

ART. 1st. The grant made by the Governor, for the time being, Don Manuel Jimeno, of the tract of land called Las Salinas and Potrero Vagi, to the person of Don Cornelio Bernal, is approved.

ART. 2d. Let this Expediente be returned to the Departmental Government for expedient purposes.

JOSE RAFAEL GONZALES,
S. ARGUELLO.

MONTEREY, May 20, 1840.

———

MONTEREY, May 22, 1840.

At the session this day, the Honorable Departmental Junta approved the two articles, wherewith the foregoing report concluded.

M. JIMENO, President.

JOSE Z. FERNANDEZ, Secretary.

On the 30th of the same month, an authenticated copy of the preceding was given to the party.

Manuel Jimeno Casarin, Chief Member of the Most Honorable Junta of the Department of California, in exercise of the government of the same :

Whereas, Citizen Cornelio Bernal has petitioned, for his personal benefit and that of his family, the place known by the name of Las Salinas, with the Potrero Viego, bounded by the Mission of San Francisco, the sea, and the lands of La Visitacion, all the steps and investigations concerning thereto having been had according to the requirements of the law and regulation, exercising the powers which were conferred upon me by the Mexican nation, I have granted to him the above mentioned tract of land, declaring to him the ownership thereof by these presents, to be subject to the approval of the Most Honorable Dept. Junta, and to the following conditions :

1st. He may enclose it, without detriment to the passages, roads, and easements, enjoy it freely and exclusively, applying it to such use or cultivation as may best suit him ; but within one year he shall build a house, and the same shall be inhabited.

2d. He shall apply to the proper officer to give him juridical possession, by virtue of this title, by whom the bounds shall be marked out, at the limits of which he shall place, besides the landmarks, some fruit or useful forest trees.

3d. The tract of land, of which mention is hereby made, consists of one sitio de Granada Mayor, a little more or less, as explained in the sketch attached to the Espediente. The officer who may give this possession may cause the same to be measured according to ordinance, the surplus thereof to remain to the nation for convenient purposes.

4th. If he shall contravene these conditions, he shall forfeit his right to the lands, and they shall be liable to be denounced by another.

Therefore, I do command that this title, being held as good and valid, record thereof be made in the book to which it corresponds, and it be delivered to the party interested, for his safety and other purposes.

Given at Monterey, on the 10th day of October, 1839.

No. XLVII.

[EXHIBIT V TO DEPOSITION OF R. C. HOPKINS.]

ESPEDIENTE OF LEESE FOR THE RANCHO LA VISITATION.

NOVEMBER, 1839.

Seal of the Fourth Class. ¼ *Real.*

Provisionally authorized by the Maritime Custom House of Monterey for the years 1838 and 1840.

ALVARADO. ANTONIO M^{A.} OSIO.

Most Excellent Señor:

The citizen Jacob Luis de Leese, with due respect, and in due form of law, represents to your Excellency, as follows: That being desirous of possessing a place suitable for raising cattle and horses, he solicits the tract known as " La Cañada de Guadalupe and Visitacion, situated in the corner (rinconadaa formed by the hill of San Bruno, being about one league from the Mission of San Francisco, in accordance with the accompanying map, excepting the " Rincon de las Salinas," which appears upon it; defining as boundaries, the said rincon on the North, on the West, the royal road as far as the " Portesuelo," on the South the ranchos of Don Francisco Haro and Don José Sanchez, and on the East the sea.

Wherefore, I beg that your Excellency will grant this my petition, thereby conferring upon me a distinguished favor, I swearing that it is not made through malice, and whatever is necessary.

MONTEREY, Nov. 14, 1839.

JACOB P. LEESE.

To the Governor of this Department.

[Marginal decree.]

SAN JUAN DE CASTRO, Nov. 16, 1839.

Let the Justice of the Peace of San Francisco report as to the contents of this petition.

Señor Prefect:

In compliance with the marginal decree of your worship, I have the honor to report, that the petitioner possesses the legal qualifications required, that the land that he solicits may be granted to him, by virtue of his having formerly received permission from the Government of the Department to occupy it provisionally.

SAN FRANCISCO, Nov. 17, 1839.

FRANCISCO GUERRERO.

SAN JUAN DE CASTRO, Nov. 19, 1839.

Let the above be transmitted to the most Excellent Governor of the Department in order that his Excellency may decide upon it, as he may deem fit.

JOSE CASTRO.

MONTEREY, July 31st, 1841.

In view of the petition which commences this espediente, the report of the Justice of the Peace of the Port of San Francisco and that of the Prefect of

the First District, with all other matters appearing, it seeming to be in conformity with the laws and regulations concerning the matter, I declare Don
Jacob P. Leese to be the owner of that tract of land known as the " Cañada
de Guadalupe, la Visitacion and Rodeo Viejo," it being bounded on the East
by the sea, on the West by the royal road (camino real) and the Portesuelo, on
the North by the rancho of Don Cornelio Bernal, and on the South by that of
Don José Sanchez. Let the corresponding dispatch issue, and be copied in the
proper book and let this Expediente be transmitted to the most Excellent
Junta Departmental, for its approval.

Señor Don Juan B. Alvarado, Constitutional Governor of the Department
of the Californias, thus order, decree. and sign, and which I attest.

Juan B. Alvarado, Constitutional Governor of the Department of the
Californias.

Whereas, Don Jacob Luis de Leese has solicited, for his personal benefit and
that of his family, the tract of land known by the names of " Cañada de
Guadalupe," " la Visitacion," and " Rodeo Viejo," bounded, on the East by
the sea, on the West by the royal road (camino real) and Portesuelo, on the
North by the rancho of Don Cornelio Bernal, and on the South by that of Don
José Sanchez, the necessary steps having been taken and investigations made,
in accordance with the laws and regulations ; by virtue of the power conferred
upon me in the name of the Mexican Nation, I hereby grant to the petitioner
the aforesaid tract of land, declaring him the owner thereof, by these presents,
subject to the approval of the most Excellent Junta Departmental and to the
following conditions :

1st. The petitioner may enclose the land without prejudice to the crossings,
roads and public conveniences (servitudes), he may enjoy it freely and exclusively, devoting it to such use or cultivation as he may see fit, but within one
year, he must build a house which shall be inhabited.

2d. He shall apply to the proper judge who will give him legal possession in
accordance with this decree, and will define the boundaries, at the limits of
which, the petitioner, besides the usual landmarks, shall plant some fruit trees,
or forest trees of some utility.

3d. The said land is two square leagues, more or less, according to the map
which accompanies the espediente. The judge who gives possession, shall have
the land surveyed, in conformity with the ordinance, and the surplus shall
belong to the nation for such purposes as may be convenient.

4th. If the petitioner violates these conditions, he shall forfeit his title to the
land, and be liable to prosecution.

Wherefore, I order that this title be considered firm and valid, a copy of it
shall be made in the proper book, and it shall then be delivered to the party
interested, for his protection and other purposes.

Given in Monterey, July 31st, 1841.

No. XLVIII.

CASTRO, PREFECT, TO THE GOVERNOR, CONCERNING LOTS AT THE MISSION, NOV. 25, 1839.

[Exhibit **O** to deposition of R. C. Hopkins, California Archives, Vol. III, Prefecturas y
Juzgados, Benicia, p. 28.]

Most Excellent Sir :

The residents of the Municipality of San Francisco, have made various *verbal*
representations through the Justice of the Peace, to the end that through this

Prefectura, they may receive the necessary license to establish themselves in the Establishment of Dolores, where they desire to form a settlement. This project is of public utility, which will result in a benefit to the inhabitants. and the government can be administered in all its branches with better results. All *are now dispersed*, and this condition of society is not the most desirable for the present age, in which civilization is one of the objects which particularly attracts the attention of the Departmental Government. I submit this proposition to your Excellency, praying you to make provisions for the inhabitants whom I represent, conceding to them the solares which they need in the said Establishment on which to build their houses.

In saying this to your Excellency, I have the honor to protest the assurances of my esteem and regard.

God and Liberty!

Pueblo of San Juan de Castro, November 25, 1839.

JOSE CASTRO.

[Marginal order of Governor on foregoing representation of *Prefect*.]

November 3d, 1839.

1st. That the Justice of the Peace of San Francisco may concede solares for house lots in the Establishment of Dolores, of the extent of 50 varas or less according to the means of the petitioners.

2d. That the inhabitants may place their stock on the lands surrounding said Establishment and may maintain them there in community as settlers, (pobladores) leaving free the lands of San Mateo, and the coast, the first place, that Indians may establish themselves there at the proper time, and the second place because the little stock that remains subsists there.

3d. That they shall not embarrass in any respect the functions of the administrator nor disturb the Indians so long as the community exists.

No. XLIX.

CERTIFICATE AND GRANT OF 50 VARAS AT THE CAÑUTAL BY GUERRERO, JUSTICE OF THE PEACE.

Francisco Guerrero, }
    to   }
John Vioget. }

[Exhibit XX in the Case.]

San Francisco, January 16, 1840.

There is no stamped paper.

The Departmental Government having expedited an order to my court on the 1st day of the month of November, of the last year, in order that a lot of one hundred varas square should be granted in Yerba Buena in accordance with the plan, and by virtue of having granted and given possession of fifty varas wide and one hundred varas long to the citizen Juan Vioget, the number of varas that he lacks are in the place called the Cañutal, to the west of the road to the Mission of San Francisco, being vacant land.

Wherefore I, Francisco Guerrero, Justice of the Peace of the Jurisdiction of San Francisco, by virtue of the power vested in me, do hereby give him the present, which will serve him as a lawful document under the same terms expressed in the articles comprised in the title expedited to said Vioget on the 15th day of the present month, of the same year. For which I give faith. Dated as above.

FRANCISCO GUERRERO.

No. L.

DOCUMENT D, P, L IN THE CASE.

[California Archives, Legislative Records, Vol. III, page 338.]

EXTRACTS FROM THE MESSAGE OF THE GOVERNOR, FEB. 16TH, 1840, RESPECTING THE PROPIOS AND EJIDOS OF THE PUEBLOS.

At the port of Monterey on the 16th day of the month of February in the year 1840, having Messrs. Manuel Jimeno Cassarin, José Castro, Santiago Arguello, and Rafael Gonzales, met in the Government Hall by summons of the Most Excellent Governor for the purpose of duly taking their oath as members of the Departmental Board, the same was solemnly done; and H. E. the Governor declared the Corporation to have been legally installed, whom H. E. subsequently informed that Messrs. Anastacio Carillo and Manuel Requena, had reported sickness as the cause of their not appearing to fulfil their duty, and that only from the member Mr. Pio Pico no answer had been received at all, and that the Board should qualify their procedure.

After which H. E. brought into the knowledge of the Board through a statement of the actual condition of the Public Administration of the Department as follows :

* * * * * * * *

COMMONS (EJIDOS).

None of the said towns, with the exception of Monterey, has its common and landed property (señalados los ejidos y terrenos de propios) marked out, which to each of the Municipality should be fixed, in order to know its legal property (fundo legal), for which reason the Government on making concession of land in the vicinity thereof, granted the same temporally, waiting for such a regulation ; and regarding the same subject proper reports have been repeatedly asked. Your H. Junta, however, in view of all this—exercising the power conferred upon you in part 1st of the article 45 of the above mentioned law, and in concert with the Government will arrange what may be deemed proper.

JUSTICES OF PEACE [PAZ].

There was a division of the Department into districts and counties, the jurisdiction of Prefect was established respectively at the principal towns over both the former and the latter ; and under the circumstances that Your Hon'ble Junta was not established, and the Ayuntamientos having to take some courses, the Government appointed for the time being a number of Justices of Peace to substitute that of the "Alcaldes" then established ; hoping that your H. Junta by power conferred by the said *Law* will determine such numbers as there ought to be, for which purpose the necessary reports have been received from the Prefect.

AYUNTAMIENTOS.

There is no Ayuntamiento whatever in the Department, for there being no competent number of inhabitants in any of the towns (pueblos) as provided by the Constitution, those then existing had to be dissolved ; and only in the Capital there ought to be one of such bodies. So Your Hon'ble Junta exercising the powers of the law will propose it, and let the Supreme Government approve a place where the same should be established. Nothing can the Government say with regard to the third district, which embraces the greatest portion of the lower California, for owing to the want of couriers undoubtedly from the great distance where the principal town lies, the correspondence of this Government with the Prefect Dn Luis del Castillo Negrete, was obstructed ; but the Government is making arrangements to have a courier to run to that place; and leading reports will be received in time.

*　　*　　*　　*　　*　　*　　*　　*

ADMINISTRATION OF JUSTICE.

The Justices of the Peace having been appointed in the towns of the Departm', those of the principal towns of the District began to exercise the judicial functions in First Instance. It has been of much pain to the Department' Governmt. to see the irregularity and faults, with which the same are managed, both from there being no able persons therein to direct them, and from the great distance, where the Supreme Court of Justice lies, which prevents displaying that desired activity and justice. The want of a Superior Court, which should have been established, has occasioned delay in the decision of criminal cases; prisoners of every class for this reason not only cannot be tried in (Court of) Third Instance, but that being long imprisoned they attract the mercy of the judges through the sufferings endured before they were adjudged; and this is a new evil, which a fair administration suffers. In the midst of such difficulties the Government did not, however cease to co-operate in the punishment of crimes for the sake of public vengeance; but that only in matters of little importance, the judicial branch being exclusively the concern of the proper court; and for which reason multitude of cases is lying paralyzed, which, being impossible to be transmitted to the Capital of the Republic for want of couriers, have to undergo an incalculable delay. The act of the 15th of July of 1839, confers upon Y. H. Junta power to appoint judges and [an] attorney general, who should exercise the judicial functions in the interior, and I do not doubt that upon a good election of such a body depends the organization of a court which in exercise of the power annexed thereto may in a short time contribute to a good so long desired—that is a fair and complete administration of justice, which up to the present time is needed in this Departm'.

MUNICIPAL FUNDS AND REVENUE (PROPIOS Y ARBITRIOS).

Proper reports have been required of the Prefect in order to ascertain the actual state of said funds—specifying the several purposes for which the same are laid out so as to bring the whole to the knowledge of your H. Junta, in order that the Junta may please to give your advice to the consultation, that upon the subject the Government may direct for the purpose of organizing such a branch; that up to the present time there has been no fixed rules to establish an inspection and economy capable of doing in fact any good, for which they are intended. I have stated above how necessary it was to have a regulation of the common lands of the towns and cities; and from hence a new resource will arise for the benefit of the funds if it is considered that the lands which may hereafter be assigned as legal property [señalados para el *fundo legal*] (of towns and cities) [de los *pueblos*] is a foundation, which periodically as it may be established, should produce a municipal ground rent, whether required of the holders thereof annually or by establishing productive landed property. This resource, I do not doubt, will in part contribute to aid the necessities existing in the towns (pueblos,) where for want of means they cannot sometimes support the prisoners in jail; and much less build proper municipal buildings, nor attend to other works of public benefit, convenience or ornament. And I entertain no doubt that Y. H. Junta, with your lights will co-operate to this object, in the persuasion that the Government will use all the means of resort for the purpose of increasing the funds in question.

I have made a statement, although substantial, of the actual estate of the principal branches of the public administration, and will now omit being extensive with other details; as every particular individual, of those composing this respective body, is aware of the palpable necessities. A new epoch of happiness has sprung to the inhabitants of the Department; and Y. H. J. with the legislative character and amidst this stormy weather of difficulties will be able to steer the vessel to a safe port; the Supreme Government is constantly recommending these sacred duties, and affording all protection dependent upon its power; and I as the near agent of the same will not spare any means whatever that is in my power to co-operate to so esteemable an object. So be Y. H. J. the first body to scatter the most abundant benefits over the country, which you represent, and receive as fruit of your tasks an eternal gratitude of its dearest sons.

I congratulate Y. H. Junta for this installation, wishing earnestly that your acts may produce the desired good results.

Which being concluded, His Excellency directed that the minutes should be drawn by the Government Secretary, there being no Secretary to the Junta, wherewith the Junta adjourned (*sine die*) H. E. the Governor and the four members first above mentioned subscribed their names hereto.

MAN^L JIMENO.

S. ARGUELLO.

No. LI.

LIST OF FOREIGNERS IN SAN FRANCISCO, MAY 20, 1840.

[Exhibit No. **10** to deposition of R. C. Hopkins; California Archives, Vol. I of Juzgados, page 305.]

List of the foreigners established in sixth section of San Francisco de Asis, who have presented their letters of security, as required by his Excellency the Governor of the Department on the 2d of the present of 1840 :

Don Jacob P. Leese, 39 years of age, married with a Mexican, a native of the United States of America, merchant, resident of the Department since the 9th of July, 1834, he came by land, presented his letters of naturalization dated Sept. 20th, 1863, by Don Nicolas Gutierrez, and letters of security by Gov. Figueroa, dated July 9th, 1834.

Don Juan C. Fuller, 43 years of age, married with a Mexican woman, a native of London, a seaman by profession, came to the country in the year 1827, he has a document certifying his matriculation given by the Señor Alcalde Don Manuel Jimeno in the year 1834, and his baptism in the Roman Catholic church, in San Blas, by Father José Antonio Espinosa.

Don Juan Calvert Davis, 31 years of age, bachelor, native of England, a carpenter by trade, came to the country by sea in the year 1834, and remained in this jurisdiction till the 14th of September, 1839, as appears by a certificate of the Captain Don José Francisco Snook, has letters of naturalization dated the 24 of September of the last year given by his Excellency the Governor Don Manuel Jimeno, and a passport given by the Señor Prefect.

Don Gregorio Escalante, 30 years of age, bachelor, native of Manilla, a mariner by profession, engaged in mercantile pursuits, came to the country in 1833 by sea, he has no document whatever, says he was admitted by the Comandante Don Man. G. Vallejo, and that he has been a dependent of the late Pedro del Castillo, and that he has petitioned for letters of naturalization.

Don Nathan Spear, 38 years of age, married in the Islands, native of the United States, engaged in mercantile pursuits, came to the country in 1832 by sea, has a letter of security given by his Excellency the President in 1836, for one year, to reside in and travel through the republic.

Don Guillermo H. Davis, 18 years of age, bachelor, a native of Oahu, merchant and clerk of Señor Spear, came by sea to the country in the year 1838 (23d of June), has no documents save a pass from his consul.

Don Daniel Sill, 41 years of age, a native of the United States of America, carpenter, came to the country by land on the 12th of February, 1835, has a passport given him by the late Gov. Figueroa and by the Señor Prefect on the 4th of April, 1840.

Don Juan Frink, 30 years of age, bachelor, a native of England, has been in the country since 1839, came by sea, has a certificate of Señor Wilson that he bears a good character, and a letter of security given by the Prefect on the 4th of April, 1840.

Henry Kirby, 31 years of age, bachelor, native of England, has been in the country since 4th of December, 1839, came by sea with Hinckley.

José Antonio Nief, 26 years of age, bachelor, native of Germany, sailor, was taken prisoner by Don Juan Cooper on the 1st of November, 1839 and liberated by General Vallejo, and is at present a servant of Leese.

Juan Benson, 19 years of age, bachelor, American, sailor, came to this country, (this jurisdiction) on the 27th of February of this year, deserter from schooner Morse, and is retained until the arrival of the Quixote, when he will be given up, as directed by Capt. Paly.

Louis Melurem, 42 years of age, a native of France, sailor, servant, came to the country in 1833, has no documents, save a certificate of the Alcalde David Spencer, Dan Manuel Jimeno and Don José R. Estrada.

Juan Vioget, 41 years of age, a native of Switzerland, merchant, came to the country in the month of October, 1839, was on the coast two years as Captain of the schooner Delmira, and has petitioned for his letters of naturalization, he obtained from the Government a solar in Yerba Buena, and has no document.

Don Juan Bausford *alias* Solis, 36 years of age, a native of Ireland, a sawyer by trade, came to the country by sea in 1829, has letters of naturalization in the Sixth House of Kinlock, presented a certificate of Señor Jimeno given at the time he was Alcalde, of his being a seaman of the third class, and by Don J. B. Cooper.

Cornelio Adam Johnson, 63 years of age, a native of Germany, married in that country, a servant of Leese, came to the country in 1826, came as a soldier from Mexico, has a certificate of the Sergeant José Maria Medrano, a functionary of the Military Comdte. of Monterey, and given on the 31st of July, 1811.

Victor Prudon, 31 years of age, bachelor, a native of France, a teacher by profession, engaged in mercantile pursuits, resident of the capital of Mexico from the year 1827 to the year 1834, when he came to the Department with the colony (of Higar) by order of the Supreme Government as a teacher, as is shown by a document which he exhibited, and a letter of security dated in the year 1828.

SAN FRANCISCO, May 20, 1840.

FRANCISCO GUERRERO.

Note. The name of Don Guillermo Richardson is not entered here, he having for some time been at Saucilito on the other side of the bay. The same remark is made in relation to the foreigners who are in the Sierra, in the neighborhood of the arroyo of San Francisquito, they pertaining to the Pueblo of Alvarado.

The name which is entered here as José Antonio Nief, is understood as applying to Henriques Richer, since he is known by both names.

No. LII.

CASTRO, PREFECT, TO SECRETARY OF STATE ABOUT LOTS
AT THE MISSION OF DOLORES, APRIL 6, 1841.

[Exhibit P to deposition of R. C. Hopkins ; California Archives, Vol. IV, Prefecturas y
Juzgados, page 230.]

Prefectura of the First District:

The Justice of the Peace of San Francisco in an official communication of
the 22d of March last, said to me as follows :

" When the Señor Prefect Don José Castro, came up to these points of the
North, an order of the Departmental Government was published conceding to
this vecindario (inhabitants) solares in the Establishment of Dolores, on account
of many representations made to the said Government by said inhabitants
(vecindario), and as after it was published, it remained to forward a copy of
said order, which perhaps on account of the pressing business of your Señoria
has been forgotten. I pray that you be pleased to order a copy of the same to
be forwarded to me as a guide, since already several lots have been granted."

Which I have the honor to transmit to your Señoria, stating that there does
not exist in the archives of this Prefectura, the order referred to by the
Justice of the Peace of San Francisco, and praying that a duplicate of the
same may be furnished from the office under your charge.

I reiterate the assurances of my respect.

God and Liberty !

SAN JUAN DE CASTRO, April 6th, 1841.

No. LIII.

MIRAMONTES, JUSTICE OF THE PEACE AT THE MISSION OF
DOLORES, ASKS TO BE RELEASED FROM HIS OFFICE.

[Exhibit Q to deposition of R. C. Hopkins.]

Vincente Miramontes to Prefect of First District.

AUGUST 18TH, 1841.

To the Prefect of the First District:

Vicente Miramontes, Justice of the Peace, suplente, in the Pueblo of Dolores,
Jurisdiction of the Port of San Francisco, before your *Señoria*, with all due
respect represents : That in the year 1839, he was appointed to said office, and
in consideration of his having fulfilled the term of his appointment, he prays
your Honor through this petition to have the goodness to grant him his discharge, since the holding of this office for the last two years has been of much
detriment to himself and family. He also represents to your Honor, that it is
impossible for him properly to discharge the duties of said office for the want
of the necessary intelligence for the same, and when it has happened that in the
absence of Francisco Guerrero, he has been compelled to exercise his functions,
he has been much embarrassed, and as there is no secretary in the Juzgado, who
might assist him in difficult points, he has been compelled to employ one and
pay him out of his pocket.

Wherefore he prays your Honor to be pleased to accede to his petition, etc.

Pueblo of Dolores, August 19th, 1841.

VINCENTE MIRAMONTES.

No. LIV.

ACCOUNTS OF FULLER, SYNDIC OF SAN FRANCISCO, FROM 1839 TO 1842.

ACCOUNT MADE OUT BY DON JUAN FULLER, AS SINDICO OF THE MUNICIPALITY OF SAN FRANCISCO.

Amounts Received. To Wit:

1839.

		S	rls.
Aug.	Don David Cooper, paid for two bbls. Agn'te,...........	6	00
	For License for 1 month, according to decree.............	4	00
	Don Francisco De Haro, for 1 bbl country wine,.........	3	00
	Don Josefa Sal "	3	00
	Don Nathan Spear, "	3	00
	Don Vincente Miramontes, "	3	00
	Don Nathan Spear, paid piso and license,..............	2	4
	Don Guillermo Richardson, for the solar of Don Antonio Ortega, owing to my predecessor,..............	10	00
Sept.	Guillº. Smith, for cigaros,...........................	3	00
	Jesus Noe, for barrel mescal,.......................	3	00
	Juana Ruines, back dues,...........................	1	4
	Nathan Spear, for license,...........................	1	00
Oct.	Nathan Spear, for license and goods,..................	2	00
Nov.	Juan Matarin, for sales,............................	2	00
	Juan Vioget, for solar of 100 yards in length by 50 in breadth, according,.........................	12	00
	Juan Davis, for solar of 100 yards square,.............	25	00
	Gregario Escalante, for liquors and license,............	15	00
Dec.	Victor Prudon, for one barrel,.......................	3	00
	License for one month, paid in goods,.................	1	00
	Juan Fuller, for 2 barrels country wine,...............	6	00
1840.			
Jan'y.	Juanita Malarin, for 1 barrel,.......................	3	00
	" for 1 month license,.................		4
	Juanita Malarin, license 1 month, Señor Gegino,.........	1	00
	" sale of 4 gallons,....................		6
	Jose de la Cruz Sanchez, 1 barrel,....................	3	00
Feb'y.	Victor Prudon, fined 10, by order of Judge, for permitting gambling in his house,.......................	16	00
March.	Nathan Spear, for license and 1 barrel of Aguardiente, last month,..................................	4	4
	Nathan Spear, 10 beaver skins and 3 of otter, at 4 —,....	6	00
	Tiburcio Vasquez, for 1 barrel,.......................	3	00
April.	Juan Davis, for do and 1 month's license,..............	3	4
	Gregerio Escalante, license,.........................		4
May.	Nathan Spear, barrel aguardiente and license,..........	3	4
	Juana Briones, 1 barrel and month's license,...........	3	4
	Juan Anto. Vallejo, paid for 1 solar of 50 yds.,.........	12	00
June.	Manuel, portugues,.................................	3	4
	License,..		4
July.	Nathan Spear, liquors and license,...................	7	00
Aug.	J. P. Leese, for registry of brand and mark,...........	1	4
	Don Ml. Miramontes,...............................	1	4

		$	rls.
Aug.	J. P. Leese, barrel country wine,	3	00
	Gegino Escalante, solar of 50 vs.,	12	4
Sept.	Nathan Spear, license for store,	1	00
	David Cooper, 2 barrels aguardiente,	6	00
Oct.	" license, 2 mos.,	1	00
	Do. of Don Nathan, 1 month,	1	00
	Do. of Juanito, "		4
Nov.	Nathan Spear, license,	1	00
	Don Juanito,		4
Dec.	Nathan Spear, license,	1	00
	Geraldo Bijorquez, 1 barrel,	3	00
	Juan Finich, or Davis, for license 3 months and 3 barrels aguardiente,	10	4
	David Cooper, 1 barrel,	3	00
	License,		4
	Gregino Escalante, 1 barrel and license,	3	4
1841.			
Jan'y.	Jesus Noe, for 2 barrels muscat,	6	00
	Tiburcio Vasquez, 1 barrel,	3	00
Feb'y.	For 2 month's license, Nathan Spear,	2	00
	Juan Davis, do.,		4
	Escalente, do.,		4
March.	License, Nathan Spear,	1	00
	Davis and Escalente, at 4 rls.,	1	00
	J. P. Leese,	1	00
Oct.	From the 1st of March to the 10th of Oct. paid for Municipal duties on Aguardiente and other liquors by Juan Vioget,	44	7
	Don Nathan, paid up to 23d of June, from 1st of April, for license,	3	00
	For 1 barrel of aguardiente,	3	00
	Juan Vioget, paid for license, 1 barrel aguardiente, November and December,	8	00
	Collected by Judge, in absence of Sindico Juan Fuller— Nathan Spear, paid for license of store,	5	00
	Capt. Hinckley and Spear, for 5 barrels of aguardiente, sold to individuals in this place and to others, as appears by account rendered on last of December, 1841,	15	00
	Juan Davis, for license 5 months and 2 barrels of aguardiente,	8	4
	Gregorio Escalante, paid for 1 barrel,	3	00
Dec.	Mr. Fil, for license 5 months	5	00
	Mr. Rae, for license 4 months,	6	00
	Jesus Noe, 2 barrels muscat,	3	00
	Nathan Spear, for 1 solar, petitioned for by Perry,	12	4
	Ten dollars paid by Hinckley on goods, under law of 1834,	10	00
	Mr. Rae paid on 1st of January on 92 packages of goods, and one real for three dollars given to Francisco Sanchez,	11	4
	Sum total,	$379	1

SAN FRANCISCO, January 10th, 1842.
Correct.   JUAN FULLER.

Paid from Municipal Fund.

	$ rls.
Expenses of opening road,	9 00
November 2d, 1839, for 1 ream of paper for Juzgado,	8 00
For ink, $2 ; for wax, &c., $2,	4 00
January 15th, 1840, paid Francisco Sanchez, by order of Alcalde,	25 00
January 15, 1840, paid to Don Juan Davis twenty-six dollars, for 1 sopero and masita for the archives	26 00
For expenses stationery and clerk for Sindicaturo,	6 00
In February, 1840, by order of Alcalde, Don Francisco Sanchez,	10 00
For 1 ream of paper, re-cut for letters on 20th February, 1840,	7 00
On the 15th of March, 1840, returned to Don Jose de la Cruz Sanchez, 15, he having paid $18 for one barrel of aguardiente,	15 00
On same day returned to Jacinto Malarin,	15 00
On the 18th of April, paid to the Juan Neophyte thirteen dollars for two saddles, which were lost when the foreigners were taken prisoners,	13 00
Paid to the same, by order of Alcalde, seven dollars, for a horse which was lost,	7 00
For one bullock, killed for the use of the prisoners by order of the Judge,	8 00
On the 9th May, 1850, returned to Juan Vioget $12 4, he having paid twenty-five for a solar of 100 vs., which was only 50 vs. wide and 100 vs. long,	12 4
On the 10th of May, by order of the Judge, to Victor Prudon, for services in Juzgado,	14 00
For the two pair of fetters used on prisoners,	8 00
For sundry articles furnished to prisoners,	5 00
On 5th of November paid to Soleto for carrying express,	6 00
Nov. 18, for ink, &c.. for Juzgado,	4 00
Aug. 29, by order of Francisco Sanchez,	10 00
For candles for prisoners,	2 00
September, paid on order for table cover for Juzgado,	8 00
September 18, paid for inkstand and two candlesticks for Juzgado,	3 00
For payment made to Catalina for two gross of large wax candles (gruesas de toches) and for the solemnization of the 16th of September, according to order of the year 1839,	30 00
Paid for gunpowder and licenses for the solemnization of the 16th of the present month, according to order of to-day, 24, 1840,	26 00
For one ream of paper and wax for Juzgado,	9 00
Paid to persons who went in search of the carpenter of the Leonidas and brought him to Juan Maturin,	
March, 1840, the Diezmo, as a reward to the sailors who carried the express for the Señor General,	8 00
On the 3d of the present month paid for a candado for use of the jail,	2 00
Sept. 29, to Daniel Sill, for two chains with handcuffs,	10 00
March 11th, 1841, paid to Don Francisco Sanchez,	10 00
Three dollars given to Alcalde Francisco Sanchez,	3 00
Paid to conductors of the ropero,	1 00
Sum total,	$349 1

Due to the Municipal Fund.

Mr. Bari,	18 00
The Sindico Blas Angelin, since his term,	21 1
The Sindico Jose Rodriquez, since his term,	16 00

$ rls.

All the individuals, according to the accounts, who have not paid the fines imposed upon them by the Judge, paid to the citizen Cayetano Juarez, and remitted by him,................. 55 4

Señor Prefects, herewith are presented the docs which show the credits (Esgresos) numbered from 1 to 32, including an account forwarded by Señor Hinckley for 4 pipes, (of liquor) which was introduced and the most of it sold outside of the Demarcation. And Mr. Rae has not paid any duty on aquardiente, which he has introduced, it not having been sold ; and Don Jose Limantour has not paid anything, and he established his store on the 24th of December of the last year.

SAN FRANCISCO, Jan'y. 1st, 1842.

Correct.   JUAN FULLER.

Comparison.

Amount of Ingresos,..........................$379 1

"   of Exgresos, ... 149 1

Amount on hand in cash, $ 30

Because the Sindico Procurador of the Municipal Fund of this Demarcation has gone to the Points de Reyes and Baulines, without giving notice of the same, he loses his right to the five per cent. which belonged to him. Thus I, the Justice of the Peace, ordered and determined.

SAN FRANCISCO, Jan'y. 2d, 1842.

FRANCISCO GUERRERO.

Received the amount on hand above set forth.

FRANCISCO SANCHEZ.

No. LV.

CENSUS OF SAN FRANCISCO IN 1842.

[Exhibit No. 9 to Deposition of R. C. Hopkins.]

" Padron," Containing the Inhabitants of Both Sexes, in the Jurisdiction of San Francisco, for the Present Year.

Name.	Birthplace.	Occupation.	Age.
Tiburcio Vasquez	Sn José Gpl	Laborer	49
Alvira Hernandez	Monterey	"	37
Juan José Vasquez	Sn José Gpl	"	17
Barbara Vasquez	"	"	15
Josefa Vasquez	"	"	13
Siviaca Vasquez	"	"	11
José Ma. Vasquez	"	"	10
Purificacion Vasquez	San Francisco	"	9
Luciano Vasquez	"	"	8
Francisco Vasquez	"	"	6
Francisco Vasquez	"	"	4
Pablo Vasquez	"	"	2
José Corn. Bernal	"	"	46
Carmen Sibrian	San Juan	"	38

Name.	Birthplace.	Occupation.	Age.
José de Jesus Bernal	San Francisco	Laborer	13
Fran. Llagas, Neofito*	Pulgas	Domestic	57
Concordio, Neofito	San Pablo	"	54
Ma. Feda, Neofita	"	"	46
Gertrudis, Neofito	"	"	13
José Antonio, Neofito	San Francisco	"	16
Teresa, Neofita	Sonoma	"	20
Francisco Guerrero	Tepic	Laborer	31
Josefa de Haro	San Francisco	"	17
Spot. Ay. de Guerr'o	"	"	—
Anto. Abad, Neofita	Costa	Domestic	37
Lorenza, Neofita	Sonoma	"	23
Alejo, Neofita	San Francisco	"	35
Vicente Miramontes	Mission de San José	Laborer	32
Jesus Hernandez	San Francisco	"	27
J. Ma. Miramontes	"	"	4
Benita Miramontes	"	"	2
Mariana Miramontes	"	"	—
Pablo, Neofito	"	Domestic	18
Francisco, Neofito	Sn Mig'l	"	20
Cadido Valencia	Sn Clara	Laborer	38
Paula Sanchez	San José Gpl	"	32
Eustag. Valencia	"	"	14
José Ramon Valencia	San Francisco	"	13
Ma. de los Aug. Valencia	"	"	10
Lucia Valencia	"	"	9
Tomaso Valencia	"	"	5
Ma. Josefa Valencia	"	"	1
Jesus Valencia	Sta. Clara	"	35
Julia Sanchez	"	"	30
Catarina Valencia	San Francisco	"	7
Riso Valencia	"	"	5
Francisco Valencia	"	"	—
Francisco de Haro	Composta	"	50
Francisco de Haro	San Francisco	"	15
Ramon de Haro	"	"	15
Rosalia de Haro	"	"	14
Natividad de Haro	"	"	13
Prud. de Haro	"	"	11
Cat. de Haro	"	"	9
Carlota de Haro	"	"	9
Dolorez de Haro	"	"	6
Jesus Felipe de Haro	"	"	2
Alonzo de Haro	"	"	—
Anast. Ramirez	San Juan	"	11
Junipero, Neofito	San Francisco	"	43
José Ysidro Sanchez	"	"	24
Teodora Alviso	Sta. Clara	"	23
Dolorez Sanchez	San Francisco	"	5
Ysabel Sanchez	"	"	2
Narsisa Sanchez	"	"	—

* The words Neofito and Neofita denote Indian catechumens, male and female, respectively. It will be observed that these neophytes have no surnames, and that they all seem to have been named from the Saints in the calendar of the Roman Catholic Church.

Name.	Birthplace.	Occupation.	Age.
José de los Santos, Neofito.	Tulares	Laborer	10
Leander Galindo	San Francisco	"	55
Domingo Allaman	Sta. Clara	"	34
Seferino Galindo	"	"	12
Maria Galindo	"	"	9
Ant. Galindo	Santa Clara	"	7
Francisco Galindo	San Francisco	"	4
Gregoria Galindo	"	"	3
Genaro Galindo	"	"	2
Mariano Galindo	"		—
Jesus Noe	Puebla	"	37
Guadalupe Gardaño	"	"	30
Miguel Noe	Mexico	"	9
Dolorez Noe	Sta. Clara	"	6
Esperidion Noe	San Francisco	"	4
Ma. Concep. Noe	Sta. Clara	"	2
Candelaria, Neofita	Sonoma	Domestic	17
Francisco, Neofita	Sta. Cruz	"	28
Concep., Neofita	"	"	21
Lorenzo, Neofito	"	"	26
Juan Fuller	England	Merchant	40
Concepcion Arila	Mont'y		26
Ma. Concep. Fuller	Monterey		6
Santiago Fuller	San Rafael		4
Nicolasa, Neofita	Sacramento	Domestic	13
Carlos, Neofito	"	"	10
Pedro Serbia	Denmark	Merchant	26
Juan, Neofito	Sacramento	Domestic	11
Natan Spear	America	Merchant	42
Juana Miss Spear	Ys. Sanduic		27
Tomas, Canaca	"	Domestic	9
Carlos, Indiga (Indian)	Sacramento	"	18
Isabel, " "	"	"	11
Daniel Sill	America	"Depend."	46
Fran. Grño Ynkly	"	Merchant	35
Susana Suart	San Francisco		16
Juan Canaca	Y Sanduic	Domestic	20
Yspecanoe Canaca	"	"	23
Manaria, Neofita	Sacramento		12
Guillermo Reed	New Orleans	Merchant	32
Señora Reed	"		24
Juan Reed	"		3
Maria Reed	"		2
Eloisa Reed	San Francisco		—
Knittes	"	Domestic	—
Pedro, Canaca	Ys. Sanduic, (Sand. Isl.)	"	50
Mijalda, Canaca	" " "		22
Opunul, Canaca	" " "		20
José, Canaca	" " "		21
Tomas ——	France	"	30
Juan C. Davis	America	Carpenter	32
Juan Fricher	"	Blacksmith	36
Antonio	Peru	Domestic	19
Fredrico, Neofito	Sonoma	"	11
Gregorio Escalante	Manila	Merchant	34

Name.	Birthplace.	Occupation.	Age.
Mr. F. Andrews	America	Carpenter	26
Apolino Miranda	San Francisco	Laborer	47
Juana Briones	Sta. Cruz		39
Presentacion Miranda	San Francisco		20
Gomes Miranda	"		13
Narsisa Miranda	"		12
Refugio Miranda	"		10
José de Jesus Miranda	"		7
Manuel Miranda	"		5
Paulina, Neofito	Sacramento	Domestic	16
Candel. Mirantes	Guadalajara	Laborer	53
Guadalupe Briones	Sta. Cruz		49
Miguel Miramontes	San Francisco	Laborer	23
Rodolfo Miramontes	"	"	22
José Arciano Miramontes	"		18
Ma. Dolores Miramontes	"		19
José de los Stos. Miramontes	"	Laborer	16
Raymundo Miramontes	"	"	13
Juan Jc. Miramontes	"	"	12
Guadalupe Miramontes	"	"	11
Carmen Miramontes	"	"	10
Luz Briones	Sta Cruz	"	43
José Ramon, Neofito	San Francisco		16
Marcario, Neofito	Sonoma	Domestic	16
José Rodriguez	Monterey	Laborer	35
Romana Miramontes	Sta Cruz	"	30
Francisco Rodriguez	San Francisco	"	5
Ma. Rodriguez	"	"	4
Ma. Rodriguez	"	"	2
José Rodriguez	"	"	—
José Antonio Sanchez	Sonora	" Harcendo "	67
Ysidro Jc. Sanchez	San Francisco	Laborer	23
José Feliz	"	"	15
Felipe, Neofito	Tulares	Domestic	12
Raymundo, Neofito	Sonoma	"	16
Manuel Sanchez	San Francisco	Laborer	30
Francisco Sotelo	P. de los Angeles	"	24
Manuel Sanchez	San Francisco		11
Rosario Sanchez	"		5
Dolores Sanchez	"		4
Juan Fran. Sanchez	"		1
Jc. de la Ce. Sanchez	"	Laborer	40
Ma. Josefa Merido	San Diego	"	32
Solidad Sanchez	San Francisco	"	19
Concepcion Sanchez	"	"	12
José Ma. Sanchez	"	"	8
Ricardo Sanchez	"	"	5
Francisco Sanchez	"	"	—
Josefa, Neofita		Domestic	14
Eduardo, Neofita	Santa Cruz	"	40
Francisco Sanchez	San José	Laborer	35
Teodora Higuera	San Francisco	"	26
Luisa Sanchez	"	"	8
Luis Don Sanchez	"	"	6
Dolores Sanchez	"	"	4

Name.	Birthplace.	Occupation.	Age.
Pedro Sanchez	San Francisco	Laborer	—
Consolacion, Neofita	"	Domestic	12
Ygnacio, Neofita	"	"	53
Dunas, Neofita	"	"	49
Forcuata, Neofita	"	"	40
José (a) Segnio, Neofita	"	"	16
Domingo Felis	"	Laborer	22
Anto, Felis	"	"	19
Angela Rusa	"	"	19
Luis Felis	"	"	16
Juan Coopinger	Dublin	Sawyer	30
Luis Soto	San José	"	23
José, Neofito	Tulares	Domestic	10
Santiago Henysy	Scotland	Sawyer	91
Roberto McCalister	Cork	"	29
Tomas Gerbert	London	"	33
Juan Mereno	Holland	"	40
Guillermo Handes	Boston	"	42
George Williams	England	"	39
Recardo Maltok	"	"	23
Jqs. Mirantes	Sta. Clara	Laborer	31
Mr. Ignacio Martinez	San Francisco	"	23
Ma. Miramontes	Sonoma	"	—
Maria, Neofita	"	Domestic	9
Francisco Miramontes	San Francisco		9
Maria, Neofita	San Rafael	Domestic	33
José D., Neofito	San Francisco		3

WI. San José, 155.

RESUMEN.

	Men.	Women.	Boys.	Girls.	Totals.
1a. Columna	15	11	8	6	40
2d. "	11	7	11	16	45
3d. "	24	11	8	5	48
4a. "	18	11	11	8	48
5a. "	8	2	4	1	15
	76	42	42	36	196

Establecemiento de Dolores, 31 de Obre, de 1842.

FRANCISCO SANCHEZ.

No. LVI.

GOVERNOR MICHELTORENA'S PROCLAMATION RESPECTING THE MISSIONS, MARCH 29, 1843.

[See the same, *without the preamble:* Halleck's Report, Appendix, No. 19; 1 Rockwell, 469; Jones' Report, page 71.]

Manuel Micheltorena, General of Brigade of the Republic, Adjutant General of the Plana Mayor, Governor of the same, Commanding-General and Inspector of both Californias:

It being one of the ample or complete instructions or orders, with which is invested the undersigned General and Governor, viz. : to examine into the situation of all the Missions in his government at the present moment, their prospects and resources, in order to regulate them, and the Supreme National Government having transmitted all its powers, [delegated to him all its powers,] according to the supreme order made February 11, 1842.

On deliberation, and with the assent of the most Reverend Fathers, Fray José Joaquin Jimeno, Fray José Ma. de Jesus Gonzales Rubico, who have been made personally to appear before the government, as Presidents of other Missions, as well as in the name of, and to represent the most Rev. Father, Presidential Vicar, the absent Fray Narciso Duran, being fully impressed with, and having well reflected upon all things requisite.

That the vast and immense landed property formerly belonging* to the Missions had been scattered or partitioned out to individuals, which at the epoch it was done was caused by the exigencies of the country.

That the pious and charitable institutions of social order, for the conversion of the savages to Catholicism and to an agricultural and peaceful life, are reduced to the huertas and inclosures of the churches and buildings.

That the most Most Rev. Ecclesiastics have no support but charity, and that the divine religion not prospering, barely sustains itself.

That the Indians, naturally lazy, from additional labor, scarcity of nourishment, and in a state of nudity, having no fixed employment or appointed Mission, prefer to keep out of the way and die impenitent in desert woods, to escape a life of slavery, filled with all privations and without social joys.

That this continued emigration of the natives from the service of individuals to that of Missions, and from that of the Missions to that of individuals, or to the woods, retards more and more agriculture, and frightens off, instead of drawing together the Gentiles from without the pale of our Holy Religion.

That in the administration of the Missions, there have been committed some frauds and notorious extravagance, which every inhabitant of California laments.

That as there is no other method of reanimating the skeleton of a giant like the remains of the ancient Missions, without falling back upon experience and fortifying it with the levers of Civil and Ecclesiastical power.

Now, everything well considered and naturally reflected upon, I have determined to decree the following articles:

No. 1. The Government Department decrees to be "delivered up or restored" to the Most Rev. Fathers (who shall name the Ecclesiastic to be placed respectively in charge) the Missions of San Diego, San Luis Rey, San Fernando, Santa Barbara, San Antonio, San José, San Juan Capistrano, San Gabriel, San Buenaventura, Santa Cruz, La Purisima, Santa Clara; which shall con-

---

[* *Appurtenant* is a better translation of *pertenecientes*—the word "belonging" is equivocal. The word "Fray," which is not translated, signifies "Brother" of a regular order, a "religioso," as the *secular* priests were called "Padres"—Fathers.]

tinue for the future to be governed by the Most Rev. Fathers (they taking charge of the natives) in the same manner as they were before.

No. 2. The government considers what has been done to this date as irrevocable: the Missions can reclaim none of the lands granted prior to this date; and in reclaiming the cattle, chattels, and instruments of agriculture loaned by the Rev. Fathers, Curators, or Superintendents, they shall grant sufficient time and arrange with the debtors or holders, amicably.

No. 3. They shall likewise take care to collect the scattered neophytes or converts. First, those lawfully exempted by the Supreme Departmental Government. Second, those who at the date of this decree are provided for by individuals, it being, however, understood, that if any of both classes wish and prefer to return to their respective Missions, they shall be admitted and received, with cognizance of the masters and the Most Rev. Missionaries.

No. 4. The Departmental Government, in whose possession up to this day have been the Missions, in virtue of the most ample powers with which it is invested, and referring to the aforesaid considerations, authorizes the Most Rev. Fathers to apply the products of the Missions to the necessary expenditures of the reduction, food, clothing, and other temporal wants of the Indians; and they shall likewise take from the same fund their own support, for the salary of the Mayordomo, and for the support of the divine religion, under the condition that they shall remain obligated by their word of honor and conscience, to deliver to the Treasury, upon notice to the Rev. Fathers, of this government, and the express order, in writing, of the undersigned Governor, Commanding-General, and Inspector of relief, sustenance, and clothing of the troops and observances of the civil employees, the *eighth part* of the whole annual produce of every kind; keeping for the guidance of its Ecclesiastics a true and exact account at the end of the year, of the number of their converts, possessions real and personal, and of every description of produce or its corresponding value, which may belong to such Mission.

No. 5. The Departmental Government, which glories in religion, as well as the whole of California, and in the same manner being interested as well as all and every one of the inhabitants of both Californias in the advancement of the Holy Catholic Faith and in the prosperity of the country, " dedicates itself," (or places at the disposition of "all its power,") in aid of the Missions, and in quality of General commanding, the power of its arms to protect, and defend, and sustain them, and in the possession and preservation of all the lands they may hold from this day, they shall be the same as the possessions and guarantees enjoyed by private persons, *binding itself to make no new grants without the information of the respective authorities of the Most Rev. Ministers, notorious non-occupation, non-cultivation, or necessity.*

Dated 29th day of March, 1843.   MANUEL MICHELT^{NA.}
FRANCISCO ARCE, Secretary.

No. LVII.

EXHIBIT No. 11 TO DEPOSITION OF M. G. VALLEJO.

Order for election of Ayuntamientos and Alcaldes, Nov. 14, 1843.

Citizen Manuel Micheltorena, General of Brigade of the Mexican Army, Adjutant-General of the Staff of the same, Governor, Comandante-General, and Inspector of the Department of the Californias.

{ Govt. Seal. }   Although Justices of the Peace have been established in the towns of this Department in conformity with the law of March 20, 1837, which gives them the powers and obligations which the Ayuntamientos have, yet it is observed that in the Courts of the chief towns of the Districts matters of various kinds are daily brought which prevent the Justices from dedicating themselves to the duties which correspond to them, for want of Ayuntamientos, and moreover the Prefectures of this Department having to be discontinued for the coming year, and as the most excellent Junta has passed resolutions on the matter, by the powers conferred on it by the Organic Bases, I have decided the last law for elections of Ayuntamientos of April 27, 1837, be put in force under the following rules:

1st. They will proceed to verify in Monterey and the city of Los Angeles, as chief towns of the Districts, the elections of Ayuntamientos, composed each one of First and Second Alcalde, four Regidores, and one Sindico.

2d. In the Pueblos of San Diego, Santa Barbara, San Juan, Villa de Branceforte, Pueblo de San José, San Francisco, and Sonoma, elections will be held to appoint two Alcaldes, of first and second nomination.

3d. In consequence, on the second Sunday of the coming December, the residents of their respective towns will appoint in one session seven Arbritrators (compromisarios) who will meet on the Friday preceding the third Sunday in December, presided over by the civil authority of the District, for the purpose of electing the Ayuntamiento and Alcaldes, as the foregoing Articles direct, observing in the necessary part the provisions of the law of Elections, of January 19th of the present year, under the rubric (rubro) of secondary elections, and the other articles of the same which may tend to the purpose.

4th. The first Alcaldes of which these dispositions speak, will perform the duties which correspond to the Judges of First Instance in conformity with the decree of July 15th, 1839, and they will also take charge of the Prefecture of their respective Districts.

5th. On the first day of January of the coming year, the persons newly appointed will enter upon the duties of their office, receiving from those going out an exact inventory of all the espedientes, books, and whatever there may be pertaining to said corporations, transmitting a copy of it to the Government in order to pass it to the Departmental Assembly.

And that it may come to the notice of all, I order that it be published by proclamation in the pueblos of the Department, and it be fixed in the accustomed places.

MONTEREY, November 14, 1843.   MICHELTORENA.
MANUEL JIMENO, Secretary.

No. LVIII.

EXHIBIT No. 15 TO DEPOSITION OF M. G. VALLEJO.

Secretary of State to Alcalde of the Port of San Francisco, January 20, 1844.

OFFICE OF THE SECRETARY }
OF THE GOVERNMENT OF THE CALIFORNIAS. }

Your note dated the 9th inst. has been received, in which you transmit the inventory of the things pertaining to your Court, and His Excellency having examined it, orders me to answer it, as I now do.

God and Liberty!

MONTEREY, January 20, 1844.   MANUEL JIMENO.

Señor First Alcalde of the Port of San Francisco, }
    Citizen GUILLERMO HINCKLEY. }

No. LIX.

EXHIBIT No. 14 TO DEPOSITION OF M..G. VALLEJO.

[The Governor addresses the same officer as Alcalde of Yerba Buena and Alcalde of San Francisco, March 3d, 1844.]

{ Seal of Departmental } { Government. }

I this day say to the Ensign Don Juan Prado Mesa, the following :

" So soon as you receive this order you will march with twelve or fifteen men of the company of your command, and present yourself to the Alcalde of first nomination of Yerba Buena, placing yourself at his disposition for the purpose of restraining a disturbance which has happened with some countrymen, causing the authority of said Alcalde to be respected, acting yourself with the greatest judgment and prudence, and under your own responsibility."

And I transcribe [this] to you for your information, recommending that you bear yourself with prudence and judgment, acting in everything under your own responsibility, forming the corresponding summary upon the fact referred to in your official communication of the 3d inst., which I answer, reporting to this Government.

God and Liberty !

MONTEREY, March 11, 1844.

MANUEL MICHELTORENA.

Señor Alcalde of San Francisco.

No. LX.

ESPEDIENTE OF THE DE HAROS FOR THE POTRERO NUEVO.

EXHIBIT No. 11 TO TESTIMONY OF R. C. HOPKINS IN THE CASE.

Espediente instigated by the citizens Francisco and Ramon De Haro, in claiming the tract called " Potrero de San Francisco."

Most Excellent Señor Governor of the Californias :

Francisco De Haro, Ramon De Haro, in the name of our family, Mexicans by birth, and living in the Ex-Mission of San Francisco de Asis, before your Ex. with greatest submission appear and represent, that being compelled to remove from the ranch of the deceased José Antonio Sanchez, the portion of cattle belonging to our deceased mother, and as we wish to tame the same, we beg your Excellency, in the exercise of your authority (or powers) to grant us a small piece of land called Potrero de San Francisco, in extent from North to South 2,288 varas, and from East to West 2,508 varas, measuring up to the " Lomerias," (or Range of Highlands), " because there is no competent person to do it, according to the annexed diseño," which we submit to your Ex., and as said parcel of land can be enclosed, we intend to place in it the tame cattle, because the range of our father's cattle is insufficient and all occupied, and he has given us due permission to make a petition, as we are under parental power and control.

Therefore we entreat Y. E. to grant us this benefit, whereby we shall receive favor and grace, making oath that we are not instigated either by malice or bad motives.

There being no sealed paper here we could not use it.

SAN FRANCISCO, April 12, 1844.

RAMON DE HARO,
FRANCISCO DE HARO.

___

MONTEREY, April 29, 1844.

Let the Official Secretary make the necessary report.

MICHELTORENA.

___

Señor Governor :

The Mission of San Francisco now has no property (bienes) whatever, and therefore the Potrero petitioned for is vacant, as the petitioners have shown by the report of the respective justice, and as the ejidos of said establishment are to be designated, I think that in the meanwhile, the interested parties may occupy the land by a provisional license which your Excellency may be pleased to give them, it being no prejudice to the community, nor to any individual whatever. The determination of your Excellency will be most proper.

MONTEREY, April 29th, 1844.

[Signed]

MANUEL JIMENO.

MONTEREY, April 30th, 1844.

Agreed.
[Signed]

MICHELTORENA.

___

MONTEREY, April 30th, 1844.

" In view of the petition with which this Espediente commences, the foregoing reports, with all matters presenting themselves, and necessary to be considered, in conformity with the laws and regulations governing the matter, I declare Francisco and Ramon De Haro favored in that they may occupy provisionally, the land named Potrero of San Francisco, of the extent of one half of a square league ; its boundaries being the Esteros of the entrance (boca) of the Potrero, and the hills that surround the same. Let the corresponding dispatch issue, and registry be made of the same, and let a communication be directed to the person in charge of said establishment. His Excellency the Sr. Governor thus ordered, decreed and signed, which I attest."

Fourth Seal Two Reales.

" Provisionally authorized by the Maritime Custom House of the Port of Monterey, in the Department of the Californias, for the years 1844 and 1845."

MICHELTORENA.

PABLO DE LA GUERRA.

[L. S.]

___

" The citizen Manuel Micheltorena, General of Brigade of the Mexican Army, Adjutant General of the Staff of the same, Governor Com^to, General and Inspector of the Department of Californias.

Whereas, the citizens Francisco and Ramon De Haro have petitioned for the concession of the Portrero which is named San Francisco, from the mouth of the Esteros to the Lomaria which surrounds the same, and the proceedings having been taken, and the investigations concerning the same having been made, as required by the laws and regulations in relation to the matter, I have determined in use of the authority conferred upon me, in the name of the Mexican Nation, to permit them the occupation of the said Potrero, subject to the measurement which may be made of the Ejidos of the Establishment of

San Francisco, (sujetandose á la medicion que se haya de los ejidos del Establecimiento de San Francisco,) and to the following conditions :

First. They cannot by any title sell it, nor alienate it without prejudice to
some property (bienes) which the Establishment of San Francisco should have.

Second. They shall not obstruct the crossings, roads and servitudes, devoting
it to cultivation, and to the property (bienes) which they design to introduce,
but within one year it shall be occupied.

The land of which mention is made, is one half a square league, and if they
violate these conditions, they will lose their right to this provisional concession,
which is delivered to the interested parties for their security and further ends.

Given in MONTEREY, on the first of May, 1844.

MANUEL MICHELTORENA.

MANUEL JIMENO, Secretary.

NO. LXI.

EXHIBIT NO. 12 TO DEPOSITION OF M. G. VALLEJO.

Election of First Alcalde in 1844.

DIVISION OF SAN FRANCISCO.

In the Secondary elections of this day the citizen Electors being assembled
in the Court room, you resulted elected for Alcalde of first nomination, that
you may appear the first day of the year 1845, for the purpose of taking the
customary oath in order to take charge of the Administration of Justice, in
conformity with the laws.

All which I have the honor to communicate to you for the purposes mentioned, offering you the sincere considerations of our esteem.

God and Liberty.

SAN FRANCISCO, December 22, 1844.

President,
FRANCISCO GUERRERO.
Vice President,
FRANCISCO SANCHEZ.
1st Secretary,
JESUS NOE.
2d Secretary,
JUAN N. PADILLA.

Citizen JUAN N. PADILLA,
Alcalde Elect of 1st nomination.

No. LXII.

[TRANSLATION.]

DECREE OF THE DEPARTMENTAL ASSEMBLY OF MAY 28TH, 1845, RESPECTING THE RENTING OF SOME OF THE MISSIONS, AND CONVERTING OTHERS INTO PUEBLOS, ETC.

[See the same, Halleck's Rep. App. 20; 1 Rockwell, 471; Jones's Rep. 72.]

ARTICLE 1. The Departmental Government shall call together the Indians (*los
Neofitos*) of the Missions of San Rafael, DOLORES, Soledad, San Miguel and La

Purisima, which are abandoned by them, by means of a proclamation, which it will publish, allowing them the term of one month from the day of its publication in their respective Missions, or in those nearest to them, for them to reunite for the purpose of occupying and cultivating them; and they are informed that. if they fail to do so, said Missions will be declared to be without owners (*mostrencas*)* and the Assembly and Departmental Government will dispose of them as may best suit the general good of the department.

ART. 2. The Carmelo, San Juan Bautista, San Juan Capistrano, and San Francisco Solano shall be considered as pueblos, which is the character they have at present; and the government, after separating a sufficient locality for the Curate's house, for churches, and appurtenances, and court-house, will proceed to sell the remaining premises at public auction in order to pay their respective debts; and the overplus, should there be any, shall remain for the benefit and preservation of divine worship.

ART. 3. The remainder of the Missions, as far as San Diego, inclusive, may be rented out at the option of the government, which will establish the manner and form of carrying this into execution, taking care in so doing that the establishments move prosperously onward. These respective Indians will consequently remain in absolute liberty to occupy themselves as they may see fit, either in the employment of the renter himself, or in the cultivation of their own lands which the government will necessarily designate for them, or in the employ of any other private person.

ART. 4. The principal edifice of the Mission of Santa Barbara is excepted from the renting mentioned in the foregoing article; and the government will arrange in the most suitable manner, which part thereof shall be destined for the habitation and other conveniences of his Grace the Bishop and his suite, and which for the Reverend Missionary Padres who at present inhabit said principal edifice. And likewise one-half of its total rent of the other property of the Mission shall be invested for the benefit of the church, and for the maintenance of its minister, and the other half for the benefit of its respective Indians.

ART. 5. The products of the rents, mentioned in Article 3, shall be divided into three equal parts, and the government shall destine one of them for the maintenance of the Reverend Padre Minister and the conservation of divine worship; another for the Indians; and the last shall necessarily be dedicated by government towards education and public beneficence, as soon as the legal debts of each Mission be paid.

ART. 6. The third part mentioned in the 5th Article as destined for the maintenance of the priests and help towards divine worship, shall be placed at the disposal of the Reverend Prelates, for them to form a general fund, to be distributed equitably in the before-mentioned objects.

ART. 7. The authorities or ecclesiastical ministers, should there be any in the Missions referred to in Article 1, or those in the nearest Missions, or persons who may merit the confidence of government, will be requested by said government to see that the proclamation above mentioned be published, and to give information immediately whether the said neophytes have presented themselves or not, within the period fixed, in order that, in view of such documents, the necessary measures may be taken.

ART. 8. Government will, in the strictest manner, exact the amount owing by various persons to all the Missions in general, as already ordered by the Most Excellent Assembly in its decree of the 24th August, 1844, and dispose of the same for the object mentioned in the last part of the 5th Article.

---

* [*Mostrencas,* means more properly, public property. Salva defines it: "property which has no known owner, and therefore belongs to the sovereign or community."]

No. LXIII.

PROCLAMATION FOR THE SALE OF THE MISSIONS.

OCTOBER 28, 1845.

[See the same, Halleck's Rep. App. 21; 1 Rockwell, 472; Jones' Rep. p. 75. This was not an "Act of the Departmental Assembly," as it has sometimes been styled, but a proclamation of Governor Pico in execution of the Act of May 28, 1845, as will seen on consulting the original.]

PIO PICO, GOVERNOR AD INTERIM OF THE DEPARTMENT OF THE CALIFORNIAS, TO THE INHABITANTS THEREOF, KNOW YE:

That, in order to give due fulfilment to the resolution of the Excellent Departmental Assembly of the 28th of May last, relative to the leasing and alienating of the Missions, and being authorized by the aforesaid Excellent Body, I have thought proper to issue the following

REGULATION FOR THE SALE AND LEASING OF THE MISSIONS.

OF ALIENATION.

ARTICLE 1. There will be sold in this Capital, to the highest bidder, the Missions of San Rafael, Dolores, Soledad, San Miguel, and La Purisima, which are abandoned by their neophytes, (que se hallan abandonados de sus neofitos.)

ART. 2. Of the existing premises of [in, *en*] the pueblos of San Luis Obispo, Carmelo, San Juan Bautista, and San Juan Capistrano, and which formerly belonged to the Missions, there shall be separated the churches and appurtenances; one part for the Curate's house, another for a court-house, and a place for a school, and the remainder of said edifice shall be sold at public auction, where an account of them will be given.

ART. 3. In the same manner will be sold the property on hand belonging to the Missions—such as grain, produce, or mercantile goods—giving the preference for the same amount to the rentors, and deducting previously that part of said property destined for the food and clothing of the Reverend Padre Minister and the neophytes until the harvest of next year.

ART. 4. The public sale of the Missions of San Luis Obispo, Purisima, and San Juan Capistrano shall take place on the first four days of the month of December next, notice being previously posted up in the towns of the department inviting bidders, and three publications being made in the Capital at intervals of eight days one from the other before the sale. In the same manner will be sold what belongs to San Rafael, Dolores, San Juan Bautista, Carmelo, and San Miguel on the 23d* and 24th of January, next year.

ART. 5. From the date of the publication of these regulations, proposals will be admitted in this Capital to be made to government, which will take them into consideration.

ART. 6. The total proceeds of these sales shall be paid into the departmental treasury, to pay therewith the debts of said Missions; and should anything remain, it will be placed at the disposal of the respective Prelate for the maintenance of religious worship, agreeably to Article 2 of the decree of the Departmental Assembly.

OF RENTING.

ART. 7. The Missions of San Fernando, San Buenaventura, Santa Barbara,

---

* [This is a mistake, first made in Halleck's report, and copied by Jones and Rockwell. It is "2d, 3d, and 4th." See official original.]

and Santa Ynez, shall be rented out to the highest bidder for the term of nine years.

ART. 8. To this end bidders shall be convoked in all the departments, by fixing advertisements in the town, in order that by the 5th December next they may appear in this Capital, either personally or by their legal agents.

ART. 9. Three publications shall be made in this Capital at intervals of eight days each, before the day appointed for the renting, and proposals will be admitted on the terms expressed in Article 5.

ART. 10. There shall be included in said renting all the lands, out-door property, implements of agriculture, vineyards, orchards, workshops, and whatever according to the inventories made, belongs to the respective Missions, with the mere exceptions of those small portions of land which have always been occupied by some of the Indians of the Missions.

ART. 11. The buildings are likewise included, excepting the churches and their appurtenances, the part destined for the Curate's house, the court-house, and place for a school. In the Mission of Santa Barbara no part of the principal edifice shall be included which is destined for the inhabitants of his Grace the Bishop and suite, and the Reverend Padres who inhabit it; and there shall be merely placed at the disposal of the rentor, the cellars, movables and workshops, which are not applied to the service of said Prelates.

ART. 12. As the proceeds of the rent are to be divided into three parts to be distributed according to Article 5, of said decree, the rentor may himself deliver to the respective Padre, Prefect, or to the person whom he may appoint, the third part destined for the maintenance of the Minister and the religious worship; and only in the Mission of Santa Barbara, the half of said rent money shall be paid for the same object, in conformity with the 4th Article of the decree of the Departmental Assembly.

ART. 13. The government reserves to itself the right of taking care that the establishments prosper; in virtue of which it will prevent their destruction, ruin or decline, should it be necessary during the period of renting.

ART. 14. The renting of the Missions of San Diego, San Luis Rey, San Gabriel, San Antonio, Santa Clara, and San José, shall take place when the difficulties shall be got over which at present exist with respect to the debts of those establishments, and then the government will inform the public; and all shall be done agreeably to these regulations.

ADVANTAGES AND OBLIGATIONS OF THE RENTORS.

ART. 15. The rentors shall have the benefit of the usufruct of everything delivered to them on rent according to these regulations.

ART. 16. The obligations of the rentors are: 1st. To pay promptly and quarterly when due the amount of rent. 2d. To deliver back, with improvements, at the expiration of the nine years, whatever they may receive on rent, with the exception of the stills, movables and implements of agriculture, which must be returned in a serviceable state. 3d. They shall return at the same time the number of cattle which they receive, and of the same description, and of such an age as not to embarrass the procreation of the following year. 4th. They shall give bonds to the satisfaction of government before they receive the establishments, conditioned for the fulfilment of the obligations of the rentors—one of which is the payment of the damages which the government may be obliged to find against them, agreeably to Article 13.

OF THE INDIANS.

ART. 17. The Indians are free from their neophytism, and may establish themselves in their Missions or wherever they choose. They are not obliged to serve the rentors, but they may engage themselves to them, on being paid for their labor, and they will be subject to the authorities and to the local police.

Art. 18. The Indians radicated in each Mission shall appoint from among themselves, on the first of January in each year, four overseers, who will watch and take care of the preservation of public order, and be subject to the Justice of the Peace to be named by government in each Mission, agreeably to the decree of 4th July last. If the overseers do not perform their duty well, they shall be replaced by others, to be appointed by the Justice of the Peace, with previous permission from government, who will remain in office for the remainder of the year in which they were appointed.

Art. 19. The overseers shall appoint, every month, from among the best of the Indians, a sacristan, a cook, a tortilla-maker, a vaquero, and two washer-women, for the service of the Padre Minister, and no one shall be hindered from remaining in this service as long as he choose. In the Mission of Santa Barbara, the overseers will appoint an Indian to the satisfaction of the priest, to take care daily of the reservoir and water conduits that lead to the principal edifice, and he shall receive a compensation of four dollars per month, out of the rent belonging to the Indians.

Art. 20. The Indians who possess portions of land, in which they have their gardens and houses, will apply to this government for the respective title, in order that the ownership thereof may be adjudicated to them, it being understood that they cannot alienate said lands, but they shall be hereditary among their relatives, according to the order established by law.

Art. 21. From the said Indian population, three boys shall be chosen as pages for the Priest, and to assist in the ceremonies of the church.

Art. 22. The musicians and singers who may establish themselves in the Missions shall be exempt from the burdens mentioned in Article 18, but they shall lend their services in the churches, at the masses, and the *funciones* which may occur.

OF THE JUSTICES OF THE PEACE.

Art. 23. The Justices of the Peace shall put in execution the orders communicated to them by the nearest superior authority; they will take care that veneration and respect be paid to matter appertaining to our religion and its Ministers, and that the 18th and 20th articles, inclusive of these regulations, be punctually fulfilled; they will see that no one be hindered in the free use of his property; they will quiet the little disturbances that may occur, and, if necessary impose light and moderate correction; and if the occurrence should be of such a nature as to belong to the cognizance of other authorities, they will remit to such authorities the criminals and antecedents.

And in order that it may come to the notice of all, I command that this be published by public edict in this capital and the other towns of the Department, and that it be posted up at the customary public places, and that it may be sent to whomsoever it may concern.

Given at the City of Los Angeles, on the 28th day of October, 1845.

PIO PICO.

Jose Maria Covarrubias, Secretary.

No. LXIV.

ESPEDIENTE OF NOE FOR THE RANCHO SAN MIGUEL.

Exhibit W to Deposition of R. C. Hopkins.

His Excellency the Governor ad interim of the Department of California:

José de Jesus Noé, a Mexican by birth and a resident of San Francisco de Asis represents to your Excellency that being the owner of a number of cattle and horses, which stock is increasing, and not having a suitable place upon which to put them, he begs that your Excellency, by virtue of your powers, will grant him a square league of land, on the tract, now vacant, to the West and Northwest of the Establishment of Dolores, bounded by the ranches of the citizens Francisco de Haro, Robert Riddle, and José Cornelio Bernal and bordering on the sea, on the West, according to the map accompanying this petition.

The petitioner respectfully solicits that your Excellency will grant this petition, as he has a large family; this not being on stamped paper on account of having none, swearing what is necessary, etc.

SAN FRANCISCO, May 28th, 1845.

J. DE JESUS NOE.

[Marginal decree.]

AUG., June 14th, 1844.

Let this be transmitted to the Justice of San Francisco for his report, let the said Judge notify the owners of the adjoining estates of this petition, that their property may receive no prejudice, also ascertain whether any other petition is pending, respecting the tract of land in question, and having done this, return this document to the Government.

PICO.

2d Constitutional Justice's Court of Yerba Buena.

In view of the preceding Superior decree and in compliance with its dictates, I have to report : That having given notice to the owners of the estates adjoining the land petitioned for, and having compared their respective maps, it appears that no injury will result to them. The said land is recognized as the property of the Ex-Mission of San Francisco (es de los que se reconoce por de su propiedad la Ex-Mission de S. Francisco,) and is now unoccupied ; it is near that solicited by Don Benito Diaz, whose petition is now pending, and which having been compared with this petition, does not conflict with it.

The petitioner possesses the qualifications required by law. All which is submitted to the superior understanding of your Excellency, in compliance with the preceding decree and for the necessary purposes.

YERBA BUENA, Aug. 28th, 1845.

J. DE LA C. SANCHEZ.

ANGELES, Dec. 23d, 1845.

In view of the petition commencing this Espediente, the report of the 2d Alcalde of San Francisco and other things referring to the matter : In conformity with the law of August 18th, 1824 and the regulations of the 21st of November, 1828, I declare Don José Jesus Noé the owner of a square league of land in the immediate neighborhood of the Mission Dolores, being adjoining the lands of Don Francisco Haro, Robert Riddle and Josè Cornelio Bernal. Let the necessary title issue and the espediente be retained to be submitted to the Most Excellent Departamental Assembly, for its approbation. Pio Pico, provisional Governor of the Californias has thus ordered, decreed, signed and duly attests.

PIO PICO.

JOSE MARIA COVARRUBIAS, Secretary.

Pio Pico Senior Vocal of the Departmental Assembly and Provisional Governor of California :

Whereas, Don José Jesus Noé has solicited, for his individual benefit and that of his family, a piece of land in the immediate neighborhood of the Ex-Mission of Dolores, one square league in extent : the customary investigations having been made, by virtue of the powers conferred upon me. in the name of the Mexican Nation, I do by this decree, grant the aforesaid land to the petitioner, declaring him, by these presents, the owner thereof, in conformity with the law of August, 18th, 1824, and the regulation of Nov. 21st, 1828, subject to the approval of the most Excellent Departmental Assembly and to the following conditions :

1st. The petitioner may enclose the land, without interfering with the crossings, roads and public conveniences, and he may enjoy it freely and exclusively, devoting it to such purposes as he may see fit.

2d. He shall apply to the proper Judge to place him in lawful possession, in accordance with this decree, and the said Judge will define the boundaries and the necessary landmarks.

3d. The land granted, is one square league in extent, according to the map which accompanies the Espediente, and borders on the lands of Don Francisco Haro, Robert Riddle, and José Cornelio Bernal. The Judge who gives possession will have the land measured in conformity with the ordinance.

I therefore order that the present title, being considered firm and valid, shall be registered in the proper book, and shall be deliver,d to the petitioner for his protection and other purposes.

Given at the city of Los Angeles, on ordinary paper, for want of stamped paper, this 23d day of December, 1845.

PIO PICO.

Jose Maria Covarrubias, Secretary.

This title has been duly registered in the proper book.

Angeles, May 8, 1846.

This Espediente having been submitted in session of to-day to the Departmental Assembly, it was referred to the Committee on Vacant Lands.

PIO PICO,

Agustin Olvera, Deputy Secretary.   President.

The Committee on Vacant Lands has carefully examined the Espediente relative to the land in the immediate neighborhood of the Ex-Mission of Dolores solicited by José de Jesus Noé, which was granted by the Superior Departmental Government, in accordance with the laws concerning the matter, and it now has the honor of submitting the following report to your Excellency's consideration.

It approves of the grant made to José de Jesus Noé of the tract of land in the immediate neighborhood of the Ex-Mission of Dolores, one square league in extent, according to the title issued on the 23d day of December of the past year, this being entirely in conformity with the law of August 18th, 1824, the article of October 5th, and the regulation of Nov. 21st, 1828.

Given in the Hall of Commissions, in the City of Los Angeles, May 22d, 1846.

S. AGUELLO.

Angeles, June 3d, 1846.

In session of to-day the most Excellent Departmental Assembly approves of the contents of the preceding decree.

No. LXV.

SUB-PREFECT GUERRERO INSTRUCTS THE JUDGE OF FIRST INSTANCE OF THE PORT OF SAN FRANCISCO RESPECTING THE DEFALCATION OF SYNDIC SHERREBACK, FEB. 7, 1846.

[Exhibit 16 to deposition of R. C. Hopkins.]

Sub-Prefectura of the }
  2d District. }

In view of your note of the 3d of the present month, in relation to the accounts of the Sindicatura of Don Pedro Sherreback, and of the refusal of this (that) gentleman to reply to two official communications from your predecessor, asking a rendition of accounts. Wherefore, I require you to cause him to be summoned to appear before the Juzgado under your charge, and that he present the accounts, you first examining the same, and if they are not made out as they should be, showing corresponding vouchers, with the necessary entries of amounts received, so as to detect any bad faith, if any has been practiced; and if they are not so found, you shall attach his property, if he have any, and if he have none, you shall imprison him till he make payment, or be sent to the public works.

Which I have the honor to say to you in reply,

God and liberty. YERBA BUENA, Feb. 7th, 1846.

FRANCISCO GUERRERO.

To the Judge of 1st Instance, }
  of the Pueblo of San Francisco. }

No. LXVI.

PETITION OF FITCH AND GUERRERO FOR LANDS AT THE PRESIDIO.

MAY 13, 1846.

[Exhibit No. 8 to Deposition of R. C. Hopkins.]

To the Most Excellent Governor of the Department of the Californias:

Henry Fitch, naturalized in the Mexican Republic, and Francisco Guerrero, a Mexican by birth, residing in the Department, before your Excellency with due respect, represent: That finding a place in the point of the Presidio of San Francisco, which up to the present time, has not been occupied by any person; that an arroyo which is found almost in the centre of said place, being suitable for the establishment of machinery for a mill, and other pieces for sowing purposes and the greater part Chimesal and Monte, as your Excellency will see by examining the accompanying diseño; the said land being two and a half sitios a little more or less; bounding in the South with the Ranchos of the citizens Francisco De Haro and José de Jesus Noé, on the S.S.E. with the Mission of San Erancisco; on the East with Yerba Buena, and on the North and West with the sea shore; the petitioners making known to your Excellency that they do not desire to prejudice the interests of any person whatever, who may be seeking to obtain, or who may already have obtained a title; in that case they will only receive the favor (of a grant) for three thousand varas, which may be on said arroyo, for the purpose of establishing said machinery, and then they can make an agreement *with whoever may be the owner, and if your Excellency should be pleased to grant to the petitioners the favor they ask, subject to the ejidos of the poblacion of Yerba Buena, although they have not yet been designated (dejando en salvo hasta los ejidos de la poblacion de Yerba Buena aun que no estan nombrados) since in the concession of the land, some persons will be benefited, and the petitioners not being prejudiced by another who may obtain in property, some part of the said lands, of small extent, in pieces of desirable land, or of much monte or sand hills (arenales).

Wherefore they earnestly pray your Excellency to be pleased to concede to them that which they ask, if it be may be convenient to do so, remaining satisfied with the determination of your Excellency, swearing to what is necessary; writing this upon common paper, for want of that which is sealed.

YERBA BUENA, May 13th, 1846.

FRAN^{co}. GUERRERO,
H. D. FITCH.

FRAN^{co}. GUERRERO,
H. D. FITCH.

———

(*Certificate of the Justice of the Peace.*)

José de Jesus Noé, Justice of the Peace of the Jurisdiction of Yerba Buena.

I certify, in relation to the petition of the citizens Francisco Guerrero and Henry D. Fitch, that the part of land asked for is vacant at this time, although there are other petitioners for the same, whose petitions are pending. The object of the last petitioners being to establish a mill which will be useful to the community, and besides the petitioners limit themselves to a certain number of varas, it will not be prejudicial to other parties, if the Government should think proper to grant to one or another the lands indicated. And for the necessary ends I give this in Yerba Buena, on the 13th of May, 1846.

J. DE JESUS NOE.

No. LXVII.

[From 1 DeMofras' California, etc., page 320.]

COMPARATIVE TABLE OF THE MISSIONS OF UPPER CALIFORNIA,

UNDER THE RELIGIOUS ADMINISTRATIONS IN 1834, AND UNDER THE CIVIL ADMINISTRATION IN 1842.

Names of the Missions; Going North From the South.	Epoch of their Foundation.	Distance from the Preceding.	Number of Indians.		Number of Horned Cattle.		Number of Horses, Mules, etc.		Number of Sheep, Goats and Hogs.		Crops of Wheat, Maize, &c.
		Leagues.	1834.	1842.	1834.	1842.	1834.	1842.	1834.	1842.	1834. Bushels.
San Diego	16 June......1769	17	2,500	500	12,000	20	1,800	100	17,000	200	13,000
San Luis Rey	13 June......1798	14	3,500	650	80,000	2,000	10,000	400	100,000	4,000	14,000
San Juan Capistrano	1 November..1776	13	1,700	100	70,000	500	1,900	150	10,000	200	10,000
San Gabriel	8 September..1771	18	2,700	500	105,000	700	20,000	500	40,000	3,500	20,000
San Fernando	8 September..1797	9	1,500	400	14,000	1,500	5,000	400	7,000	2,000	8,000
San Buenaventura	31 March......1782	18	1,100	300	4,000	200	1,000	40	6,000	400	2,500
Santa Barbara	4 December..1786	12	1,200	400	5,000	1,800	1,200	160	5,000	400	3,000
Santa Inés	17 September..1804	12	1,300	250	14,000	10,000	1,200	500	12,000	4,000	3,500
La Purisima Concepcion	8 December...1787	8	900	60	15,000	800	2,000	300	14,000	3,500	6,000
San Luis Obispo	1 September..1771	18	1,250	80	9,000	300	4,000	200	7,000	800	4,000
San Miguel	25 July......1797	13	1,200	30	4,000	40	2,500	50	10,000	400	2,500
San Antonio	14 July......1771	13	1,400	150	12,000	800	2,000	500	14,000	2,000	3,000
N. S. de la Soledad	9 October...1791	11	700	20	6,000	"	1,200	"	7,000	"	2,500
Mission del Carmelo	3 June......1770	15	500	40	3,000	"	700	"	7,000	"	1,500
San Juan Bautista	24 June......1799	14	1,450	80	9,000	"	1,200	"	9,000	"	3,500
Santa Cruz	28 August...1791	17	600	50	8,000	"	800	"	10,000	"	2,500
Santa Clara	18 January..1777	11	1,800	300	13,000	1,500	1,200	250	15,000	3,000	6,000
San José	18 June......1797	7	2,300	400	24,000	8,000	1,100	200	19,000	7,000	10,000
Dolores de S. Francisco	9 October...1776	18	500	50	5,000	60	1,600	50	4,000	200	2,500
San Rafael	18 December..1817	8	1,250	20	3,000	"	500	"	4,500	"	1,500
San Francisco Solano	25 August...1823	13	1,300	70	8,000	"	700	"	4,000	"	3,000
21 Missions on a line of.....262 legs.			30,650	4,450	424,000	28,220	62,500	3,800	321,500	31,600	122,500

No. LXVIII.

Statement showing respectively the names of all the Indian pueblos in New Mexico, with their localities, populations, wealth, etc., and the time when their land claims were confirmed by Congress, and when surveyed, and the areas thereof.

[From Executive Doc. No. I, U. S. Senate, 2d Session 37th Congress, (Dec. 1861); President's Message, etc., Vol. 1, pp. 581, 582; Report of Sec. of Interior.]

No.	Name of Pueblo	Designation in this office.	Locality—County.	Population—census of 1860.	Personal estate owned in Pueblo.	Claim when confirmed.	Claim when surveyed. 1859.	Area of Claim.	Remarks.
								Acres.	
1	Jemez	A	Santa Ana	650	$159,662	Dec. 22, 1858	August	17,510.45	On Jemez River.
2	Acoma	B	Valencia	523	42,782	do	August		On a rock 500 feet high, 15 miles south-west of Laguna; nearest water, 1 mile.
3	San Juan	C	Rio Arriba	341	14,850	do	July	17,544.77	On Rio Grande.
4	Picuris	D	Taos	360	8,385	do	July	17,460.69	On Rio Picuris.
5	San Felipe	E	Santa Ana	360	27,200	do	Nov. & Dec.	34,766.86	On Rio Grande.
6	Pecos	F	San Miguel			do	July & Aug.	18,763.33	Pueblo deserted; remnant of people now living at Zuñi and Jemez.
7	Cochiti	G	Santa Ana	172	114,538	do	Aug. & Sept.	24,256.50	On Rio Grande.
8	Santo Domingo	H	do.	261	18,580	do	November	74,743.11	On Rio Grande.
9	Taos	I	Taos	363		do	July	17,360.55	Value of personal property included with that of Picuris.
10	Santa Clara	K	Rio Arriba	179		do	July	17,368.52	Value of personal property included with that of San Juan.
11	Tesuque	L	Santa Fé	97	2,500	do	June & July	17,471.12	On Tesuque Creek, 6 miles north of Santa Fé.
12	San Ildefonso	M	do.	154	2,610	do	June & July	17,292.64	On Rio Grande.
13	Pojoaque	N	do.	37	820	do	June	13,520.38	On Pojoaque Creek, 15 miles north of Santa Fé.
14	Zia	O	Santa Ana	117	2,035	do	August	17,514.63	Near the Pueblo of Jemez.
15	Sandia	P	Bernalillo	217	30,956	do	November	24,187.29	On Rio Grande.
16	Isleta	Q	do.	440	7,080	do	October	110,080.31	On Rio Grande.
17	Nambé	R	Santa Fé	103	5,510	do	June	13,586.33	On Nambé Creek, 3 miles east of Pojoaque.
18	Laguna	S	Valencia	927	44,972	June 21, 1860			West of Albuquerque 45 miles, on San José River.
19	Zuñi		do.	1,300	13,106				On Zuñi River; no claim filed.
20	Santa Ana		Santa Ana	316	15,665				Lands on Rio Grande; pueblo 5 miles west; no claim filed.

No.	Name	Location	Lat./Long.	Population			Remarks
21	San Xavier	Arizona		170	6,325	....	Pápago Pueblo, 9 miles south of Tucson; old Jesuit Mission.
	Pima and Maricopa reservation.						
22	Sacaton	do.		144			On the Gila River; the first two pueblos inhabited by Maricopa Indians, and all the others by the Pimas; they are an agricultural and stock-raising people. (*Vide* sections 3 and 4 of the Act "making appropriations for the current and contingent expenses of the Indian department," &c., approved Feb. 28th, 1859, making reservation of 100 square miles for the confederated bands of the Pimas and Maricopas.)
23	Hueso Parrado	do.		250			
24	Agua Raiz	do.		527			
25	Corrito	do.		258			
26	Arenal	do.		577			
27	Cachanilla	do.		503	129,290 Feb. 28, 1859. In 1859	64,000.00	
28	Hormiguero	do.		510			
29	Casa Blanca	do.		339			
30	Cerro Chiquito	do.		232			
31	Llano	do.		385			
	Moqui pueblos.		Lat. 35° 45', Long. 110° 30'.				
32	Oraiva	do.		*800			Comparatively very little is known of these Indians; they have occupied the pueblos from time immemorial; not known whether they have or ever had any written title to their lands. Their pueblos, like that of Acoma, are situated on the tops of high rocks or hills.
33	Shomonpavi	do.		*600			
34	Iano	do.		*250			
35	Cichomovi	do.		*100			
36	Opijiqui	do.		*300			
37	Moshanganabi	do.		*250			
38	Shapanlobi	do.		*200			
	Pápago pueblos.						
39	Cunaro	Arizona					The Pápagos inhabit the country between Tucson and the Colorado of the West and between the Gila and the international boundary line, and are similar in nearly all respects to the Pimas, speaking the same dialect, &c.
40	Tecolote	do.					
41	Charco	do.					
42	Pirigua	do.					
43	Ocaboa	do.			*3,500	*125,000	
44	Cojite	do.					
45	Coca	do.					
46	Santa Rosa	do.					
47	Cahuavi	do.					
48	Llano	do.					
				16,922	772,766	517,427.48	

* Estimated.

SURVEYOR-GENERAL'S OFFICE,
Santa Fé, New Mexico, August 29th, 1861.

A. P. WILBAR, *Surveyor-General.*

No. LXIX.

A.D. 1836.

EXTRACTS RESPECTING PREFECTS, SUB-PREFECTS, AYUNTAMIENTOS, ALCALDES, AND JUSTICES OF THE PEACE, FROM THE SIXTH CONSTITUTIONAL LAW OF MEXICO. ADOPTED DECEMBER 29TH, 1836.

[Bases y Leyes Constitutionales de la Republica Mexicana, decretados por el Congreso general de la nacion en el año de 1836. Mexico: Imprenta del aguila, José Jimeno, 1837.]

ART. 1. The Republic shall be divided into Departments, in conformity with the eighth organic (constitutional) base. The Departments shall be divided into Districts, and the Districts into Partidos.

*   *   *   *   *   *   *   *   *   *

ART. 16. In each chief town (capital, cabecera) of a District there shall be a Prefect, nominated by the Governor and confirmed by the General Government, who shall hold office for four years, and may be re-elected.

*   *   *   *   *   *   *   *   *   *

ART. 18. It belongs to the Prefects: 1st. To maintain order and public tranquility in their Districts, with entire subjection to the Governor. 2d. To execute and cause to be executed the orders of the respective government of the Department. 3d. To watch over the fulfillment of their duties by the Ayuntamientos, and in general over everything pertaining to police (al ramo de policia).

ART. 19. In each capital (cabecera) of a Partido there shall be a sub-Prefect, nominated by the Prefect and approved by the Governor, who shall hold his office four years, and may be re-elected.

*   *   *   *   *   *   *   *   *   *

ART. 31. The functions of Sub-Prefect in the Partido are the same as those of the Prefect in the Districts, subject to the Prefect, and through him to the Governor.

ART. 22. There shall be Ayuntamientos in the capitals of Departments; in those places (lugares) where there were such in 1808; in sea ports with a population of four thousand souls; and in those pueblos which have a population of eight thousand. In those which do not possess the above population (que no haya esa populacion) there shall be Justices of the Peace (Jueces de Paz), also entrusted with police (policia), in such number as may be designated by the respective Departmental Juntas, in concert with the Governor.

ART. 23. The Ayuntamientos shall be elected by the people in districts (terminos), to be fixed by a law. The number of Alcaldes, Councilmen (Regidores) and Syndics shall be determined by the respective Departmental Juntas, in concert with the Governor, except that there cannot be more than six Alcaldes, twelve Regidores, or two Syndics in the same Ayuntamiento.

*   *   *   *   *   *   *   *   *   *

ART. 25. The Ayuntamientos shall be charged with the care of public health and accommodation, (literally, *convenience,* policia de salubridad y *comodidad,*) to watch over prisons, hospitals, and benevolent institutions which are not of private foundation, primary schools sustained by public funds, the construction and repair of bridges, highways, and roads, the raising and expenditure of public moneys from taxes, licenses, and the rents of municipal property, (la recaudacion é inversion de los propios y arbitrios,) to promote the advancement of agriculture, industry, and commerce, and to assist the Alcaldes in the preservation of peace and public order among their inhabitants (vecindario), under absolute subjection to the laws and regulations.

ART. 26. It shall be the duty of the Alcaldes to exercise in their pueblos the office of conciliators, to decide oral litigations, to take the necessary proceedings in urgent lawsuits in which recourse cannot be had to Judges of the First Instance; and, in the same case, to take the preliminary proceedings in criminal cases; to conduct such proceedings as are entrusted to them by the respective tribunals or judges; and to watch over public tranquility and order, subject, in this respect, to the Sub-Prefects, and, through them, to the respective superior authorities.

ART. 27. Those Justices of the Peace who are also charged with police powers [see ante, Art. 22], shall be proposed by the Sub-Prefect, nominated by the Prefect, and approved by the Governor; hold office one year, and be re-eligible.

*   *   *   *   *   *   *   *   *   *

ART. 29. Such Justices shall exercise in their respective pueblos the same powers which are designated for Alcaldes and Ayuntamientos, subject, in respect to these powers, to the Sub-Prefects, and, through them, to the respective superior authorities. In those towns (lugares) where there are not a thousand inhabitants, the functions of Justices of the Peace shall be restricted to watching over the public peace, and to the administration of police, and to exercising judicial functions, both civil and criminal, in cases whose urgency does not permit a resort to the nearest respective authorities.

ART. 30. The official trusts (cargos) of Sub-Prefects, Alcaldes, Justices of the Peace charged with police administration, Regidores, and Syndics, pertain to the Pueblo,* and cannot be resigned without a legal excuse, approved by the Governor, or, in case of a re-election.

ART. 31. A secondary (supplemental) law shall detail everything relating to the exercise of the duties of Prefects, Sub-Prefects, Justices of the Peace, Alcaldes, Regidores, and Syndics, etc., etc.

No. LXX.

A.D. 1845.

ESPEDIENTE OF BENITO DIAZ, FOR THE POINT OF LOBOS.

[California Archives, Irregular Espediente, No. 255.]

ANGELES, May 24th, 1845. Let it be transmitted to the respective Judge, and await the Military Commandant, to say what he may deem convenient, so that, in view of all, when it shall be returned to the Government, the same may resolve what may be convenient to the party who petitions. PICO.

Most Excellent Senor Governor :—Benito Diaz, a native of the Californias, and a resident of San Francisco, before your Excellency as may be most acceptable, and with due respect represents : That having some head of large cattle, and not having a place whereon to put them for the increase thereof, and as there is a vacant place in the jurisdiction of San Francisco, known by the name of Punta de Lobos, bounded on the north by the sea running toward the port of San Francisco, on the south by the high land lying back of the Mission of San Francisco, known by the name of the Serro de la Laguna Honda, on the east by the high hill, and on the west by the Point of Lobos, which may be comprehended, a little more or less, two square leagues (sitios de ganado mayor), adverting that the ruins of the Presidio

---

* NOTE.—"Los cargos de Sub-Prefectos, Alcaldes, Jueces de Paz encargados de policia, Regidores y Sindicos son *concejiles.*" CONCEJIL, adj. Lo perteneciente al concejo, ó lo que es comun á los vecinos *de un pueblo.* SALVA Dic. Esp. in verbo. See Argument, § 13.

of San ranci sco and castle (fort) which lie within the place, are not included in this petition, unless the Government should wish to grant me said ruins, obligating myself, if it be effected, to build a house at the port of San Francisco, for the Military Commandant, to be twenty-five varas long and six wide. Wherefore, I request your Excellency to take into consideration my petition and grant me the land I ask, which I hope, from the well-known goodness of your Excellency, by which I will receive a favor, swearing that which is necessary, etc.

BENITO DIAZ.

YERBA BUENA, April 3d, 1845.

———

In view of the preceding Decree relating to information of the land which the petitioner asks, I will say that it is vacant, and that said petitioner possesses the necessary requisites, according to the law in the matter; but as to the place occupied by the military point, I cannot give information, because I know nothing of its commons (ejidos).

PUEBLO OF SAN FRANCISCO, August 16th, 1845.

J^E. DE LA C. SANCHEZ.

———

OFFICE OF MILITARY COMMANDANT OF SAN FRANCISCO, }
October 18th, 1845. }

In conformity with the preceding superior Decree, issued by the Most Excellent Señor, Governor *ad interim* of this Department, on the 24th of May of the present year, I have to say, that the land which the interested party asks, being vacant, I believe can be granted to him without including in the concession the two military points of the Presidio and castle (fort) which are comprehended in his petition.

FRAN^{co}. SANCHEZ.

———

No. LXXI.

A.D. 1844. APRIL.

THE INHABITANTS OF THE MISSION OF (DOLORES OF) SAN FRANCISCO COMPLAIN THAT THEIR SETTLEMENT HAS NEVER BEEN RECOGNIZED AS A PUEBLO, AND ASK THE GOVERNOR TO EXTINGUISH THE NAME OF MISSION AND DECLARE IT A PUEBLO FOR THE FUTURE. THE GOVERNOR DECLINES TO ACT.

[California Archives ; Unbound Documents.]

[TRANSLATION.]

Let the Secretary of State report, first giving the matter due consideration.
MICHELT^A.

MOST EXCELLENT SIR : The undersigned, all residents (vecinos) of the jurisdiction of San Francisco de Asis, and established in the ex-Mission of this name, before your Excellency, respectfully and in due form, represent, that all of us being desirous to do all that we can for the increase and advancement of this settlement (poblacion); also, to promote the branches of industry, agriculture, and commerce, as far as it is in our power. Up to the present time, in spite of the data which proved the contrary, this place is still hitherto commonly recognized as a Mission (se reconoce aun y corre por Mision), and notwithstanding the data to which we refer, which show that it ought to be held and recognized as a PUEBLO, such as the Bando issued by his Excellency the Governor D. Juan

B. Alborado, on the 27th of February, 1839, in which this establishment was named as a "cabecera de partido," (seat of the partido government) that the one issued by your Excellency on the 25th April, 1843, in which this was excepted in the order to return the Missions to the Fathers ; and lastly, according to that of the 28th of September, of the same year, issued also by your Excellency, the 2d article of which required 1st and 2d Alcaldes to be appointed for the place, among the others which your Excellency thought proper to distinguish with this honorable designation. Wherefore, in consideration of said data, for the extinction of such title of Mission, as well as that the same be recognized IN FUTURE as a PUEBLO, and in order to avoid controversies, that the office of mayordomo which exists, although with a small number of Indians of both sexes in COMMUNITY (en comunidad) ; also, that by the authorities a proper impulse may be given, and a due observance of the decrees and regulations of police (policia) and good government ; and, finally, in order that the public may be undeceived in relation to the title that it now has, and that the difficulties and obstacles that have embarrassed the settlement and prosperity of the said settlement (poblacion), may in the future be avoided. Wherefore, we apply to the ample powers of you Excellency, in order that in the use of the same, and in consideration of what has been set forth, you may be pleased to declare in due form the same to be a PUEBLO, and in consequence of its being such, by your superior approbation, permit us to ratify the same, which act will be duly solemnized in accordance with our authorities, making due acknowledgments to your Excellency for this favor. Wherefore, we earnestly pray you to look propitiously upon our petition (solicitud) and to admit this on common paper, there being no sealed paper in this place.

S. FRANCISCO DE ASIS, April 8, 1844.

FRANCISCO DE HARO, T. DE LA C. SANCHEJ, FRAN'CO GUERRERO, FRAN'CO SANCHEZ, F. DE JESUS NOE, MANUEL SANCHEZ, CAND'LLO VALENCIA, RAMON DE HARO, BISENTE MIRAMONTES, JOSE JESUS, FRAN'CO M. HARO, YSDRO T. SANCHEZ, FELIPE SOTO, DOMINGO FELIS, JOSE BERNAL—[something obscure here.]

———

NOTE.—This is in the hand-writing of Francisco Arce, the then Secretary of State, but not signed by him.   The preceding paper, subscribed by some citizens (algunos vecinos) of San Francisco : I understand that it is not of such urgency as to require you to determine the matter until you have the condition in which the Mission is, which is indebted to some merchants, and these have asked that the same be satisfied with some of the property of the Mission. Therefore, your Excellency can determine what is proper as soon as you make the visit that you have resolved upon.

MONTEREY, 29th April, 1844.

———

MONTEREY, April 30, 1844.

In accordance with the opinion of the Secretary of State, and as the Governor has determined, let it be known to the gentlemen who subscribe, assuring them that the Government can never desire anything but their welfare, consistently with the general good (publico general), which it is his duty to promote.

MICHELTOᴿᴬ.

NO. LXXII.

A.D. 1847. MARCH.

GENERAL KEARNY, MILITARY GOVERNOR OF CALIFORNIA, RECOGNIZES THE CORPORATE TOWN OF SAN FRANCISCO, AND GRANTS IT BEACH AND WATER LOTS.

[Executive Document No. 17, House of Rep., 1st Sess. 31st Cong., page 146.]

I, Brigadier-General S. W. Kearny, Governor of California, by virtue of authority in me vested by the President of the United States of America, do hereby grant, convey, and release unto the town of San Francisco, the people, or corporate authorities thereof, all the right, title, and interest of the Government of the United States and of the Territory of California, in and to the beach and water-lots on the east front of said town of San Francisco, included between the points known as the " Rincon " and " Fort Montgomery," excepting such lots as may be selected for the use of the Government by the senior officers now there : Provided the said grant hereby ceded shall be divided into lots, and sold at public auction, to the highest bidder, after three months' notice previously given ; the proceeds of said sale to be for the benefit of the town of San Francisco.

Given at Monterey, capital of California, this 10th day of March, 1847, in the 71st year of the independence of the United States.

S. W. KEARNY,
Brig.-Gen. and Governor of California.

No. LXXIII.

A.D. 1849. MARCH.

THE CITIZENS OF SAN FRANCISCO INSTITUTE A " DISTRICT LEGISLATURE."

[Executive Document No. 17, House of Rep., 1st Session 31st Cong. (1849-50) pages 728, etc.]

No. I.

A public meeting of the citizens of the town and district of San Francisco was held in the public square on Monday afternoon, the 12th instant, in accordance with previous notice.

The meeting was organized by calling Mr. Norton to preside, and S. W. Perkins to act as secretary.

The chairman, after reading the call of the meeting, opened it more fully by briefly but succinctly stating its object ; when Mr. Hyde, on being invited, after some preliminary remarks, submitted the following plan of organization or government for the district of San Francisco :

Whereas, we, the people of the district of San Francisco, perceiving the necessity of having some better defined and more permanent civil regulations for our general security than the vague, unlimited, and irresponsible authority that now exists, do, in general convention assembled, hereby establish and ordain :

ARTICLE I.

Section 1. That there shall be elected by ballot a Legislative Assembly for the district of San Francisco, consisting of fifteen members, citizens of the district, eight of whom shall constitute a quorum for the transaction of business ; and whose power, duty, and office shall be to make such laws as they in their wisdom may deem essential to promote the happiness of the people, provided they shall not conflict with the Constitution of the United States, nor be repugnant to the common law.

Sec. 2. Every bill which shall have passed the Legislative Assembly shall, before it becomes a law, be signed by the speaker and the recording clerk.

Sec. 3. It shall keep a journal of its proceedings, and determine its own rules.

Sec. 4. The members of the Legislative Assembly shall enter upon the duties of their office on the first Monday of March.

ARTICLE II.

Section 1. That for the purpose of securing to the people a more efficient administration of law and justice, there shall be elected by ballot three justices of the peace, of equal though separate jurisdiction, who shall be empowered by their commission of office to hear and adjudicate all civil and criminal issues in this district, according to the common law, as recognized by the Constitution of the United States, under which we live.

Sec. 2. That there shall be an election held, and the same is hereby ordered, at the Public Institute, in the town of San Francisco, on Wednesday, the 21st of February, 1849, between the hours of eight A. M. and five P. M., for fifteen members of the Legislative Assembly for the district of San Francisco, and three justices of the peace, as hereinbefore prescribed.

Sec. 3. That the members of the said Legislative Assembly, and the three justices of the peace elected as hereinbefore prescribed, shall hold their office for the term of one year from the date of their commissions, unless sooner superseded by the competent authorities from the United States Government, or by the action of a provisional government now invoked by the people of this Territory, or by the action of the people of this district.

Sec. 4. Members of the legislature and justices of the peace shall, before they enter upon the duties of their respective offices, take and subscribe the following oath :

I do solemnly swear that I will support the Constitution of the United States and government of this district, and that I will faithfully discharge the duties of the office of ———, according to the best of my ability.

Mr. Harris moved the adoption of the plan entire, which was seconded ; when Mr. Buckalew moved to supersede the plan of government presented by submitting the subject to a committee to be appointed by the meeting, and whose duty it should be to report to an adjourned meeting. Thereupon an animated discussion ensued. Mr. Buckalew's motion having been seconded, was lost by vote ; when the question recurred on the original motion of Mr. Harris, which was carried almost unanimously.

On motion of Mr. Hyde, it was

Resolved, That the judges of the election to be held on the 24th instant shall meet at the Public Institute, in the town of San Francisco, on the 22d instant, at 10 o'clock A. M., to present to the justices of the peace their commissions, and administer to them their oath of office.

On motion of Mr. Per Lee, it was determined that every male resident of the age of twenty-one years or upwards shall be entitled to vote at the said election.

On motion of Mr. Roach, it was

Resolved, That the persons who were elected on the 27th of December last to serve as a town council for the year 1849, and those who were elected for the same purpose on the 15th of January, 1849, be, and are hereby, requested to tender their resignations to a committee selected by this meeting to receive the same.

Messrs. Ellis, Swasey, Long, Buckalew, and Hyde were elected such committee.

On motion, it was

Resolved, That these proceedings be published in the " Alta California."

On motion, the meeting then adjourned.

MYRON NORTON,
President.

T. W. PERKINS,
Secretary.

No. II.

SAN FRANCISCO, March 23, 1849.

I do hereby certify, that at an election held for justices of the peace and for members of the district legislature, on the 21st day of February, 1849, Myron Norton, Heron R. Per Lee, and William M. Stewart, were elected justices of the peace; Stephen A. Wright, Alfred J. Ellis, Henry A. Harrison, George C. Hubbard, George Hyde, Isaac Montgomery, William M. Smith, Andrew J. Grayson, James Creighton, Robert A. Parker, Thomas J. Roach, William F. Swasey, Talbot H. Green, Francis J. Lippitt, and George Hawk Lemon were elected to the district legislature.

W. GILLESPIE,
One of the Judges, and Inspector of Election.

No. III.

I hereby certify that I administered the oath of office to the members of the legislature of the district of San Francisco, on the 5th of March, 1849.

H. R. PER LEE,
Justice of the Peace.

SAN FRANCISCO, March 20, 1849.

No. IV.

MONDAY EVENING, March 5, 1849.

The Legislative Assembly of the district of San Francisco met the first time at the Public Institute. Present: Messrs. Creighton, Ellis, Grayson, Green, Harrison, Hubbard, Hyde, Lemon, Lippitt, Montgomery, Parker, Roach, Smith, Swasey, and Wright.

The oath of office was administered to the aforesaid members elect by his Honor Judge H. R. Per Lee.

Mr. Hyde was then appointed chairman *pro tempore*.

The members then proceeded to elect, by ballot, their officers, Messrs. Roach and Smith having been appointed tellers, who, after counting the votes, declared Francis J. Lippitt duly elected as speaker of the house, and J. Howard Ackerman clerk. Accordingly, Mr. Lippitt took the chair.

On motion, a committee of three were appointed to draw up rules of proceeding, to report at a special meeting to be held on Tuesday evening, at 7 o'clock. Messrs. Harrison, Hyde, and Roach, committee.

Mr. J. Cade was appointed sergeant-at-arms, and Mr. E. Gilbert printer for the house.

On motion, a special committee of three were appointed to act in connection with the judges of the district, to report a code of laws as soon as practicable.

On motion, Mr. Lippitt was added to the committee. Messrs. Hyde, Harrison, and Creighton, committee.

The following resolution was presented by Mr. Hyde, which, after some discussion, was carried unanimously :

Resolved, That Mr. Frank Ward be appointed the treasurer of the district of San Francisco, to act temporarily until properly superseded by law, and who shall be empowered to receive all bonds, mortgages, notes, and money or moneys now in the hands of any officers existing under the late authority, and report the amount to this house.

Moved by Mr. Smith, and seconded, that a suitable place be provided in which the magistrates elect may hold a court.

On motion, a committee of three were appointed to confer with the judges on the subject. Messrs. Parker, Wright, and Ellis, committee.

On motion, the meeting adjourned until Friday evening, at 7 o'clock.

FRANCIS J. LIPPITT,
Speaker.

True copy from the minutes :

J. Howard Ackerman, Clerk.

No. LXXIV.

A.D. 1849. June 4.

GENERAL RILEY, MILITARY GOVERNOR OF CALIFORNIA, DENOUNCES THE "LEGISLATIVE ASSEMBLY OF SAN FRANCISCO."

[Executive Document No. 17, House of Rep., 1st Session, 31st Congress, page 773.]

PROCLAMATION.

To the People of the District of San Francisco.

Whereas, proof has been laid before me that a body of men styling themselves " the Legislative Assembly of the District of San Francisco," have usurped powers which are vested only in the Congress of the United States, by making laws, creating and filling offices, imposing and collecting taxes, without the authority of law, and in violation of the Constitution of the United States, and of the late treaty with Mexico :   Now, therefore, all persons are warned not to countenance said illegal and unauthorized body, either by paying taxes or by supporting or abetting their officers.

And, whereas, due proof has been received that a person assuming the title of sheriff, under the authority of one claiming to be a justice of the peace in the town of San Francisco, did, on the 31st of May last, with an armed party, violently enter the office of the 1st Alcalde of the District of San Francisco, and there forcibly take and carry away the public records of said district from the legal custody and keeping of said 1st Alcalde : Now, therefore, all good citizens are called upon to assist in restoring said records to their lawful keeper, and in sustaining the legally-constituted authorities of the land.

The office of justice of the peace in California, even where regularly constituted and legally filled, is subordinate to that of Alcalde ; and for one holding such office to assume the control of, and authority over, a superior tribunal, argues an utter ignorance of the laws, or a willful desire to violate them, and to disturb the public tranquility. It is believed, however, that such persons have been led into the commission of this rash act through the impulse of the moment, rather than any willful and settled design to transgress the law ; and it is hoped that on due reflection they will be convinced of their error, and unite with all good citizens in repairing the violence they have done to the laws. It can hardly be possible that intelligent and thinking men should be so blinded by passion, and so unmindful of their own interests and the security of their property, after the salutary and disinterested advice and warnings which have been given them by the President of the United States, by the Secretaries of State and of War, and by men of high integrity and disinterested motives, as to countenance and support any illegally constituted body in their open violation of the laws, and assumption of authority which in no possible event could ever belong to them.

The office of alcalde is one established by law, and all officers of the United States have been ordered by the President to recognize and support the legal authority of the person holding such office ; and whatever feelings of prejudice or personal dislike may exist against the individual holding such office, the office itself should be sacred. For any incompetency or mal-administration, the law affords abundant means of remedy and punishment—means which the Executive will always be found ready and willing to employ, to the full extent of the powers in him vested.

Given at Monterey, California, this 4th day of June, in the year of our Lord 1849.

B. RILEY,
Brevet Brig.-Gen. U. S. A., and Governor of California.

Official :
    H. W. HALLECK,
        Brevet Captain, and Secretary of State.

No. LXXV.

A.D. 1849. JUNE 5TH.

GOVERNOR RILEY, UNITED STATES MILITARY GOVERNOR OF CALIFORNIA, RESTORES THE AYUNTAMIENTO OF THE PUEBLO OF SAN FRANCISCO.

[Executive Document No. 18, House of Rep. 1st Sess. 31st Congress, page 774.]

STATE DEPARTMENT OF THE TERRITORY OF CALIFORNIA,
Monterey, June 5, 1849.

GENTLEMEN : I am directed to send you the enclosed appointment as judges and inspectors, to give notice and hold a special election for filling certain vacancies in the district and town of San Francisco.

The growing importance of your town, and the immense amount of business transacted there, render it important for the security of property and of the rights of citizens, that it should not be kept without regular and legally-constituted officers for the administration of justice, and the management of the affairs of your Municipality. It is therefore hoped that an election will be held, with no more delay than may be necessary in order to have the notice generally known in the town and district.

It is the opinion of all eminent legal authorities which have been consulted, that all laws of California which existed at the time this country was annexed to the United States, and which are not inconsistent with the Constitution, laws, and treaties of the United States, are still in force, and must continue in force till changed by competent authority. The powers and duties of all civil officers in California, except so far as they may have been modified by the act of annexation, are therefore the same as they were previous to the conquest of the country. As the laws touching the subject of Town Councils (Ayuntamientos) may not be of convenient reference, I am directed to subjoin a few of their provisions. The number of members for each town cannot exceed 6 alcaldes, 12 councilmen (regidores), 1 collector, and 2 treasurers, (or 2 syndicos ;) to change, however, from their number previously established, requires the assent of the Governor. For the town of San Francisco, such assent is hereby given for any number not exceeding the provisions of the law.

The council is charged with the police and good order of the town, the construction of roads, the laying out, lighting, and paving of streets, the construction and repair of bridges, the removal of nuisances, the establishment of public burying grounds, the building of jails, the support of town paupers, the granting of town licenses, the examination of weights and measures, the levying of municipal taxes, and the management and disposition of all municipal property. The council appoints its own secretary, who, as well as the members, before entering upon their respective duties, must take the usual oath of office. Each member of the Council is bound to assist the alcaldes in executing the laws, and is individually liable for any mal-administration of the municipal funds, provided he voted for such mal-administration. A full account of the receipts and expenditures of the council must be kept, and at the end of each year submitted to the prefect or sub-prefect of the district, who, after his examination, will transmit them to the Governor, for file in the government archives. In case of the death or removal of any member of the council, the vacancy may be supplied by a special election ; but if such vacancy occur within three months of the close of the year, it will not be filled till the regular annual election. In case of the suspension of the members of the council, those of the preceding year may be reinstated, with their full powers.

As questions are frequently asked respecting town lots, I am directed to say that the most recent law on the subject, that can be found in the government archives, gives to the council (ayuntamiento) power to sell out in building lots (solares) the municipal lands (propios) which have been regularly granted to the town ; but the common lands (egidos) so granted cannot be sold without special authority. All public lands without the limits of the town form a part of the public domain, and can be disposed of only by authority of Congress.

The laws require that the results of elections be transmitted to the Governor for his approval and placed on file in this office. This is not always a useless form, for in some cases it is necessary to accompany legal papers with certificates of the Governor or Secretary of State that certain officers have been duly elected and qualified—which certificates cannot be given unless the requisite evidence of election is deposited in the government archives.

By order of Governor Riley :

H. W. HALLECK,
Brevet Captain, and Secretary of State.

Messrs. R. A. Parker, Frederick Billings, John Servine, W. S. Clark, Stephen Harris, B. R. Buckalew, William H. Tillinghurst, A. J. Grayson, J. P. Haven, San Francisco.

No. LXXVI.

Comparative Table of the Population of the Pueblo of San Francisco and of the Mission of Dolores.

PRESIDIAL PUEBLO OF SAN FRANCISCO.   INDIAN NEOPHITES AT DOLORES.

A. D.	Men.	Wom.	Boys.	Girls.	Total.	Men.	Wom.	Boys.	Girls.	Total.
* 1794	46	33	38	26	143	* 355	369	110	79	913
† 1800	79	49	46	49	223	† 315	260	32	37	644
‡ 1815	125	92	74	82	373	‡ 542	391	90	92	1115
§ 1830	59	46	13	13	131	§ 140	53	13	13	219
¶ 1842	...	...	...	...	160	** ...	...	...	...	50
‖ 1842	...	...	...	to	100	†† ...	...	...	to	37

SOURCES OF INFORMATION.

* California Archives, State Papers, Vol. II Missions, page 35.
†   ''   ''   ''   III   ''   '' 278.
‡   ''   ''   ''   IV   ''   '' 372.
§   ''   ''   ''   V   ''   '' 297.
¶ Census of San Francisco, A. D. 1842, ADDENDA, No. LV, page 78.
‖ 1 DeMofras, page 318.
** 1 DeMofras, page 320. ADDENDA, No. LXVII, page 97.
†† ADDENDA, No. LV, page 78. There were only 37 Neophytes.

No. LXXVII.

EARLY OFFICERS OF SAN FRANCISCO.

It will be convenient to have in a complete form a list of the early officers of San Francisco, with the dates of their terms of service. The following list is one prepared by James W. Bingham, Esq. the present City Clerk.

On the third of November, 1834, the Departmental Legislature of California passed an act authorizing the election of an Ayuntamiento in San Francisco; in pursuance of which, Francisco De Haro was elected First Alcalde.

The second election took place November 27th, 1835, when José Joaquin Estudillo was elected First Alcalde. The succeeding Alcaldes under Mexican authority (but who, in many instances, were Justices of the Peace exercising the functions of Alcaldes) were:

Francisco Guerrero...................................	1836.
Y. Martinez..	1837.
Francisco De Haro..................................	1838.
* Francisco De Haro................................	1839.
Francisco Guerrero.................................	1840.
Francisco Guerrero.................................	1841.
Francisco Guerrero.................................	1842.
Jesus Noe...	1842.
Francisco Sanches	1843.
Guillermo Hinkley..................................	1844.
Juan N. Padilla....................................	1845.
Jesus De la Caz Sanchez...........................	1845.
José De Jesus Noe.................................	1846.

On the eighth day of July, 1846, San Francisco was formally taken possession of by Captain John B. Montgomery, commanding the United States sloop of war "Portsmouth," by whom Lieut. Washington A. Bartlett was appointed Chief Magistrate, or Alcalde, which appointment was subsequently ratified by a formal election by citizens. Mr. Bartlett held the office, with a brief interval, until February, 1847. His successors were:

Edwin Bryant.....................February 22d to June, 1847.
George Hyde.......................June, 1847, to April, 1848.
J. Townsend........................April to September, 1848.
T. M. Leavenworth...........September, 1848, to August, 1849.
John W. Geary...................August, 1840, to May, 1850,

The two Ayuntamientos immediately preceding the incorporation of the city were composed as follows:

---

*Note.—The first official survey of the vicinity of the landing, or water front, appears to have been made in 1836, by Capt. John Voiget, by direction of the then Alcalde, and included that portion of the present city lying between Montgomery, Pacific, Dupont and Sacramento streets; Montgomery Street being the then water front.

AUGUST 6TH, 1849, TO JANUARY 10th, 1850.

Horace Hawes, Prefect.
Joseph R. Curtis, } Sub-Prefects.
Francisco Guerrero, } Sub-Prefects.
John W. Geary, First Alcalde.
Frank Turk, Second Alcalde.

COUNCILMEN.

Thos. B. Winston,	Wm. M. Stewart,	Rodman M. Price,
Samuel Brannan,	Henry A. Harrison,	Stephen R. Harris,
Alfred J. Ellis,	Bezer Simmons,	John Townsend,
Wm. H. Davis,	Gabriel B. Post.	Talbot H. Green.

Frank Turk } Secretaries.
Henry L. Dodge, } Secretaries.

JANUARY 11TH TO MAY 8TH, 1850.

John W. Geary, First Alcalde.
Frank Turk, Second Alcalde.

COUNCILMEN.

Samuel Brannan,	Wm. H. Davis,	Mathew Crooks,
Alfred J. Ellis,	Wm. M. Stewart,	A. M. Van Nostrand,
Hugh C. Murray,	F. C. Gray,	Frank Tilford,
Jas. S. Graham,	Jas. Hagan,	Talbot H. Green.
		Henry L. Dodge, Secretary.

Jonathan Cade, Sergeant-at-Arms.

No. LXXVIII.

SCHEDULE OF GRANTS BY MUNICIPAL AUTHORITIES OF SAN FRANCISCO, BETWEEN THE YEAR 1835 AND JULY 7TH, 1846.

Date of Grant.	By whom signed.	Grantee.	Quantity.	Description, etc.
1836.				
June 2	Estudillo, Alcalde..	W. A. Richardson..	100	No. In Yerba Buena
July 8	" " ..	J. P. Leese........	100	No. 56 "
1837.				
Mar. 14	Martinez, Alcalde..	J. Fuller..........	100	No. 24 "
Nov. 8	" " ..	F. Sanchez........	100	No. 76 "
Dec. 7	" " ..	J. Feil............	200 x 50	No. ? "
1838.				
Mar. 30	De Haro, Alcalde..	F. Casares........	100	No. 49 "
Dec. 1	" " ..	W. Gulnac	200 x 50	No. 49 "
1839.				
Jan. 18	" " ..	S. Vallejo........		No. ? "
April 18	" " ..	J. Pena..........		No. ? "
Dec. 1	Guerrero, J. de P...	W. Hinckley	100 x 50	No. 19 "
9	" " ..	J. C. Davis......	100	No. 18 "
1840.				
Jan. 15	" " ..	J. P. Leese.......	100	No. 7 "
15	" " ..	J. A. Vallejo......	50	No. 3 "
15	" " ..	J. B. Cooper.......	100	No. 50 "
15	" " ..	J. Vioget..........	100 x 50	No. 23 "
16	" " ..	J. Vioget....	100 x 50	Back Leese house "
Aug. 4	" " ..	G. Escolante.... ..		In Yerba Buena
Nov. 18	" " ..	L. Galindo	50	At Dolores
18	" " ..	C. Valencia........	50	"
18	" " ..	F. Gomez.........	50	"
1842.				
Mar. 8	Sanchez, J. de P...	W. Hinckley.......	50	"
8	" " ..	G. Allen..........	50	No. 21 Yerba Buena
May 1	" " ..	P. Sherback.......	50	No. 20 "
Oct. 12	" " ..	C. Moreno........	50	M. Dolores
1843.				
April	" " ..	V. Miramontes.....	50	No. 55 In Yerba Buena
April	" " ..	F. DeHaro........	50	No. 31 "
14	" " ..	J. Noe............	50	No. 51 "
15	" " ..	D. Felis..........	50	No. 32 "
15	" " ..	J. Bautista........	50	No. 33 "
July 3	" " ..	W. A. Leisdesdorff.	100 x 50	Nos. 49, 30 "
Aug. 15	" " ..	B. Valencia	50	No. 16 "
20	" " ..	D. Felis..........	200	In Dolores
Oct. 15	" " ..	G. Escolante.......	50	No. 15 In Yerba Buena
Nov. 15	" " ..	F. Guerrero	50	No. 4 "
Dec. 15	" " ..	T. Malla..........	50	No. 154 "
Dec. 15	Sanchez, J. de P...	H. Bee............	50	No. In Yerba Buena
15	" " ..	J. Castaneda.......	50	No. 53 "
15	" " ..	T. Maya..........	50	No. 54 "
27	" " ..	J. Martin..........	50	No. 35 "
1844.				
Mar. 10	Hinckley, Alcalde..	C. W. Fluge.......	100	No. 26 "
April 1	" " ..	J. Briones.........	50	"
July 12	" " ..	R. Ridley	50	No. 139 "

8*

Date of Grant.	By whom signed.	Grantee.	Quantity.	Description, etc.
1844				
July 12	Hinckley, Alcalde..	J. R. Berry........	50	No. 138 Yerba Buena
19	" " ..	B. Dias & J. P. Mesa	50	No. 17 "
Nov. 13	" " ..	C. Glien...........	50	No. 7 "
Dec. 1	" " ..	E. T. Bale.........	50	No. 136 "
15	" " ..	J. Rose...........	50	No. 83 "
15	" " ..	A. A. Andrews	50	No. 104 "
17	" " ..	G. Reynolds.......	50	No. 84 "
17	" " ..	E. S. Bernal.......	50	No. 37 "
21	" " ..	J. P. Dedmund....	50	No. 58 "
24	" " ..	W. Johnson.......	50	No. 134 "
24	" " ..	W. Richardson.....	50	No. 59 "
1845.				
April 9	Padilla, Alcalde....	R. Haro...........	50	No. 174 "
18	" " ..	T. Smith..........	50	No. 66 "
May 3	" " ..	J. Pena..........	50	No. 161 "
10	" " ..	E. Sota...........	50	No. 44 "
10	" " ..	L. Pena...........	50	No. 86 "
Aug. 10	C. Sanchez, Alcalde.	F. Sanchez........	50	No. 25 "
22	" "	F. Le Page........	50	No. "
Oct. 20	" "	W. Fisher.........	50	No. 61 "
Nov. 25	" "	P. Estrada.........	50	No. "
30	" "	M. Pedrorena......	50	No. 74 "
Dec. 4	" "	S. Smith..........	100 x 50	No. "
7	" "	G. Briones........	50	No. 5 "
1846.				
April 2	" "	R. T. Ridley.......	100	In San Francisco
22	Noe, J. de P.....	W. Leidesdorff.....	50	No. In Yerba Buena
22	Sanchez, J. de P...	J. A. Forbes.......	50	Nos. 183, 184 "
May 14	Noe, J. de P...	H Fitch	50	No. 22 "
15	" "	F.Haen & G.Dopling	50	No. 189 "
20	" "	W. Hinckley	50	No. 27 "
22	" "	E. Grimes.........	50	No. 140 "
22	" "	M. Fernandez......	50	No. 195 "
25	" "	Hensley...........	50	No. 191 "
28	" "	Reading...........	50	No. 8 "
29	" "	W. Hinckley.......	100 x 50	No. "
30	" "	L. Galindo........	50	No. 190 "
June 3	" "	S. Smith..........	50	No. 52 "
6	" "	J. M. S. Maria.....	50	No. 6 "
18	" "	M. E. McIntosh....		No. 196 "
19	" "	D. Garcia.........		No. 273 "
19	" "	F. Hoen...........		No. 62 "
19	" "	J. Allig...........		No. 63 "
20	" "	J. Yuvain.........		No. 60 "

No. LXXIX.

COLONIAL GOVERNORS OF CALIFORNIA.

From the First Spanish Governor on Record to 1849.

1. SPANISH GOVERNORS.—1767–1822.

1.	Gaspar de Portala	from —— 1767	to	——	1771
2.	Felipe Barri	from —— 1771	to	Dec.	1774
3.	Felipe de Neve	from Dec. 1774	to	Sept.	1782
4.	Pedro Fajes	from Sept. 1782	to	Sept.	1790
5.	José Antonio Romeu	from Sept. 1790	to	April,	1792
6.	José Joaquin de Arrillaga	from April, 1792	to	May,	1794
7.	Diego de Borica	from May, 1794	to	——	1800
8.	José Joaquin de Arrillaga	from —— 1800	to	——	1814
9.	José Arguello	from —— 1814	to	——	1815
10.	Pablo Vincente de Sola	from —— 1815	to	Nov.	1822

2. MEXICAN GOVERNORS.—1822–1846.

1.	Pablo Vincente de Sola	from Nov. 1822	to	——	1823
2.	Luis Arguello	from —— 1823	to	June,	1825
3.	José Maria de Echeandia	from June, 1825	to	Jan'y,	1831
4.	Manuel Victoria	from Jan'y, 1831	to	Jan'y,	1832
5.	Pio Pico	from Jan'y, 1832	to	Jan'y,	1833
6.	José Figueroa	from Jan'y, 1833	to	Aug.	1835
7.	José Castro	from Aug. 1835	to	Jan'y,	1836
8.	Nicolas Gutierrez	from Jan'y, 1836	to	May,	1836
9.	Mariano Chico	from May, 1836	to	——	1836
10.	Nicolas Gutierrez	from —— 1836	to	——	1836
11.	Juan B. Alvarado	from —— 1836	to	Dec.	1842
12.	Manuel Micheltorena	from Dec. 1842	to	Feb.	1845
13.	Pio Pico	from Feb. 1845	to	July,	1846

3. AMERICAN MILITARY GOVERNORS.—1846–1849.

1. COMMODORE JOHN D. SLOAT hoisted the American flag at Monterey July, 7th, 1846, and, by proclamation, took formal possession of California in the name of the United States Government.

2. COMMODORE ROBERT F. STOCKTON.—Proclamation dated at Los Angeles, August 17th, 1846.

3. COLONEL JOHN C. FREMONT.—Appointed by Commodore Stockton January, 1847.

4. GENERAL STEPHEN W. KEARNEY.—Proclamation dated at Monterey, March 1st, 1847.

5. COLONEL RICHARD B. MASON.—Proclamation dated at Monterey, May 31st, 1847.

6. GENERAL BENNET RILEY.—Became Military Governor April 13th, 1849.

The treaty ceding California and New Mexico to the United States was dated at the City of Guadalupe Hidalgo, February 2d, 1848 ; exchanged at Queretaro, May 30th, 1848 ; ratified by the President, March 16th, 1848 ; and proclaimed by the President, July 4th, 1848. The State Constitution adopted November, 1849 ; went into effect December 15th, 1849.

31901050803966

CPSIA information can be obtained at www.ICGtesting.com
Printed in the USA
243395LV00007B/7/P